Hearthstones in the Hills

Hearthstones in the Hills

*People and Places in
the North Wales Heartland*

STOWERS JOHNSON

ROBERT HALE · LONDON

© *Stowers Johnson 1987*
First published in Great Britain 1987

ISBN 0 7090 2966 7

Robert Hale Limited
Clerkenwell House
Clerkenwell Green
London EC1R 0HT

British Library Cataloguing in Publication Data

Johnson, Stowers
  Hearthstones in the hills : people and
  places in the North Wales heartland.
  1. Snowdonia (Wales)—Social life and
  customs
  I. Title
  942.9′250857′0924   DA740.S6

Photoset in North Wales by
Derek Doyle & Associates, Mold, Clwyd.
Printed in Great Britain by
St Edmundsbury Press, Bury St Edmunds, Suffolk.
Bound by WBC Bookbinders Limited.

Contents

List of Illustrations

PICTURE CREDITS

Clwyd County Museum Service: 8

1 West Winds from Snowdon

I knew from the expression on the face of the garage manager that he had something serious to tell me. As he pressed a button, my Bedford Dormobile gradually rose from the workshop floor to head height.

'Look,' he said, 'you'd better know the truth and see for yourself!' Taking out his penknife, he pushed it through the steel girders of the chassis, penetrating and sprinkling dirty flakes of rust. 'Corrosion!' he growled. 'Rusted away! How does it hold together on hardly an inch of steel? And I'll show you the other one just as bad!'

But I stopped him, fearful of the final straw that broke the fabled camel's back. My Dormobile! Alas, my Dormobile that had taken me to Mount Ararat and on another journey had been my friend all across Russia through Kiev to the Caucasus Mountains.

'Another chassis?' I suggested. But he shook his head. A lump came into my throat.

'For myself,' he declared gloomily, 'not I, nor one of my boys would drive that thing out of this workshop. We are not making any charge, but we don't want it left here. Oh no, and you must take it away yourself!'

Then I remembered. It was the model with the extra two feet of length – yes, a large chassis, perhaps not strong enough for all the weight I would use. I recalled strange experiences on the motorway from Birmingham, when the rear of the vehicle would begin to sway at speed and sway as a caravan would in reaching speeds towards sixty miles per hour. Of course! That was the rear of the Dormobile wanting to sever connection with the two front wheels and the driver above them!

On Eastern Avenue, from force of habit, I fell into my usual speed and was passing fifty miles per hour when suddenly that swinging motion intruded from the rear. Now I understood its cause, it became a thousand times more terrifying. If I did not dispose of my old friend it would dispose of me. The roads of the eastern London suburbs are lined with car dealers' stands. In such a mood I drove among the dealers, eschewed Dormobiles and caravans and traded my vehicle making up the price with cash to obtain a nice little Ford Escort.

As for my custom of independent Continental travel, surely I could secure that with camping. Salesmen at the Camping Show at Earls Court were quick to assure me this was really so and lost no time in selling me a trailer tent, a French pattern which erected itself, or almost so, as they demonstrated. There it was on its platform, up and down again, packed away so simply a child might understand it. It provided a luxury double-lined home that would trail safely and afford a modern bungalow of linen electrically lit. The contraption could rise anywhere with a few turns of the wrist and one or two easy adjustments to be completed in less than ten minutes at the most.

There and then I bought the trailer tent. Did I see a glance of guilt-stricken conscience on the part of the girl who assisted those super hand-shaking salesmen who helped me to part with my cheque in such a friendly way?

Unfortunately, as I planned new and adventurous enterprises, I was forced into realization that my circumstances had changed. The explanation of those whirling sways of the Dormobile on the motorways, the revelation that life and limb had depended on rusty diminishing half inches of metal, had cost me the confidence of my wife. She now regarded my motoring projects with suspicion. My impulses to tow a trailer into remote parts of Europe, to erect a tent anywhere on mountain or lakeside, there to leave it unattended for excursions to cities or celebrations, gave her no joy, and she became suspicious. I proved how easy it would be by erecting it on our front lawn. I towed it here and there. She became more and more doubtful. It must be tried out in Britain first and well tested under the terms of its guarantee.

I found she had been in touch with her Welsh cousin whose husband knew farmers in Denbighshire and had in fact been headmaster of a school in those mountains. He promised to arrange a camp site on a farm there. Diffidently I agreed. After a week of trial we would be sure. Then we would go. Down south into Spain for a start, perhaps Morocco later.

While I made preparations for Spain, regarding the Welsh interlude as a mere pipe dream, I was suddenly presented with a *fait accompli*. It had all been arranged! We were committed. Dates had been fixed – mid August – a site arranged on Mr D.J. Davies's farm and a pleasant welcome promised for us. The neighbouring farmer in Pandy Tudur had also been told. We were expected. Only one week, my wife explained, and then we could be sure, really sure, and away to Spain.

The day before departure I had what was intended to be a casual rehearsal on the front lawn. Time, however had elapsed. Joints, locks and catches seemed different even when read against the instruction book. Unexplained difficulties cropped up and then, when at last erected, the contraption seemed averse to immediate dismantling. In fact, it repeatedly disobeyed the instruction book, but eventually under much pressure condescended to come down all of a creaking heap with one ominous crack! I contented myself by reflecting that if it could be put up when in Wales it could stay up while its engineering was investigated *in situ.*

Nevertheless, not till next midday did we leave Brentwood and it was an hour till twilight before we turned north at Pentre Voelas to pass Nebo. Long storm-clouds were massing above the Snowdon ranges, gathering to threaten rain across that breath-taking landscape of dark moorland, giving a grim hint that midsummer was long gone and night, cold mountain night was near.

Excellent directions had been provided for us. Every house and farm had been named in detail, so we sped with confidence up the hill and into the farmyard of Ty Gwyn. Alas, we had become so far behind time that we had been given up as non-arrivals. The folk at Ty Gwyn had gone to the coast. Even the neighbouring farmer, Mr Griffiths, we learned, had waited some time at the field and he too had departed. Ty Gwyn was empty, the doors were shut, the windows closed.

They had told us to choose our own site, perhaps taking it for granted we would pick a sheltered place near the farmyard but hills attract me, a man of the plains, so I chose to go onward, higher and higher. The farm track, neatly asphalted, led from the second field above to a ridge that commanded the landscape. The trailer tent had windows which the salesman had extolled as making 'a room with a view', so up we went to obtain full use of that view from a prime site with a thick hedge sheltering from the north and a thinner one to the west, but a glorious though darkening aspect over the wild Hiraethog moors.

The grass was long, quite uncut. The groundsheet refused to lie flat upon it but no item in the camping equipment was defective so in the darkening twilight the frame consented to be erected. The canvas was pulled across, the polythene windows were laced down, and stays and tent-pegs were driven into position.

Just before the evening shower began, amid our hasty unloading of gear and provisions, the farmer drove up the hill. Poor Mr D.J. Davies, how perturbed he was to find we had arrived in his absence! Having noticed the car lights and the activity on the hilltop, Mr Griffiths came next.

As it eventually happened, the voices of our hosts did die away as they went down the hillside. The fluorescent lamp was connected to the car battery, the tent interior blazed with light. The curtains could be drawn and, after a pleasant meal and cups of tea to reassure us against the dark night outside, we settled to the prospect of a peaceful slumber.

But that was not to be. After midnight the wind began, a steady, raging wind that blew from the west where I knew was Snowdon. It steadily pressed the canvas, which stood against it, but now and again in a raging gust of fury blew harder, fiercer, so that the tent frames creaked. As they creaked, they moved increasingly so that sleep was impossible. Throughout the midnight and early morning I found myself creeping outside, tightening tent-pegs, loosening some, hammering in others, adjusting the stays, flexing the joints in the frame, listening to these metallic, straining protests, hoping for silence. For possibly five minutes at a time, after stiffening everything against that steady, relentless blast that came roaring from the west, I could think I had succeeded, but then unaccountably, with a nod of defiance the whole tent would shake and the creaking begin again. Not till I was so exhausted that I would hear nothing except the heavy rain falling on the roof could I fall asleep.

The very next moment, as it seemed, I was awake. There was not a breath of wind, the sun was shining and, as I sat shaving beside the car mirror, Moel Siabod, that great shoe-shaped spur of Snowdonia, came peeping through the clouds. It was weird on the top of that hill in a sort of high mystery land for as the sun rose Siabod seemed to move and begin its wandering through the skies, yet it was always there behind rain and sunshine like the hub of the world, for perhaps we ourselves were moving, recovering our place from which the wild wind had blown us.

Every day after that the buzzard flew mewing, higher it seemed than Siabod, travelling towards the Glyders across the far Conwy river, too high to be mobbed by magpies or crows and keeping time, regular time for all the mountains, never altering his clock, pursuing a regular aerial patrol.

The farmer's daughter, Beryl, came with offers of eggs and milk, yes, and we could have fresh vegetables as well, for Mr D.J. Davies was a genuine agricultural contractor. His family had all been concerned about us for we were very high up in that place, much too high for camping. We might find it better to move down beside the farmhouse, nestling far below, sheltered by that very hill, its actual farm buildings grouped to ward off the elements while the woods and scrub of old quarries gave still more protection. On the southern slopes it basked in the mature sunshine of late summer. Its site had never such significance to me as now. Far above it as I was, I could stare to the further horizons to revel from the sweep of the Hiraethog heatherlands to the range of the Snowdonia Glyders, enjoying the pleasure of that little valley of the River Galen below.

Days began to go by easily, almost sleepily for when the sun shone that wind would seem to falter and vanish. In brooding over the far-away moorland I would forget the wakeful night and the creaking tent-frame.

The road from Llansannan to Pandy Tudur swept downhill in the grand modern semicircle of a new road, bypassing the older highway which was so steep it had used to serve for testing merit and quality in horses, sometimes becoming an improvised racecourse. Every day as I watched, a couple of men wandered down the meadows within that semicircle, filling sacks as they descended. It was mushroom time and they had found a secret supply, ripe for picking. As my binoculars travelled on, sweeping the long limestone ravines that intersect the moorlands, I perceived how all the farms hid away in the hollows, crouching maybe from old-time predators but most from the weathers of these Snowdon winds.

In the centre of the far landscape there was one cottage that defied them all, a lonely building with a wall before and a huge spreading sycamore close to westward. The cottage appeared to take possession of that panorama. It was empty, a fragment of the roof had gone, the chimney remained but not the glass nor even the frames of the windows. Five miles away as it was, it grew larger as the morning wore on and the shining air sparkled. I coveted it, for it had walls, wonderful stone walls that would stand against the wind. And it seemed permanent. Perhaps it had been there for ever, permanent as the heather around it.

I had developed a reluctance to take my tent up daily and move away gypsy fashion. Quality of experience was more life enhancing than variety. In such a cottage I could be master of the weathers rather than slave. Such a cottage garden the birds would visit, the buzzard would wheel above it and the wild flowers bloom in all their seasons.

The determination came to me to buy that cottage. Derelict and deserted as it was, it must be for sale, only awaiting a purchaser.

2 *Prospecting for a Cottage*

We did not remain many more days obstructing the wind on that hill.
It had come to the end of August when days were becoming shorter.
Although I had stopped most of the tubes from creaking in the tent-
frame, it seemed there was little more to learn about using a trailer
tent. I had been revisiting a landscape of which I had been a lover
from boyhood so I well knew how its seasons could close as sharply
as the shutting of a door. When we actually moved away it was
already September and then the last look at that lonely cottage
clinched our decision to buy it, to have it for our own. Long before we
reached the motorways, our decision was firm. We had come under
the hypnotic influence of those mountains as they conjured with the
clouds across the Conwy river, receding or advancing according to
the sunlight and the wind. With just a wave of a cheque book we
would acquire that cottage and at leisure we could return to lounge in
comfort, to bask before the panoramas of those ever extending Glyder
ranges and tramp those miles of heather on the Hiraethog moorlands.

But the cottage was not for sale and would not, could not be bought
or sold! My wife's cousin telephoned to tell us. Her husband had been
kind enough to seek out the owner. It was a cottage well known in
those parts. Owls had lived in that sycamore tree and the old man in
the house had died long ago, so now it belonged to the nearest farmer
who might one day repair it for his sons. Most definitely he did not
want people he could not control living there! We both agreed there
were other cottages. Why bother?

Opposition, however, renewed my keenness. Back in Essex the
heather honey scent of the moors, the fresh, clean wind from the hills
became more alluring in memories. Then, when turning the pages of a
Sunday newspaper, I noticed the advertisement of an abandoned
cottage for sale at Gyffylliog with the asking price of £6,000 in which
a 'magnificent barn', glorious views and the possibility of a planning
permission grant were included. Gyffylliog was on the far side of the

Clocaenog Forest, that vast, depopulated blanket of dark green fir trees all planted in our own lifetime without thought for the splendour of the Welsh oak or fear of the funereal morbidity of conifers in the mass. Snowdon could not be seen from that valley. While I hesitated the cottage re-appeared in the advertisements with the gruff and angry addition: 'Re-advertised due to a time waster.' Somebody else had hesitated and withdrawn.

I also, however, could advertise for such a dream cottage and I fondly thought, take my choice. Into the *North Wales Weekly News* went my offer to buy a cottage. No price inducement was included and I chose the anonymity of a box number. While I awaited the host of replies I constructed imaginary pictures of Snowdon views seen from cosy windows, of mountains arising across and above the valley mist, all in the serene stillness of heather-clad moors.

Only one letter arrived, pathetic and pleading from a woman in Abergele who lived with her sister and was lonely there. She begged to meet the anonymous advertiser and gave details of her dreary life from which she hoped to be rescued if only for brief intervals. There were two pages of close written unhappiness which I heartlessly threw away, glad that my anonymity had prevented any direct approach and selfishly retreating from psychiatric altruism. She had not even read the advertisement, or had she? Did she think someone who could buy a mountain cottage had also a moneyed stream that could be tapped? No other reply arrived in all the three weeks of insertions, nor did I find anything tempting in the advertisement columns. How strange! No one had a mountain cottage to sell, although from the top of the hill at Ty Gwyn and from my memories of the Snowdon valleys the mountain meadows had seemed littered with derelict dwellings.

For several years I had been used to spending part of each summer in Llanrwst not merely dreaming on the mountains but fishing along the River Conwy below the Gwydir woods, watching the tantalizing glides of that cold stream. Sometimes I had the exasperation as I went down in mid-morning of meeting Crosville omnibus men coming away with a salmon apiece. Their garage was opposite the river so they would be up at dawn, long before their shift was due, trailing a shrimp bait to catch fish newly arrived from the estuary.

There was a lonely cottage which even then allured me. Called 'Oerfa' after the mountain behind it, signifying 'cold place', it stood high and back from the Nebo road, and its window could have surveyed a magnificent view of all the Snowdon mountains. An old lady lived there then and had been alone those many years, as my landlady, Miss Owen of Llys Cernyw averred. When she passed away, Miss Owen declared, the cottage would stand empty. No one else would live there, in that cold place, alone, so far from the shops. Why, the old lady had not even a garden in which to grow vegetables, supposing they would grow up there! That was told me twenty or more years ago. The old lady might be there still and perhaps be glad to sell and move to a warmer location, or perhaps the cottage was now empty.

I had passed it on the way back, where it stood even now, shuttered, built of huge boulders and alone, like the old lady who had been reputed to live there. There were no remaining outbuildings, just the cottage with the bare splendour surrounding it, the moorland of Hiraethog and, across the Conwy, all Gwydir Forest extending below a vast backdrop of the highest mountains of Wales and Snowdon itself. Sadly, both Miss Owen sisters had passed away and I could not enquire of them, but every time I had driven by Oerfa, shutters, chimney and close-fastened door had declared it as without a tenant.

October had come by now. It became obvious that if I wanted a cottage I must search the chosen countryside myself. Back to Wales I went and found that 'Cold Place' on the way to Nebo. Yes, definitely it was untenanted and it stood on land obviously the property of the farm opposite and below the road, called, as I remember, Briniog.

I left my car and walked around that cottage. Shuttered as it was, standing alone with its boulders straight up from the meadow grass and without trace of any garden, its bleakness was accentuated by barbed wire. The weathers had beaten upon it, leaving their own marks of incipient destruction. The paint on the shutters was peeling. Everything was locked and barred. Resolving to visit the farmer who possessed that ubiquitous name of Davies, I took my car down to the farmyard.

To my surprise, it was full of sheep, hundreds of them. They crowded the pens, the barns and sheds and jam-packed the whole yard. As I tried to force my way beyond, two lads came forward to help. Someone else shouted and a message went on to the farm. I was encouraged, almost lifted forward, as if I were an expected visitor. Extricating myself from all that bleating, crushing and hot odour of sheep, I found a reception party waiting round the kitchen table. Tea was poured, sandwiches were passed. I could not even begin to talk for all the discussions, lectures indeed, upon the weather. They were pleasant farming folk and in rustic working clothes, whereas I was dressed in a smart city suit, so I put it down to that, but it was an awkward experience. I did not deserve such a welcome. Who was I, so unannounced, to be so received. After the weather, the discussion was forcibly led by my hosts and travelled to my journey there. They were so solicitous, but surprised I had come from Llandudno. They thought I came from Chester! A second sandwich was offered before I could get to the point of my visit. Empty cottage! Oerfa! Everyone stopped drinking tea. The silence in that kitchen sharply contrasted with the sheep bleating beyond the window panes.

So I was not the vet from the Agriculture Department? So I did not want to see the sheep? The Agricultural Inspector was due. They had thought it was funny if he came from Llandudno. The family all gathered there concealed the mistake by their gracious hospitality, accepting the mistaken identity as if they had insulted me, thereby smoothing away some of the confusion. So I was not a friend of the Inspector?

I told my story ruthlessly, abandoning any commercial palaver. I wanted to buy Oerfa and would give a good sum for it. They could name their price. Mr Davies took charge now, the others faded from the table.

'I cannot sell,' he declared apologetically. 'That cottage is kept for my sons when they come on holiday or after term time.' No, not though I tempted him in rising four figure amounts. He shook his head and rose from the table. Oerfa was now part of his farm. Fine for his sons, maybe, but he did not want others there with dogs, children and the like. 'No, no,' he protested as he shook hands at the door. 'You should have telephoned and it would have saved you the journey and I would have known who you were. No, indeed, no, I would never part with the cottage even to let it.'

The sheep had grown quiet while I stood there thanking him. Another car could be heard approaching, probably the one expected and I left with further apologies – not, however, before he had told me who owned the other derelict cottages along that high and lonely road.

The first on the western side just down from Oerfa possessed no more than four substantial walls and a chimney but had once been two storeys high. The wall with attached chimney lurched slightly. The fierce winds coming over the hill had flung out the roof rafters and even the floorboards and they lay idly within the walls among fallen building-stones. There were no slates at all and never a sign humanity had reposed there; even the old doorway was blocked up. A swift stream of transparent water came under the road to run below alongside the house, crystal clear and lending a charm to the location, the meadow, the sloping bank, seeming to purify the old ruin itself. I could make a seat by that brook and sit through the brighter days, while the clouds drove along the valley below. The stream purled, tumbling swiftly over stones it had been rolling for centuries and the beauty coloured in its rocks made the ugliness of the stark old walls attractive. Across the meadow the land fell down miles and miles to the Conwy river but all the Forest of Gwydir rose there beyond, a green base from which the Snowdon mountains seemed to rise into the autumn air.

Mrs Kerry, the owner, lived in the centre of Llanrwst where she let sites on a caravan park. I arrived at the best of times for she was in the garden by the gate, tending the flowery urns that made a guard of honour to welcome arriving caravans.

'Yes,' she agreed, 'Tan-y-ffordd belongs to me. I know it from years ago. The old lady who lived happily there used to wash her linen in that stream. Very good drinking water, too, except when it froze up. But you can't buy it!'

'I will give a very good price. Full market value!'

'Market value! Do you know there are twelve acres in that holding. I have already been offered £12,000 for it and refused outright. Several people are wanting that and offering now and again, but I'm not selling.'

'It is only the cottage I want.'

'The cottage? That is a ruin! They have pinched all the slates from it and everything else they can take. It is the land people want, land!'

'Not I. I wouldn't know what to do with the land,' I argued. 'Only sell me the cottage. Suppose mountain land is £1,000 an acre. Sell me the cottage for £2,000, then you continue to possess your holding at its value of £12,000. You said it was a ruin. If most of it is stolen, the remaining ruin is worthless, surely.'

She regarded me curiously, then suspiciously. 'Why do you want such a place? Since my husband died I have decided not to sell anything at all. In any case, I am thinking of going in for ponies up there. Ponies are the thing now in Wales and my daughter can deal with that.'

'£5,000 then, for the cottage alone?'

She hesitated, almost tempted, but shook her head.

'Since my husband died, I will not sell a thing,' she declared. 'It will be months before everything is straightened out.'

I was shocked for I had not noticed she was wearing a definite black.

'Of course,' I agreed. 'Well, it is most kind of you to give me this attention. Let us say the offer is open and I will ask my solicitor to write to you confirming my intention, to which you can decide at your convenience.'

During a comfortable lunch in Llanrwst my expectations seemed to fade like the autumn afternoon. I could not rely upon Mrs Kerry changing her mind. The owner of the most distant cottage was a Mr Evans up above Melin-y-Coed, only some two miles away. I would have just enough time to see him before the afternoon vanished. The road to his address was steep and narrow, built to overlook the Conwy Valley and its bluebell woods, but that route swept me into some forecourts of mansions like suburban palaces, embarrassing one into a belated and reversing recognition that none of them was a farmer's dwelling. Each was deserted, however, so higher and higher I drove till a scrambling of defiant dogs assured me I had come into a genuine farmyard.

Mrs Evans came out of her farmhouse and commanded the dogs away. They did not leave but skulked silently and prowled around with a savage menace.

'Why Tyn-y-Bryn?' she demanded, interrupting my enquiry. 'There's nothing there, nothing left, nothing. You can only see the walls!'

I explained how I had been to Mr Davies to buy Oerfa but he would not sell because he wanted it for his sons. My words inflamed her.

'Sons!' she cried. 'I've got sons. Sons, indeed! Who has not got sons?'

Just then her husband arrived. She announced my visit in angry Welsh to him and went inside. He was much more conciliatory. When I explained how, though I was English, my wife was Welsh, yes and Welsh-speaking withal, he protested he had nothing against the English. There was a lot that could be said for them, indeed he knew there was, but his brother was ill and could not be approached, was very ill and in hospital, likely to be there for some time. No, he could not be approached, nor could he make any decisions about anything, especially about selling, indeed. As for Tyn-y-Bryn, it was finished. You could not make a cowshed out of it.

I disagreed and suggested a price which staggered him.

'If you give that,' he continued, magnanimously, 'better make it "subject to planning permission".' Then as he thought about the offer, speaking slowly and meaningfully, 'If my brother ever gets better, you will not get anything neither. Planning permission is a funny thing in these parts. No, you will not get anywhere with this.'

When I made my way homeward to Essex, I could not resist taking the high road over the hills towards Nebo so as to take another look at the ruins which kept themselves so tantalizingly out of my reach. The four walls of Tyn-y-Bryn especially attracted me as they stood just below Oerfa on the fringe of the moor where Moel Seisiog gradually rose above the heather to its 1,534 feet of height. Only one old oak lintel remained above the door. Cattle and sheep were its tenants now. Even the fallen stones and boulders had been cleared away. Beyond a disused quarry stood two empty farmhouses, half hidden along a green track, each without either windows or doorways but used as hay barns. They were well built, their appearance strangely romantic. Ancient well-heads of stone made thousands of years ago protected their water supply, and each crouched away from those west winds which had torn down the cottages. Maintaining either in good repair would mean endless building contracts apart from the initial outlay and entail the troublesome worry of dealing with far-away workmen.

As for the four walls of Tyn-y-Bryn cottage, they stand even today sheltering their black mountain cattle, and it came to pass that I wrote letter after letter enquiring after the health of Mr Evans's brother, but he never got better, he never got worse, until I ceased to write and forwent any thoughts of those cottages along the Nebo road. Instead I wrote to W.J.I. Owen of David Thomas Owen & Co, solicitors in Ancaster Square, who my wife's cousin assured me had the reputation of being one of the most reliable solicitors in that valley.

And so he proved, for a reply soon came from him agreeing to act on my behalf but advising me to obtain a surveyor's report before contemplating purchase of any building aged over ten years. He strongly recommended Dewi Jones, manager of the firm Bob Parry & Co Ltd as most of the agricultural and private properties in that area came under their notice and they could be thoroughly relied upon.

There was of course little use in engaging a surveyor for the kind of property I had in mind, so I replied confessing my offer for the roofless cottage of Mrs Kerry and asking him to convey my intention to make a purchase proposal. In a few days, however, back came a letter all the way from Wales to tell me that that very solicitor had just had an appointment with Mrs Sarah Kerry in connection with the estate of her late husband: She was not interested in selling either the cottage on its own or the cottage and smallholding. Mr Owen described her as a charming lady, but a lady who knew her own mind. 'She is not the sort of person I could possibly try to persuade against her own better judgment,' he wrote, 'and therefore I said no more but promised I would write to you.'

Mr Evans now wrote that his brother was still not well enough to discuss matters of importance but 'I wonder if you would be interested in renting a house?' I was not, of course, but the offer alerted me and when I researched the Welsh Tourist Board's booklet *Where to stay in Wales*, the cause of my difficulties became apparent. No wonder farmers would not sell their empty cottages! Spread across the booklet's map was marked a sprinkling of old-time abandoned farmhouses now listed as little villas to let, looked after and managed by the owner of some larger farm into which the smaller farm property had been amalgamated. All over the countryside farmers had a clandestine and profitable industry, alien to Wales maybe but supplementary to the vicissitudes of farming and providing for their wives domestic interest and variety against the dull routine of agriculture. Of course no one would sell! Even an empty derelict building blinked its promise of conversion into a little gold-mine at some future date.

One more letter came from the solicitor in which he enclosed a circular from Bob Parry Ltd describing a cottage obviously not owned by any farmer nor suitable for such a *Where to Stay* sideline. It detailed a dwelling called 'Coddau' at Llangernyw. Priced at £4,750, it had 500 square yards of ground, including a small orchard with a variety of fruit trees. There were three ground-floor and three first-floor rooms to the house which was 'built of stone, rendered under a slated roof and is semi-detached to a small chapel. It is basically a sound little cottage and is ideal for renovation purposes, having plenty of scope' etc, etc.

With the help of my relative Trevor Jones, I sought out 'Coddau' on the map and found it high above Llangernyw on that wide open moorland south of Colwyn Bay. The orthodox Welsh spelling proved to be 'Codau'.

Was the chapel included as part of the sale? Visions of conversion into an art gallery, a theatre and lecture room, a studio, a celebration centre perhaps – dazzling expectations crowded into one's dreams. But no, it was not. That chapel had its niche in local religious history. Anniversaries, commemorations of past events, even funeral ceremonies were still held there. I shuddered as Trevor Jones told me, and shivered yet more when he telephoned to say the house could be damp. The slope of the hill fell towards it. 'Semi-detached to a small chapel' – I could become the caretaker? The lay preacher? People would knock at my door for spiritual guidance, for commiserative prayer or for loans of cash. Towards all rural aspirations such as these I felt a want of competence.

Later I inspected the place myself and peeped through the windows to see half-opened bibles and hymnbooks lying derelict upon dusty furniture neglected by man, while, unobserving of God, grass crowded upon the walls. This was really nothing to go by, for years later, in 1982, it transpired the chapel had been dusted, cleaned and polished. The interior had been festooned with flowers from the nursery gardens at Glan Conwy and some two score folk had gathered to celebrate the 150th year of its existence in a demonstration to prove that, though the chapel might be closed, the Church it represented lived still. The list of the forty people gathered there showed names from as far away as New Zealand and in itself was a testimony to the depopulation of that immediate countryside. The local paper gave a stirring account not merely of the sermons but of the recollections of those pilgrims as they remembered walking hand in hand with parents to worship in times when the chapel was always full. They had comforted themselves with declarations that their church consisted in more than a building. I reflected how moving it must have been on that 11 June when the voices of the elderly congregation had resounded upon the surrounding moors from the tall windows, re-echoing their faith in the strains of the ancient language.

Now closed it may be, but even today that chapel is not for sale, standing as a monument to invoke future commemorations.

Some buyer more urgent, perhaps less sensitive than I, did acquire the house adjacent, painted and renovated it. I passed his large Jaguar and its smaller companion when recently I crept up to look again through the chapel window. Thick dust was once more cloaking the furniture, hymnbooks lay idly about, half open as if to reproach some departed choir. The shiny cellulose of that Jaguar car repelled me, making the place only half solitary and myself an intruder, though it was years later, and as I glance now at the newspaper photographs of those folk grouped upon the steps, I feel some kind of regret not to have shared their memories and embraced their friendships as perhaps I might have done had I responded to the solicitor's offer to live 'semi-detached, adjacent to a small chapel'.

When I rejected the purchase for such a small price I am afraid Mr Owen washed his hands of me. The advice he had already given about employing a surveyor indicated he regarded me as a type heading for disaster. Future correspondence was plainly to show he had this settled conviction. Moreover in my letter to him I had declared I required something 'less civilized' and with the Snowdon ranges in view.

The best thing to do, it seemed, was to visit Bob Parry Ltd, to go there personally, seek advice and have my name listed among the clients and nurse such expectations as that firm could arouse. These bi-monthly journeys to North Wales from Essex were becoming expensive, their lack of success more irksome, the more so now that autumn was passing. Bob Parry's premises were close to the centre of Llanrwst and there within, employed as clerk, I recognized Dafydd's wife from the next farm to my camping place of Ty Gwyn, but she was working so busily in the background that I could not presume to claim her acquaintance. They had nothing in that estate agency to suit me. Small terraced houses in villages, lonely bungalows deserted by retired folk along the inland roads, but views of Snowdon – impossible! Such places went straight off the market, so great was the demand, and for high prices.

I protested. There were plenty of ruins and deserted farmhouses. I had seen them and I would buy and restore. Bob Parry's assistants stopped work and listened to the argument at the counter.

'Oh, no, we have no such properties. There are difficulties. Farmers will not sell, and other difficulties prevent progress with this type of property.'

'What kind of difficulties?'

The clerk shrugged his shoulders deprecatingly. 'Planning difficulties – impossible difficulties.'

He made a note of my name and address but carefully warned me that he could not advise me to purchase any ruin or disused property. The prospectus for 'Codau' was produced. It was easy to perceive that the fact I had already received it from the solicitor was taken as some guarantee of my earnestness as a client.

I enquired who was the landowner who might own the cottages on farms rented by his tenants. Was it Colonel Wynne Finch? A *frisson* went through that office. Nobody crossed himself, but I might just as well have invoked the Deity. A patronizing smile deprecated this approach. I had better enquire of the individual farmers, it was tactfully suggested. I could not, however, go from farm to farm making such an enquiry. It had been bad enough asking along the Nebo road about Oerfa.

'Try asking at the pubs,' I was advised. 'There is one at Capel Garmon. You can get views of Snowdon from there. Have a drink and ask around. And there's a post office at Nebo. Post offices are good places. If you are not pressed for time and can wait, we will send our circulars for anything that comes on the market.'

I had outlived my welcome there. Behind the sympathetic attention I was given, I was conscious I was wasting Bob Parry Ltd's time.

Capel Garmon was a fascinating village not far from Betws-y-Coed. I knew it from having visited the famous prehistoric burial chamber now well preserved as an Ancient Monument, so off I went to arrive about midday at its public house, an old-time hostelry in that characteristic Welsh façade of black and white with flowerboxes somewhere here or there.

I entered and went to the bar for a drink. There must have been a dozen or more customers, obviously locals. Though voices continued their conversation, they dropped out of my hearing. I knew I was under observation. The barman was bluff and friendly and knowledgeable about the weather. He wanted to ask where I was staying. His curiosity was shared by his locals who craned forward to listen. No, this was not the first time I had visited Capel Garmon. Yes, I had been before and often. I wondered, should I boldly announce my quest? My eye wandered over his locals. None of them looked as if they might be peddling a cottage. I drank the lager more quickly than I intended.

'Will that be all?' prompted the barman, still as curious.

'Yes,' I stammered, and, plucking up courage, began, 'I suppose houses around here go through Bob Parry, Llanrwst?'

'Yes, they do that. Bob Parry, indeed they do! Houses hereabouts indeed.'

'Ah!'

I had asked, but provoked nothing relevant in response. 'Bob Parry!' I echoed, as I left my lager and made for the door. Everyone had heard and as I strolled away I caught the reverential but inquisitive murmur, 'Bob Parry?'

I had failed. I was no sort of door-to-door salesman, buyer or seller. My query seemed ridiculous one for such a townsman as I to put before those hard-bitten locals, sheep-men of the mountains. I waited a moment or two in the car in case some one should come out and begin the anticipated probing conversation. But the pub door stayed shut, so I drove towards Nebo village by the higher road that reveals all the splendour of the Carneddau Range, of Siabod, and like a far jewel both beyond and among them, of Snowdon itself.

Nebo post office was open where it stood on the east side of the road just like any other village post office might be anywhere in Britain, nor was there at that time anything distinctly Welsh to differentiate it from any other post office. The usual wire mesh grating protected Her Majesty's goods from the greengroceries and provisions. Just to be on a friendly footing, to advertise myself also as a potential client, I bought some odds and ends of foodstuffs and oranges, and then as I settled the account broached the real object of my visit, introducing it in an off-hand, sidelong manner, as of no great importance, for I expected a rebuff or at least a shake of the head. The postmistress was from Lancashire, plump, calm, middle-aged and equable. She had time on her hands. Lots of people from England came to live in Nebo but they did not stay long. The winters settled that for them.

'If you are not chapel, what is there for you to do? And for your people, nothing. And if you are retired, it is just waiting to die and there are warmer places.' She might go back to Lancashire one day, she speculated wistfully.

In Nebo there were good houses. One just opposite had been bought by a member of the Royal Philharmonic Orchestra. He had spent an additional £16,000 making it pleasant. I saw the house as she pointed it out. It possessed magnificent views but was foreboding in its barren immediate surroundings. He might sell it if I had enough money to make him happy. I winced at the idea. Well then, there were two bungalows, each with a fine garden in which to sit beside the road of a summer time, waiting to go away home for the winter. They were modern erections no more than roughly built shacks.

Well then, if I were particular, I could do as some were doing. I could have the house built to my own liking. The owner of the Betws-y-Coed Waterloo Hotel was doing just that, and I could see the fine mansion Mr Trevor Roberts was building for him. Oh yes, Trevor Roberts was the builder working at Nebo, but he would not build houses unless they were sold in advance.

'In advance?'

'Oh yes. He has several plots of land here, but he won't build houses on them unless they are paid for in advance. You pay, and then he'll start building.'

Though this sounded rather mysterious and not what I was expecting, I took note of his address and went to look at the plots of land on which Trevor Roberts was building, especially the 'fine mansion'. These plots were unspectacular, having no grand views to match my ideal. As for the 'fine mansion', that was on the east side of the road opposite which some future builder might develop and obliterate the view.

Dark night was creeping on. I would just have time to go down to Pandy Tudur village, find the farm of Trevor Roberts and discuss possibilities with him.

3 *Frustration and Discovery*

The way up to Llwyndu-uchaf, the home of Trevor Roberts, was then
only suitable for lorries and Land Rovers. Crumbling building
material broke upon its surface, odd bullocks strove to penetrate
fences on either side until I came to the barricades of new concrete
blocks in stacks, drain-pipes and scaffolding ladders, a veritable
builder's depot all neatly thrown about into the yard of a very old
traditional Welsh farmhouse. An antique plough was set up on the
grass, and on the wall were the peculiar round stones that emerge
from the slate rock formations. Some say they are primitive quern
stones for grinding corn into flour, others see them as missiles once
used in Roman siege catapults. Never do I find them on these Welsh
door-steps without a sense of reverence.

Mrs Gwenda Roberts came to the door and at once proffered an
invitation to take tea. Tea it was in that warm, cosy farmhouse with
gooseberry pie and bread baked locally in the Pandy Tudur shop,
baked by Mr Jarman himself in his own bakehouse, the most welcome
and tasty bread one could find in the world. There was hardly a hint of
enquiry as to what I wanted, so she must have known; I seemed to be
already expected, for there was a telephone in the house and nowhere
do the phone bells ring oftener and more quickly than in these Welsh
villages.

Trevor Roberts was of a standard Welsh moorland type, rufous with
sideburns, the soft northern accent and a laconic manner of
deprecating humour as the conversation really began. Yes, of course I
knew Pandy Tudur village. My wife's cousin's husband had actually
taught Gwenda long ago in his school there. As we chatted, I felt
urgent to tell my story for I knew from the noticeboard below the farm
that Mrs Gwenda Roberts ran a little bed-and-breakfast sideline. To
avoid giving the false impression that I might be such a client, I needed
to drive straight into the point before consuming that gooseberry pie
and the other delicacies that were advancing across the large

farmhouse table, so I told my story much like one would read a book, avoiding the hospitable efforts to distract me into more friendly and sociable conversation.

There was no mistaking the interest I aroused. As I concluded, Trevor Roberts began slowly, 'Well, indeed I do have a cottage and would sell it.'

'Is there a view of Snowdon?'

'Hard to say. Between the trees you might catch a sight on a good day. But the mountains are there.'

'No,' I persisted, 'can you see Snowdon from your cottage?'

'It might not be so,' he hesitated, 'but those mountains, whichever they be, they are there. Yes and the view. It goes on and on till you get to them!'

'Oh,' I compromised, unwilling to dash away his offer. 'I only wanted to be able to see Snowdon through the cottage windows.'

He shrugged his shoulders. 'You can see through the windows very well,' he asserted. 'And the view is beautiful. It goes on and on and goes across the moor, on and on and far away.'

I shook my head. 'Pity,' he reflected. Yes, he had plots of land and would put houses on them for customers. I referred back to Tyn-y-Bryn and asked, 'If I bought a ruin, would you be able to build it up in the old style, with old materials just as it had been in the old days long ago?'

'With old materials? Second-hand?' His face lit up with interest. 'I can do that,' he declared, 'and I have the materials. Anything I have not by me, I can find it up.'

'So if I bought a site you could put back any damage – walls, roof and such?'

He nodded, but I cut his dreamy meditation short as he was continuing, 'It goes on and on, that view over the moor and over the heather.'

I had to thank Mrs Roberts for her marvellous pastry. I had to beg apologies for my intrusion. I must go and look for a farmhouse ruin on a site that would look to Snowdon. Renewing my thanks as I left them, I heard Mrs Roberts remark, 'Some day we will go to London.' Just that remark told of the far away isolation of those farms and struck reality into a casual fact mentioned as she had passed the scones. She had never been. No, she had never left Pandy Tudur, not in all her life.

I drove through the village and up the ridge that takes another parallel to overlook the Conwy Valley. Almost on the top, I noticed a cottage completely enmeshed in overgrown hedges and a tangled struggle of briar and bramble. Half ashamed, it peeped out, an empty deserted cottage, but roofed, with chimney standing, and windows, and a front door that was closed. To my astonishment there was a notice in the hedge – one of Bob Parry's For Sale notices!

Creeping through the gap remaining beside the door, I crashed through thorn tendrils and gooseberry bushes to the far side. Yes, the condition was met! Above the fields, in a line with Pandy village below, stretched a panorama of mountains: the Carneddau ranges and perhaps not Snowdon itself but the beginnings of Y Wyddfa Fawr, surely. Maybe I might forgo the capture of the peak itself as an impossible dream. Let me accept this magnificent mountain panorama that would frame the sunsets all through the changing seasons.

Now I hardly glanced at the interior. Swallows galore nested there. A bat flew below the breaking ceilings. I had faith in Trevor Roberts. Walls, windows, slates, the materials were there and waiting. Maybe the cottage was close, very close to the road, but no one, in my ignorance, could I ever imagine using that road. How fortunate that the For Sale board was out of sight. Even the hedge had overgrown it.

'There's another cottage down through the trees opposite,' suggested my wife.

It was starting to rain, fierce, heavy rain. Nevertheless I crossed and took some steps down what had once been a track but was now gone back to the wildwood. Nettles, brambles and a medley of brushwood flourished under a networked avenue of branches. The obliterated track was no more than a long pond of mud that tapered beyond the bend into an even worse chaos of undergrowth, revealing no sign of man's presence for scores of years. The track was impassable. Down came the rain and I turned back, intent on reaching Bob Parry Ltd and buying that cottage.

They were surprised to see me and also to hear the challenging accusation in my voice when I told them of the For Sale cottage which they had refrained from offering to me.

'Ah, Bryn Castell,' they said, without interest, without any apology nor sign of guilty responsibility. 'That is sold.'

'Sold? Then why is your notice still displayed in the hedge?'

'Really! Oh well, it is a long way up there. Who would have thought anyone would have seen it! But it is sold.'

I felt a doubt. No, they could not tell me who had bought it, that was against their policy.

'Well then', I persisted, 'let me know the price it fetched.'

'£5,600,' came the hesitating reply.

Could they let me have the purchaser's name? I would go higher. Such was not their method of business, however. They had no instructions from the purchasers. Tendering like that could be unwise for both parties. Yes, they had my name and address and could write to me. What could be done? Their faces plainly showed they were thwarting me, but at the time I did not know they were acting in my interest in doing so. Only long afterwards did I hear that several planning applications had been refused, the property had changed hands and how appeals had been rejected.

Gradually those words of Trevor Roberts – 'I have a cottage!' – took significance. – 'The view it goes on and on, and the mountains, they are there!' In some telepathic way the unexpectant, falling intonation of his voice caught hold of my imagination. Out of his words I built up a dream more powerful than his because unfettered by reality. Next week I telephoned him from Essex and tentatively enquired about his cottage and how much was the asking price.

'£2,000,' he replied, uncertainly.

'That's about right,' I agreed. 'Of course, I had better see it first.'

He became evasive. This would not do. I needed to have a surveyor's report before deciding. He explained exactly where the cottage was and promised to post the report to me. He thought I had better be sure I wanted the place. The mountains were there and the views went on and on, but the cottage needed 'doing up'.

No surveyor's report arrived but within three winter days my wife and I were motoring to Pandy Tudur where we arrived soon after three o'clock and made straight to see that cottage. Following his precise directions, to my amazement I found myself arrived at the beginning of that very track from which I had already turned back, giving up hope of penetrating its nettlebeds and brambles. Then it had been raining. This evening the very heavens had been let loose, pools had gathered and went on flooding everywhere as the ceaseless mountain deluge poured down, stripping the leaves and red rowan berries from the wild avenue under which we had to pass. Undeterred, we plunged through boggy mud and brushed aside the thistles and briars through a good part of half a mile of track. All had reverted to the wildwood, but there at last stood the ruin in its deserted loneliness.

I prowled around whilst my wife, exhausted, leaned against a post and appraised that scene. I caught a momentary glimpse as she waited, poised there, and saw her glance expressing in spite of the drenching rain, 'Yes, this is the site I want. This would be good for us!'

And I realized, in spite of the surrounding tumble-down dereliction, she thought well.

The ruined farmhouse had been an old Welsh longhouse of one storey, the living-rooms extended and joined the cattle stalls; these had been abandoned though the old contemporary windows of the middle rooms were still intact with original glazing bars actually containing old glass. In front of the farmhouse, as if mocking the primitive construction of the ancient building, stood a small nineteenth-century barn with good modern slates, a door and a window. It stood primly there in good order and made the long passage between house and barn appear like a little village street.

The cottage had two chimneys, both upright with good square corners. The main, central one topped the massive fireplace that was arched with its ponderous trunk of an oak tree resting upon the wall of the massive fireplace, above and athwart the hearth. The smaller chimney peered discreetly above the little bakehouse (*pobdy* is the local term) at the elevated western and beside the dairy. The heavy, antique slates were falling. The plaster on the walls crumbled away from the layers of local shale of which they were composed. The heavy rounded boulders, however, showed the building's firmer base. Smooth, shaped and massive, they lay in limbo there with curving outlines that smiled when the rain ran across them as if they remembered some grander time.

Rubbish had accumulated to rot there. Trees were invading and marching upon the walls where a vanguard of ferns and mossy grasses had taken possession. All this was no matter, a trifle compared to the danger of the water that was there with its terrible destructive power, whether winter or summer. With one wrong step I found myself knee-deep in loose mud. The cottage had become a sponge set on a muddy island. I understood how that approach track was a stream in disguise, bringing the brooks of the far mountain road to disgorge in squelchy plenty before spreading upon the surrounding meadows.

I braced myself against recognizing this menace. Did I not come from Essex where, from medieval times and even before, farmhouses have survived below high tide level on the wet marshes. A dyke, a drain, even a moat such as saved them can present an attractive charm if made a decorative feature.

My wife brushed away my enthusiasm for old stones and ancient windows. 'Let's get the site,' she urged. 'Once we own the site, we can build, or put down a caravan, or you can make a log cabin, if you like. Only let us acquire the site!'

Without doubt, since she came of a centuries-old Denbigh family, she sensed the deep tribal roots belonging to those indigenous to these parts, a *hiraeth** too powerful for even poets to express.

* *hiraeth* – yearning for homeland

4   Purchase ... 'In the Dock?'

Back we went, with the dark of a November night now upon us, to meet Trevor Roberts, who had just come in from the fields. In the farmhouse kitchen he showed me the surveyor's report, a copy of which he had actually placed in the post for me. He insisted I read it carefully before I made up my mind. I brushed his concern aside. I was the buyer, so I knew best. Nothing I could read on the closely typed report told me anything to make me consider changing my decision. I knew electricity and water supplies were close at hand. With my own eyes clearly enough I had seen 'all in need of extensive repairs'. The approach track was 350 yards long and not the surveyor's 100 yards, but this delighted me rather than the reverse. The calm, written persuasion of the surveyor, delicately touching on 'planning difficulties', was palpable, and so was 'the one condition', that the previous owner, Trevor Roberts, should be 'instructed to institute repair works/services. In this connection,' the report continued, 'I would prepare an estimate for the work involved, incorporating Bills of Quantities and using unit rates from a current Builder's Price Book. Incidentally, a plan of the existing building is available, if required.'

All this I gladly accepted, for I knew he had the reputation of being a hard-working farmer-builder. I would be glad to rely on him. Who else did I know in those parts, indeed? He was surprised at my decisiveness. Arrangements were made to meet in Llanrwst's Ancaster Square the very next morning. I mentioned my solicitor, W.J.I. Owen, which surprised Trevor Roberts for he dealt with Alwyn Jones, the junior partner in the same firm and suggested that I also deal through him. However, having been in contact with Mr Owen, I could not agree to dispense with him and thought it wiser that we kept to our own solicitors.

Next morning a bitter, wet wind was blowing in Ancaster Square. I can almost feel that November chill across the years, a damp cold from the north-west wind with flecks of sleet in the rain. Trevor Roberts was already standing there waiting, though it was I that was early. Stout farmer as he was, he kept rubbing his hands together and blowing to warm them. He was concerned. He had hoped to bring Ken Phillips, his surveyor, to tell me about Planning and the Council, but he had not turned up. We walked to and fro while we both became even colder. The name Ken Phillips continued falling on my frozen ears until I could hear it no longer and insisted on proceeding straight to Mr Owen's offices. Upstairs they were, on the first floor of the corner house, superintending, as an old-established family solicitor's premises should, the whole of that central Ancaster Square. The rooms were warm, not to say stuffy, with all that sleety cold from the Square battened out. The secretary ushered us to seats in the waiting-room but we had only to wait there for a moment, for I claimed contact with the solicitor by virtue of previous correspondence and was ushered straight into Mr Owen's sanctum.

There he stood, a grey-haired wiry Welshman. Behind him from floor to ceiling rose in red moroccan leather the magnificence of volume after volume of out of date legality in beautiful bindings that would have done credit to any bencher's or even ducal library, and certainly could be marshalled to overwhelm any litigious farmer of thereabouts.

He listened courteously and stroked one of his cheeks thoughtfully before beginning his speech from the authoritative seat behind his desk. He knew Ty'n-y-Llidiart. It was one of those abandoned farmhouses from which the land had been sold away. The Council were not willing to have such rebuilt and planning permission would be difficult to obtain, though he would reluctantly make an effort.

I told him planning permission was not required. All I wanted him to do was to convey the property to me there and then, forthwith. He sat bolt upright at this.

'It is not as easy as that,' he advised. 'These planning matters and policies are bound up with the Council. The old Hiraethog Council was extinguished. The papers and all relevant matters have by this time gone to the Colwyn Bay Borough.'

Planning permission was absolutely necessary, he insisted, but if Ty'n y Llidiart was that place above Pandy Tudur, it would never be given. That cottage was the sort that could be bought when he was young for the price of a pig. He would not see me lose my money. He must advise that I first obtain planning permission.

'I have a builder,' I explained. 'We will only repair the property.

Just arrange for me to become the owner. The vendor is here. I can pay him now.'

Mr Owen, W.J.I. Owen, senior partner of David Thomas, Owen & Co. Solicitors, felt his legal expertise was being brushed aside by an ignoramus. He rose from his desk with an accusing finger uplifted.

'Mr Johnson!' he exclaimed, 'I am going to see you in the Dock! If you talk like this, that is where you will find yourself. In the Dock! And there will be no end to the expense you will have! You will finish up with money to pay, with a worthless property, and yourself,' he paused to take breath for the significance of his final phrase, 'in the Dock!'

All the red moroccan leather tomes frowned assent from the solidity of their shelves when into the silence came Mr Alwyn Jones, the junior partner. Briskly he introduced himself as Mr Trevor Jones's solicitor.

'I have warned Mr Johnson not to purchase,' asserted Mr Owen. 'Nobody could have warned him plainer.'

The frozen smile did not lift from his partner's lips, but he looked at me doubtfully.

'I wish to have this little farmhouse conveyed to myself,' I persisted. Mr Owen sniffed and shifted papers. 'I have the cash. All I want is the site. Please convey it.'

'He intends to build,' alleged Mr Owen. 'I have warned him.'

'Very well. After all, Mr Roberts is my client and he had asked me to act for him. Would you like me to act on your behalf also?'

'No,' I replied. 'Mr Owen has advised me and I have every confidence in him. I only require to be made the owner of the place known as Ty'n-y-Llidiart, if Mr Owen would act for me.'

I heard the older partner push away the papers on his desk in astonishment. 'Very well,' he said, gruffly, 'attend to it please Mr Jones!'

Somehow or other he seemed to disappear from the scene while Mr Jones led me into his own office. Trevor Roberts was sitting there, looking rather puzzled and sheepish.

Alwyn Jones was a short, bustling man whose smile seemed to unfreeze as he became more energetic. Papers were produced, questions asked.

'Mr Ivor Owen has explained everything to you about this?' he asked, formally enough.

'He tells me planning permission is a difficult matter.'

'Ah, yes,' purred Alwyn Jones. 'Planning permission. Well, I think we have in Mr Trevor Roberts here an expert in dealing with that.

There's not much he does not know in avoiding planning permission. What do you say to that, Mr Roberts?'

'Not for me to say, indeed. I have a very good surveyor, you know.'

'Quite so, quite so.' And now came the crucial question, the significance of which I was too naïve, too frozen, too eager and optimistic to understand. If the old-fashioned word 'condemned' had been used, I would have realized the latent danger more.

'Is there a Closing Order on this house, Mr Roberts?'

'Hard to say,' came the reply. 'It used to belong to Gwilym Jones before you conveyed it to me. Then ...'

'Quite so, quite so. I will make the necessary arrangements so that Mr Johnson is acquainted.'

'I want to buy this property here and now,' I demanded, 'and I wish to pay the customary ten per cent of the purchase price for arranging a Contract of purchase. Let me write the cheque now, please.'

It seemed as if these folk were trying to stop me getting possession of this ruin. Why? Was there oil underneath? Or a gold-mine somewhere?

Alwyn Jones reluctantly took me back to Ivor Owen, where the form was signed, but my cheque was refused. Ivor Owen did not want to take it and once again grumbled off-handedly. Alwyn Jones stood diffidently in the background referring apologetically to 'my client'. Hands were shaken and I came away.

Trevor Roberts muttered to himself as we came back into the cold square. 'We must meet Ken Phillips, my surveyor. He would explain. Ivor Owen did not understand.' But Ken Phillips was not in evidence and could be found nowhere, not in the cafes nor in the newspaper shop. I could not stand about waiting for him. A long ride to London was before me on that cold November day. So I took my farewell there and then, reminding Trevor Roberts that he had sold me the cottage in the presence of those solicitors. A sale was a sale. Ken Phillips could start drawing up his contract specifying repairs and entirely renovating *my* cottage. And he could start at once. And he must do no more than put it back as it appeared in the seventeenth century.

So elated was I that I stopped to telephone my wife's cousin's husband. It proved a long conversation in which he begged me to call and see him at Rhyl on my way home.

I arrived at midday to a welcome and hospitality, but as the lunch was served, so was gloom. Trevor Jones, alarmed at my precipitation, had jumped straight from the telephone and gone to the Colwyn Bay

Council Offices to enquire about the planning status of Ty'n-y-Llidiart. After all, he had lived all his life in Clwyd and knew almost everyone, yes indeed, practically everybody. As for the clerks in the Council Departments, had he not been to school with them? They knew all about Ty'n-y-Llidiart and –

'He can't buy it!' declared Mr A. promptly.

'He has bought it,' asserted Trevor Jones.

'He can't. He has to have a solicitor.'

'He has got a solicitor. Ivor Owen, Llanrwst, and he *has* bought it!'

'This is all wrong. Ivor Owen has not done his stuff. He should have stopped him.'

Mr A. took Trevor Jones to Mr B. Both planning and health departments were consulted. The melancholy history of that cottage was disclosed. Previous planning applications had been rejected. Appeals had been rejected. There had been a site meeting on the spot – definitely rejected. In the old days of the Hiraethog Council – also rejected. 'The building is damp, the site waterlogged.' As for my idea of a ditch round the place, both the clerks insisted that, were that to be done, as the walls dried out they would crumble and the whole building would collapse.

Poor Trevor Jones, my relative! As he told me the baleful news, his face grew longer and longer. He could hardly eat his lunch. He went to fetch papers from his overcoat pocket.

'I could have stopped you,' he groaned, 'but you didn't ask me. Now there's only one thing to do.'

He produced a bundle of forms. 'Fill these in, to be completed in triplicate,' he recommended. 'Get planning permission! They both insisted you must do this.'

'Did they tell you I would get planning permission when so many have been refused?'

'Ah, no,' came the doleful reply, 'but you've got to do it before you can start building. It is all that is left to do. They insisted I had the forms.'

I looked at the printed papers with their lines, blank spaces and regulations. They were anathema to me.

'I'm not having anything to do with this,' I maintained, while expressing appreciation for his solicitude on my behalf. 'The cottage is mine. The Council have not bought it, nor repaired it as they could have done. So that is what I shall do!'

I detected a meaningful glance between my cousins, but under the force of this authoritative statement they both fell silent. My wife swiftly rescued the conversation from its problematical impasse. A pleasant lunch, a laugh or two, and I was driving back via the Horseshoe Pass and Llangollen, perhaps a more thoughtful if not a wiser man.

Faithfully Ivor Owen proceeded to carry out the searches and other work for conveying the property to me, not without further dire rumblings of legal disaster. Indeed, on 21 December he wrote offering me the opportunity to retract from the whole transaction, as he forwarded the Contract. He had found that 'An application by Mr Trevor Roberts in February 1973 for extensions and improvements to existing cottage and construction of septic tank had been refused because the proposals would result in the creation of a new dwelling in an isolated upland part of the county and would conflict with the policy of the local planning authority.' He gave his final warning in no uncertain terms:

'I must at this stage warn you that in my view you will never obtain planning permission to make the house capable of habitation. If you occupy the property without such work being carried out, then you are breaking the undertaking and will render yourself open to prosecution. You will understand therefore that in my view the investment of £2,000 in the purchase of this property is a wasted exercise and you will never be able to recoup your money. The expenditure of any further money in fighting through the courts for the amendment of the present legal position will in my view be wasted and you will not be able to sell the property for anything like what you have given for it. It is my duty to say all this.'

Though I was going to proceed diametrically against his advice, I felt grateful to him for giving it.

I did not intend to apply for Planning Permission, so I could not be refused! As for the 'undertaking', when the Closing Order was imposed it was because the house was considered unfit for human habitation, and the 'undertaking' given was that the house should not be occupied until rendered fit in every respect. Very well then. I would comply with the 'undertaking'. The house should be restored with the best conservation methods and the Council be required to withdraw their Closing Order.

I decided so to arrange with the vendor-builder, Trevor Roberts, and agreed that his surveyor Ken Phillips, could draw up a contract for repairs accordingly. Completion was settled, and payments were made.

When eventually I went to collect the little parcel of deeds from the solicitor, he was just as unpromising. I imagined I could detect the sentiment 'You'll be back' as I explained the law to him – something I now realize is about as unallowable as a patient explaining a diagnosis to his doctor.

'Yes, yes, I know all this, of course I know all this,' he remarked. 'They can't stop you repairing it, nor spending your money as you like. But they can stop you living in it. You'll see! That Closing Order is the thing. They'll stop you, you'll see!'

But I had my bundle of deeds. I was the owner of a Welsh property on the edge of Snowdonia. I would be there! And the mountains were there! And Spring was on the way. And the views, they were going on and on!

5 *Acrimonious Correspondence. Enforcement?*

The contract specifying the priced work in detail to be done by Trevor Roberts as builder on the orders of Stowers Johnson as employer duly arrived, neatly typed and set out in some legal phraseology. As I accepted it, posting it off to Ken Phillips, I realized I was making myself responsible for an outlay of £5,012.40, 'subject to employer's variations'. I suspected these would come to a great deal more, and so actually they did for I was to find eventually that the total 'adjusted value of contract (on completion)' had raced up to £6,669.28 plus an extra £20 for erecting a new gate to the track.

'The essence of the work is to RESTORE and in no way to introduce alien constructional or finishing features into the cottage, which is a typical Welsh "long-house".'

Ken Phillips had also inserted the proviso: 'No work to any section herein is to proceed UNTIL ordered by the Employer.'

I guessed from this that he doubted whether the project would ever come to fruition, but for myself I had no hesitation and arranged for a site meeting at once. Upon a frosty morning in early spring we plunged around, stumbling here and there among rubbish and waste building debris. By now I knew a great deal more about Closing Orders and kept insisting that the purpose of that contract must be 'to render the cottage fit for human habitation in every respect'.

Seth Roberts, the Colwyn Borough Environmental Health Officer was good enough to come out to the site to discuss the matter with us. Once again the old bogey of Planning Permission came up. This was a matter involving a different department from his own and he assured me that Planning Permission was essential before his department could deal with the matter, so he was glad I had the necessary forms.

Point-blank I asked him, 'If one made application, would permission be granted?' He hedged carefully – it was not his affair. 'No, no,' I cajoled, 'Tell me now. Do you know of any similar cases of

Planning Permission being granted?'

'No, I do not.'

'Tell me then. If I fill in these forms, do you think I shall get permission?'

'No, I am sure you will not. But I must stress, it is not for me to say.'

'Well?' I asked, as we watched Seth Roberts drive away. 'How far have we got?'

'Hard to say,' Trevor Roberts replied, as usual, but Ken Phillips was more definite, 'We have arrived precisely nowhere,' he declared gloomily.

'It makes no difference,' I urged. 'I have signed all your documents and I will pay accordingly. Go ahead. We do no more than repairs, but please do not linger. Do them fast!'

Back in Trevor Roberts's farmhouse, the surveyor expanded and gave me his plans that had been rejected. I did not examine them there and then, but when I spread them out in my study at home, I gasped in amazement. Here was ambition! No wonder Ken Phillips had given them to me, as an artist might show a friend a work of genius rejected by all the academies.

Here barn and farmhouse vanished, and on a level, stone-flagged site a single storey dwelling arose that projected over and commanded the landscape from all its windows. Beside walls in natural stone beautiful pillared columns arose, patios fringed rose gardens, modern porches and verandahs protected all from the weather. One could look over the paper spectacle and breathe the architect's delight. Each interior was arranged in most sumptuous style. Gracie Fields herself on Capri could have wished for no better!

But those two, Trevor Roberts and Ken Phillips, plotting and planning to bring luxury into the native Welsh fastnesses, had found no millionaires to gratify. The stern unanimity of the Planning Committee had turned them down absolutely and on appeal the gathered councillors on the site, looking from the ruined cottage, from the homely farms on the surrounding hillsides to the architectural grandeur so splendidly displayed on paper, had detected the print of the developer, the first step to wipe a new town across that beautiful landscape. They had turned it down. And in that I entirely agreed with them.

Ambition, however, still nudged at the elbow of Ken Phillips. 'You are the new owner,' he tempted me from time to time. 'You can make a new start, a little at a time; you just might pull it off.'

A day or two later more planning forms arrived from Colwyn Borough Council and also a telephone call from the cousins at Rhyl telling me I had not completed the forms, nor despatched them to the Council. I realized they were worried foreseeing disaster and disappointment. Trevor Jones had seen the planning officer, Derek Bentley.

'Impossible!' he had declared. 'He can't build there. It would be tantamount to a new building.'

'But he wants to live in Pandy Tudur. How can he if you don't give permission?'

'Let him get somewhere that is lived in! Where people are living! Then he takes over and applies for planning alterations, even possibly an improvement grant.'

My pleasant cottage, dating from the seventeenth century, that had suffered from the current policy of amalgamating small farms into larger units, an economic device resulting in depopulation of the British countryside, a farmhouse that had survived through famine and the vicissitudes of the centuries, was going to be allowed to crumble back into the earth unnoticed? Not now it belonged to me!

Once again I got in touch with Trevor Roberts, by telephone this time, to urge progress. He had a team of men working, now the site had been levelled and was clear. I asked him to cut down surrounding sycamore trees that hid much of the landscape. They do not provide for bird life. The Royal Society for Protection of Birds does not favour them. I telephoned again. Down they had come, such is the speed of the chain-saw. The branches had been burned, the logs stored in the barn. The dry weather of that early Spring had set in, making conditions for building excellent.

My next call to urge progress met with an entirely different response. It had been early March and one fine day when all the men were working at taking down and restoring the roof, Derek Bentley had come into the country from the Colwyn Bay Planning Office and arrived at the cottage. I was told he had forbidden Trevor Roberts and the men to continue and, according to Trevor Roberts, 'ran round like a wild bull'. He took photographs. He insisted a dwelling-house was being constructed that had no connection with agricultural purposes Such was not allowed by the Council. They must stop work at once! The builders were assisting in breaking the law. The team of young workmen Trevor Roberts had engaged looked and listened in bewilderment while he raged. Maybe the owner had told them to do the work! That was not good enough. The owner must be prosecuted!

The anxiety in Trevor Roberts's voice was apparent. He had noticed that Mr Derek Bentley, not content with photographing my cottage, had gone to Bryn Castell, the little ruined place opposite the entrance to my lane and photographed that as well.

'Go on working,' I urged. 'You have a contract. I will pay you. Mr Bentley will not.'

Much like a general seeing his army halted, about to disperse and scuttle in defeat, I arranged to travel to North Wales at once to rally my forces. Before I left the following letter arrived on official Borough of Colwyn paper, signed by H.D. Bentley as Planning Officer.
Dear Sir,

Ty'n Llidiart, Gwytherin

I visited Ty'n Llidiart Gwytherin yesterday and found that re-roofing this derelict structure had been begun. No application for planning permission nor for approval under the Building Regulations had been made.

Would you please let me know the extent of the works which are proposed to be carried out and the purpose for which the building is proposed to be used.

Yours faithfully,
signed.

I regarded the planning officer's object in preserving the existing charm and character of the North Wales countryside with complete approval for no one could agree with this more than myself. A sympathetic and full letter of explanation seemed called for despite what Trevor Roberts had told me, and I tried to throw in some humour in my last sentence, as I replied:

Ty'n-y-Llidiart, Gwytherin. Conservation.

Thank you for your letter of the 1st March, which arrived this morning. There has been considerable and unsolicited correspondence from your Borough under the heading of Application for Improvement Grant (Mr Barchi) as a result of which I travelled from London and met the Director of Housing on the site. I had not applied for an improvement grant but these letter headings were tantamount to an invitation to do so. I should have been most pleased to have met you personally at the same time.

I bought this property having been excited by the discovery that it is a good example of the smaller Welsh 'long-house' as described by Dr Iorwerth Peate, according to whom none now survive in Denbighshire. It is apparently also *the only example now existing within the Borough of Colwyn*, owing its survival intact to the

Closing Order put upon it in 1958.

The actual house is seventeenth century, with eighteenth century portions rebuilt before the time of the 'crogloft' alterations. There are also indications of a Roman occupation of the site. My research on these two aspects I have forwarded to the Inspector of the Historic Buildings Division for the Welsh Office for consideration at their next survey, and I also sent copies and photographs to Mr. J. Seth Roberts for the Borough Records and you should be able to see them from him.

I should greatly appreciate your interest in this matter, and particularly the help of your specialist inspector for historic buildings. It is only recently and due to Dr Peate that public interest has been stirred to realize that smaller peasant architecture has its own historical significance. Unfortunately it has almost all vanished!

... It is not proposed to alter the plans of this building in any way, nor to extend its area at all.

Ridiculous twentieth-century 'modernization' e.g. the green match-boarded ceilings that hid the timbers, and the thin new slates on the brew-house, have already been removed. These incongruous slates are being replaced by genuine antique examples.

Damage caused by storm and neglect is being made good; in particular, the roofing you mention is being treated by woodworm and rot preservative so that the old natural timbers are saved. It is anticipated that the expenses of conservation will amount to £5,000.

Old ironwork is being taken out of store, and it is hoped to furnish in true Welsh 18th century style.

The building will be used for the purpose for which it was originally built, and so has always been used. It is situated, with main services — water and electricity — on the site between Pandy Tudur and Gwytherin, being approximately a mile from either, and was the last residence of the Village Postman. It is significant that it has now also become the property of a 'man of letters', as such I can claim to be.

[Signed.]

My letter elicited no sympathy, however, but seemed to advance the matter to a further threat of disaster. Perhaps I had been unwise to use the planning officer's favourite word 'tantamount', at any rate his reply was severe and commanding. He wrote back, using the correct spelling of the property this time:

'Ty'n-y-Llidiart' is derelict, and the works required to make it habitable would be tantamount to the erection of a new dwelling. They therefore require planning permission.

I must therefore advise you not to carry out any rebuilding work without the permission of the Local Planning Authority.

I would point out that on 18 April, 1973 Denbighshire County Council refused planning permission for extensions and improvements to 'Ty'n-y-Llidiart' for the following reason: —

The proposal would result in the creation of a new dwelling is an isolated upland part of the County, and would conflict with the policy of the Local Planning Authority to secure that, except in very special circumstances, new residential development should be located within existing settlements, in order to foster the growth of such settlements, to facilitate the economic provision of necessary services and to protect the attractive characteristics of the area generally.

I propose to report on the matter to Colwyn Council in order that they may consider whether to serve an Enforcement Notice. You are entitled to make an application for permission to carry out the rebuilding works.

I enclose application forms and a leaflet setting out the Council's policy in relation to new dwellings in the countryside.

[Signed.]

The irony of it all was that I was thoroughly in agreement with these sentiments and policies. I shuffled the enclosed sample of planning permission forms. Among them was the copy of that tell-tale application from Trevor Roberts and Ken Phillips to build a Lutyens-style porticoed bungalow. Did Mr Bentley's office think I was about to spring this surprise upon them? And this shower of planning forms! If I used them and applied, I knew they would be rejected. My stance was that I was merely repairing the property to comply with the 'Undertaking' given under the terms of the Closing Order.

Of course the farmhouse itself and the land adjoining had been 'part of an agricultural holding' (Part 2 of the Certificate under Section 27, Town and County Planning Act 1971) I possessed three beehives and for thirty years have been a beekeeper, but to claim exemption under this head, the institution of an apiary, was too devious even for my enthusiasm. I hoped it would not come to that!

I answered the letter in full, and said plainly enough, having gone to the law booksellers by Lincoln's Inn and purchased all the latest publications on the subject:

I should state that I do not intend to erect a new dwelling, nor to alter the building's appearance, nor extend its area at all, nor to carry out any 'development' on the site.

I have taken legal advice and therefore do not consider the work I am undertaking requires planning permission nor will it be tantamount to the erection of a new dwelling. You refer to an Application on 18 April 1973, when Denbighshire County Council refused planning permission for 'extensions and improvements'. I must disassociate myself from this. I was not then the owner and did not even know of the building! I have no intention of making extensions nor any such twentieth-century modernizations as in that application which is the opposite of my aims.

In both your letters you employ the term *'derelict'* as if you imply abandonment of use. I would point out that it has been held that where a property has remained vacant because of compliance with a closing order, i.e., cessation of use for residential purposes in conformity with an undertaking given-to the Housing Authority, it does not amount abandonment – (1950) JPL 843; SPA XI/23 – and further, the very planning application you quote is evidence of intention, the property having been put to no other use!

Though Ty'n-y-Llidiart has been allowed to fall into some disrepair, it is not a 'derelict' building. It is a beautiful example of Welsh peasant architecture, perfect in functional simplicity and in splendid harmony with its landscape, where, shouldering away from the western gales, it has withstood the centuries.

[Signed.]

Alas, this considered reply of mine was only fuel to the fire, threatening to become a conflagration to consume both the cottage and my pocket in its flames. The Council's officials did not care about history or peasant architecture. Administration was everything: the old Welsh life and culture was something apart from them and, beyond lip service to the Welsh verbal language, they hardly knew it. To squeeze out the mountain farms, to settle the independent Welshmen as labourers or poor artisans in council houses and provide slick services, this was modernization. If the people knew the Welsh words and the Hebrew religion, what more could they want? Sport? They could collect together and shout at matches. Television? The women could watch that, and the Chapel would close the week, and indeed life itself for that matter.

I recalled how, as a lad fishing beside the Teifi River bridge at Tregaron, before that great bog was drained, at dusk one could hear from every hillside the clatter of ponies' hoofs as the farming lads and lasses rode down to make visits, and on Sundays there was the shine of black bowler hats on the mountain bridle paths as the mounted farmers set out for their distant chapels. Today a way of life has gone from the Welsh mountains which not all the power of television would bring back.

When one reads Dostoevsky one is often shown the overmastering of personality by the dominant motive which seizes possession and actually captures the human spirit itself. So it was with me. The fuel I had thrown upon the Planning Office in the Technical Services Department of Colwyn Council flared up enraged. I received such a declaration of war as was within their power to compose. Acknowledging my last letter, Mr H.D. Bentley declared himself irreconcilable as he wrote:

> The mortar and stonework of Ty'n-y-Llidiart have perished. In taking off the roof the end gables have become unstable and the eastern gable has actually parted from the lateral walls. Parts of the lateral walls have collapsed.
>
> In my opinion the building has reached such a ruinous condition due to neglect of its fabric that it has become derelict – (i.e. its use as a dwelling has been abandoned) and the works required to make it habitable would be tantamount to the erection of a new dwelling.
>
> In your letter of 4 March you stated that your intention is to use the building for the purpose for which it was originally built and I presume therefore that you are carrying out building operations to form a dwelling.
>
> If the opinion I have expressed is correct, such works require planning permission.
>
> I propose to report on the matter to a meeting of Colwyn Borough Council's Planning Committee on 30 March, and to recommend that action be taken under Section 87 of the Town and Country Planning Act 1971.

I had to answer this as well as might be, but despite my self-confidence through my obsession with being absolutely in the right, I sensed facing me the cold nonchalance of the Administration, that brisk brushing away of papers into the limbo of officialdom which cares not and cannot be moved. So nevertheless I replied, after thanking him for his letter:

> I must refer to my previous letters and reiterate that I am certainly not *'forming a dwelling'*. The dwelling is already there and has been on that habitation site for centuries.
>
> The new assertions in your opening paragraphs are contentious

and show no regard for the structural methods of native Welsh peasant architecture as illustrated in Peate's *Welsh House,* and in the more recent *Houses of the Welsh Countryside, Royal Commission 1975* pages 72-82, Chap V, and the government policy therein expressed, pages 328-331.

Where you assert, 'parts of the lateral walls have collapsed', can only refer to spaces where windows have been taken out for timber and glazing repairs, leaving temporary gaps, and any recent storm damage on the eastern side has been repaired using original materials. This should be clear from the three whole-plate photographs I enclosed in my previous correspondence with the Director of Housing, photographs which were taken of February 10.

I feel I should remind you that I have in my previous letter appealed for the help and advice of your specialist in historic buildings, but this has been ignored. He should not be left out. ... Once again, and in conclusion, I can only express absolute confidence in the legal advice I have received in this instance, and therefore must take the view that planning permission is not needed.

[Signed.]

I felt a peculiar sense of frustration. All these letters, in repetition of the one motive, to repair an interesting building representing the social history of these uplands.

Notwithstanding, beyond and above all these there was the Welsh Office, charged with the duty of caring for the heartland and the life and culture of Wales.

I would appeal to them.

6 *The Welsh Office. 'Spot Listing'*

Trevor Roberts had now ceased work towards completion of the contract. Yes, he had stopped in dismay. Ken Phillips, as surveyor, sent in his bill for all the work of planning and estimating repairs. I realized they both sensed disaster in store for me. Trevor Roberts had sold me that ruin, obviously a white elephant for him. He had no wish to see me lose more money. They were both sure I would back away from the whole affair.

Once again I travelled to meet them both on the site and urge them on. I was particularly anxious to make sure all the woodwork was heavily treated with the prescribed chemicals against woodworm and decay. Any rotten timbers would have to come out. Worm-eaten wood must have adequate defence against the dreaded beetles.

What a sight met my eyes when I stepped inside the old building! The chimney had been exposed as a massive piece of stonework going right through the roof. An athletic lad could clamber up inside to sweep it. The great oaken tree-trunk was now bare where it poised across the chimney arch, hewn probably in the beginning out of the tree growing on that very spot and lain across the stone pillars to make the chimney breast. All the green match-boarding had been stripped entirely away, exposing roof supports leaning from the walls in an ancient box construction. They met above along the roof-tree, warped as it was and the reverse of straight. All this I determined must be left visible. The previous dwellers, anxious for warmth and comfort, had covered everything with painted boarding and civilized wall-paper, making a pseudo-loft below the roof – anything and everything to keep out the cold and to make a Victorian home, sweet home.

It took my breath away, this spectacle of the old building now truly revealed, even to the mysterious alcove for placing a lantern in the end room where once the cow stalls stood. I imagined the women milking by rush light there, while the steam and breath of the cattle pervaded and warmed that far side of the house away from the great fire. I was the owner now! The dwelling was as old as I had hoped, seventeenth century perhaps, eighteenth century at least, and judging from the boulders that protruded here and there at ground level, based upon a much older structure.

'It is very good of you to take all this trouble to carry out my wishes,' I exclaimed in a burst of pleasure in recognizing this primitive roof construction.

Trevor Roberts and Ken Phillips looked at each other significantly.

'It's all right with me,' remarked the former. 'I can't lose. It's your property and your money. But you've got the Enforcement coming.'

Enforcement! If the Council backed their officers and passed that, the work would have to stop. Moreover, in the extreme of extremes, they could arrange from demolition of the work done and attempt to charge me for the exercise.

'Do you really want me to go ahead?' Trevor Roberts asked again, sadly and thoughtfully, as in his pleasant farmhouse we ate his wife's delightful pastry. Already he had lost time by deciding to wait for my reassurance.

To show him I was absolutely in earnest, I made a substantial payment as instalment on that contract. He accepted this, but in a fretful and sad gesture.

'Well, it is your money,' he repeated. 'I myself, I can't lose, can I?'

Back in London, I telephoned the Welsh Office and my tale drifted on from department to department in a long trunk call until an authoritative, urgent voice closed the conversation at last:

'In cases such as this may be, where a building possesses particular interest, intrinsic or historic, we have a system. If you can show it is under threat, we can spot-list it pending investigation.'

The speaker accepted the particulars and I undertook to set out in full and substantiate the claim of Ty'n-y-Llidiart to take its place among the significant buildings of Britain.

I now collected as many Ordnance Survey maps as referred to the district and borrowed from libraries all the relevant books I could so that I might set to work to rebuild in the mind's eye some kind of picture of the vanished history of that site. Ty'n-y-Llidiart means 'The House in the Gateway', but Gateway to what?

At first I pushed aside the more antique speculations and confined my energies to considering the building's present interest as an outstanding survival of an old-time peasant dwelling. Two books continued to fascinate me: first, Iorwerth C. Peate's treatise, *The*

*Welsh House** which I read over and over again, and which did lead me to realize that my little farmhouse might possibly not be the only one in the Colwyn Borough, for as the peasants prospered they built their newer farms in modern style while here and there the longhouse survived as an extenuated line of byre and barn adjacent to the 'new house' (*Ty Newydd* in Welsh). The second was Peter Smith's *Houses of the Welsh Countryside, a Study in Historical Geography,*† which I came to later when I was feeling more of an expert from the study of Iorwerth Peate's work. I found it a delightful treatise, full of interesting items that one would never otherwise come upon, especially the details of the conscripted castle builders taken from all over England, carpenters, stonemasons etc, snatched from homes in the Midlands and East Anglia to build those Norman castles in Wales.

As I researched, I came to realize how my little piece of the Welsh world had been left out of the records. It stood on the hilltop between the parishes of Llangernyw, Gwytherin and Llandewi (Pandy Tudur). The boundary of Gwytherin passed alongside Ty'n-y-Llidiart beside the great rocks in my lane. Hiraethog District boundary was just outside, so was the boundary of Llanrwst Rural. As far as parishes were concerned, the farmhouse, standing 965 feet above sea-level was in a kind of No Man's Land! Small wonder everything there had been passed over and left out of records. The old antiquarians, when collecting their material, likewise the Ministry officials, would go to the parish priest, the minister and the schoolmaster for records, memories and other information. My little place, however, was outside them all and so had been ignored.

With renewed energy engendered by hope as well as interest, I read on and on to make my case, seeking a niche in history for my ruin and 'derelict' building. I tried to convey some enthusiasm to Trevor Roberts, but my words fell on deaf ears. Llwyndu Uchaf, actually his wife's farmhouse, was old, historic and listed. I knew he had little regard for my one storey ruin as a symbol of Welsh social history.

I had been led on to speculate beyond the realities of peasant architecture. The high stone-banked fields, earth-ramparted, the mysterious complementary curves of the lanes leading to both Tan-y-castell and Ty'n-y-Llidiart, the double well in Cae Delyn (the Harp Field), the earth banks in the marsh below the stream flowing out of the spring, seemed to signal from a time when men were more

* The Brython Press, Liverpool 1944
† HMSO, 1974

active than just watchers of sheep. There was also the mysterious grotto with its fountain guarded by two massive standing stones far below Cae Delyn. The four right-angled crossroads outside Cefn Castell and the Roman straight roads that stretched from them, linking with the ancient road that went from Conovium to the lost city of Varis, all emphasized Roman influence; such a hilltop as was surmounted by the three remaining buildings – Bryn Castell, Cefn Castell and Ty'n-y-Llidiart, would be of military significance. Moreover, supposing the Roman camp has been superseded by a Welsh castell, the hordes of Anglo-Normans who arrived to build their castles around Snowdonia would be quick to demolish every palisade and cart away useful stones, leaving scant traces discernible today.

So I had presented my plea for historical recognition of both the site and building of Ty'n-y-Llidiart, a speculation interesting as it is more especially to those who know the local topography, not to say the humour of argumentative archaeology.

7   *Council Meeting. Decision*

How would the Welsh Office respond? Time would tell, but time was not on my side. The Council was to meet very soon – next week, in fact. The Enforcement Order would cause Trevor Roberts to stop work; the restoration, exposed to the weather, would deteriorate as everything was held up until an Appeal was heard, and even then a hostile hearing could go against me.

I grumbled to my wife's cousin Bessie.

'Well,' she advised, 'if it's the Council, you should go to a Councillor and you have a good one in your district. He is famous for helping the cause of Welsh culture. All the Eisteddfodau know of him. You tell John Hughes about it. He is on the Council as representative for Llangernyw and he is bound to be at the meeting. He is your Councillor.'

I telephoned to John Hughes. My voice went all the way to Wales and seemed to be beating the air there as I explained all the troublesome details.

'You send me the correspondence and I will read and examine it carefully. Send me the whole story,' he recommended.

'But there are pages and pages of it.'

'Never mind,' he urged. 'Send it all.'

'Please understand,' I explained. 'I have been employed in official business myself, so I know the way things are pushed through. This will come up as the last item on the agenda. Some official will say, as the meeting is about to finish and papers are being gathered: "One moment, if you please. The ruined cottage in Pandy Tudur is being built up into a modern dwelling in defiance of a Closing Order and rejection of the Council's decision on planning, where an Appeal has also been rejected. The Council cannot be flouted like this! Enforcement Order is needed. All agreed?" And the item will be passed as everyone is leaving the meeting. If I send you the details, will you please ask for the full correspondence to be read.'

'I will consider that point when I have read your letter,' John Hughes replied cautiously.

That day was Friday. I typed and typed to copy all the material but next morning when I had finished the only post had gone from Shenfield. I drove to the Brentwood main post office where I noticed that the front post box had been emptied at 12.30 pm. There was a drive-in to the rear by the side road where, at a window, a button could be pressed for enquiries. Mail from the surrounding districts was coming in by the wide doorway there. I asked if my letter could be accepted, desperately explaining how urgent it was.

'We'll see,' replied the attendant rather grudgingly.

I held my breath. The Colwyn Council meeting was on 30 March, next mid-week! That letter with slowly typed details seemed the most important I had ever composed. Suddenly I heard shouting. A tall, red-bearded man came down the post office sorting hall, like an actor commanding his stage.

'Put your letter through the front letter-box!' he ordered. 'We are not taking anything here!'

'But that postbox has been emptied.'

'Of course it has! You are too late.' There was a menace in his voice. 'We're not having people stealing in from the back.'

'This is a most important letter due to arrive before a meeting which begins next week. Please, it is vital! It needs to go today!'

'Post it at the front!'

'If I put it into that box, will you empty it, please, to catch today's post?'

'No, I won't! You are too late. You've missed the post.'

As he spoke, a postman from a rural mailvan wheeled his basket containing collected letters towards me in order to go up to the sorting benches. I flicked my foolscap envelope into his basket and was about to turn away, but that overseer, superintendent or whatever he was in command had seen the gesture. He ran forward and snatched my letter from the basket, slamming it on the ledge at my side.

'No you don't,' he bellowed. 'I said you are too late. Nothing goes now. It's the front box. Take it back and go away!'

I looked at him. A stranger he was, with his red beard and bullying voice – certainly a 'foreigner' to this town of Brentwood. My breath halted with rage. Here in my home town, I had begged a favour to have it thrown back in my teeth.

The letter I now held in my hand must go. If I had to catch a train to North Wales, it must reach John Hughes and reach him to allow time for reading before that meeting. First I would try to catch a post in London but on the way made a forlorn decision to call at the main Romford postal collecting centre. Parking my car, I showed the precious letter to a postman coming from the entrance.

'That's alright,' he said, as I told my story. 'Come along. I'll show you where to post it.' In two minutes we had crossed the yard, he had taken my letter and had handed it in! 'Yes, it would definitely go, and that very day!' His face expressed bewildered surprise at the effusion of my thanks. It seemed to me he had wrought a miracle.

John Hughes used often, in the anglicized sphere of Colwyn Borough, to be referred to as their 'mountain man'. He actually received my letter and telephoned to acknowledge the notes I sent, though he would hold out little hope. There was so much material.

Two days later he telephoned again. It had happened just as I had forecast. When that meeting was practically over, almost as people were leaving, at the end of the agenda, casually introduced, an Enforcement Order was asked for against my cottage, against building works begun without permission – an Enforcement Order being routine to which as a formality all should agree. John Hughes, arguing against protests, had insisted that the relative correspondence should be read. It was interesting, he declared; it would acquaint members with historical details. He had copies of it in his own hands. The official concerned had balefully to comply and read on and on. The meeting continued, prolonged till long after accustomed time till, when everyone was desperately anxious to depart, a unanimous vote was taken to reject the imposition of the Enforcement Order!

An enterprising journalist, Tony McIntyre, telephoned me from the *North Wales Weekly News* offices to get the story and ask permission to reproduce the photographs he had obtained from John Hughes. I was astonished, on 22 February 1978, to find the activity recorded, spreading across the page under the heading: 'How one man proved the planners wrong. The kiss of life for a country ruin.' I found myself quoted as saying: 'A ruthless planning policy that tries to extinguish buildings such as this and to press Welsh people out from their hillsides into the towns can blot out history and Welsh culture for ever, eliminating the spirit of Wales.'

On 6 April 1978 a more formal report appeared in the same newspaper, with Councillor John Hughes quoted as stoutly declaring: 'He is just repairing his own property and, if a gentleman can't repair his own property, then I would ask this Committee – "In what kind of a country do we live?" '

The Committee Vice-Chairman was reported as commenting: 'The reason this has come up like this is because it is the first time that somebody has decided to go ahead, without planning permission, and do up a derelict property – and I say more good luck to them.'

All this publicity did give me some concern, for it could appear that I was just trailing my coat in defiance of the Council's planning purposes, whereas of course I was heartily in sympathy with any effort to preserve a beautiful countryside by preventing developers sprinkling it with modern dwellings. Enough damage is already being done by alien and prefabricated farm buildings over which, as agricultural items, there is little or no control.

On 28 March the last threat had come from the Planning Officer. 'I have noted your representation about the historic interest of Ty'n Llidiart ([*sic*] for *Ty'n-y-Llidiart*). The conclusion I have reached is that the works required to establish the place as a dwelling will leave very little of the original structure.'

Now, on 4 April, from the same office, came the finality, the name of the property also misspelt in defiance of Welsh language tradition: '*re Ty'n Lidiard Gwytherin*. Further to our correspondence regarding the above. Colwyn Council's Planning Committee at their Meeting on 30 March 1978 reached the conclusion that the work you have carried out did not require planning permission.'

Nevertheless, there was in the newspaper report of 6 April 1978 a significant final paragraph obviously inspired by some official in the Council Offices: 'Although Mr Stowers Johnson has been given the all-clear to carry on with his work, Colwyn's building inspectors will be watching to see that no building regulations are broken.' There was still a Closing Order on the cottage, so I had constantly in mind the warning of the Llanrwst solicitor when he asserted, 'Ah, yes, you may be able to restore it. But they won't let you live in it! That's how they can stop you.'

8   Example of the 'Welsh Vernacular'. Listed Grade II

Parallel with this battle to resist Enforcement and its threat of costs and demolition, I was maintaining a correspondence with the Welsh Office. Of course the stimulus to Trevor Roberts and his little team when they found they were not engaged in a wild-goose chase was tremendous. Trevor Roberts had cleared the mass of slate and debris from the *pobdy* or brewhouse at the western end. As he described the result to me, it appeared an ancient oven had been discovered. Mr Phillips, our surveyor, gave a description which appeared to coincide with the oven described in Bezant Lowe's book on this very district. In *The Heart of Northern Wales* was written*

> Striking survivals of this ancient method were in existence in the hill farms of Western Denbighshire less than a century ago. As an illustration may be taken the house known as Gallt'Refail (now in ruins), about two miles south of Llanrwst, on the upper road leading to Nebo. Under the fireplace was a circular hole, about two feet in diameter and 18 inches deep. Peat was placed in this and lighted, and, after the sides of the cavity had become red hot, the ashes were raked out, and the dough was put in; this was covered with the ashes and left till it was baked.
> [Mr G.A. Humphreys saw this done in a cottage near Llyn Dulyn not 25 years ago.]
> Very frequently a peat fire was kindled in the grate at the same time, and on this was placed a 'crochan' (a three-legged iron pot), in which meat was put. This was covered with a sheet of iron, and on that more meat was put. Another example was in actual use at a farm near Nebo less than 40 years ago.

* *The Heart of Northern Wales*, W. Bezant Lowe, MA, FCS, published, W.E. Owen, Llanfairfechan, 1912

Intrigued by all this, I made the journey to North Wales to investigate the discovery. I found there was no 'ash-hole' below the floor but, in a dimension of eighteen inches square, a tunnel at floor level went under the altar-shaped stone platform from which, two feet above, a flue would take away the smoke if a fire were laid upon it. If a fire were placed within the tunnel, there was no outlet, but of course hot roasting stones could be taken from the fire above and placed in the tunnel for baking bread. The altar-like platform could also take a support for bellows to work a forge. Possibly all three purposes were once operative until in the last century the *pobdy* became a mere brewhouse for boiling cattle and pig food. Such fierce and constant use would account for the little place being re-roofed and re-slated in the nineteenth century.

When I visited St Fagans Folk Museum, I saw a reconstructed blacksmith's forge like this actually working – in reconstruction of course. But when I sent a description of the Ty'n-y-Llidiart oven to the keeper in charge of buildings there, he deprecated the item as not unusual in the last century, yet, apart from stating that gorse was used for firing he could not say how the strange altar platform with its blind tunnel was actually used and as museum folk tend to do, brushed the matter aside.

As for Trevor Roberts and his friends from Nebo, none could explain, nor could they remember anything similar. I resisted the temptation Trevor Roberts presented to me. I would not clear it away, nor make it into a kitchen annexe nor cloakroom, but kept it as it was and cherished my speculations.

I had noticed, when viewing the deserted Tan-y-Castell across the hill, an outside oven built beehive shaped so that the oven door opened into a small outbuilding, a bakehouse obviously arranged so that bread could be made and the furnace stoked in dry conditions. The vaulting was crumbling then and by now I fear it will have perished altogether.

And then, surprise, surprise. One fine sunny June day I went on the Denbigh Historical Society's visit to the excavation of the Roman site at Meliden Avenue, Prestatyn. Students and supervisors had been busy with an extensive dig to reveal this outlying station of the XIII Legion. The Society's bluff and genial secretary, W.C. Wynne-Woodhouse, conducted the party where pottery and objects displaying the Legion's wild boar emblem were on exhibition to be explained by the lecturer: but there in that exhibition tent were diagrams explaining the 'Roman Oven', an arrangement identical with that I had preserved in my own *pobdy*! On the oven platform, carefully drawn, were shown thick pottery vessels as used for baking bread, as well as other culinary operations. Now I had an explanation for the quantity of thick, broken earthenware dug up at Ty'n-y-Llidiart. Alas, I had thrown these bits and pieces away, only keeping one or two specimens, more as examples of peasant ware.

Perhaps Ieuan Jones, organizer of Pandy Tudur's literary activities made the most sensible assessment when he commented recently: 'The old people, after all, carried on practising what had been learned over the centuries without having to be taught or told. It would be just a custom for them.' I stare at my one or two blocks of earthenware sadly now, wishing I had not thrown the others away as rubbish. I might have tried to build up a more complete model, of peasant if not Roman usage.

At last the Welsh Office investigator, Miss Olwen M. Jenkins, made an appointment to inspect Ty'n-y-Llidiart and I arranged for Trevor Roberts to show her the building. She took photographs and made drawings. She wrote her notes in great detail to the wonderment of Trevor Roberts who reported that she even made drawings of the mysterious circular iron we thought had been used in the *pobdy* for use in a forge.

I had already received encouraging acknowledgements from the Welsh Office experts and also a letter telling me that urgent spot-listing of the property had been initiated, but it was not until 13 October 1978 that the building was actually listed, signed by B.H. Evans, Assistant Secretary of the Welsh Office, as a 'Building of Special Architectural or Historic Interest Ty'n-y-Llidiart Gwytherin. Grade II.' Attached to the formal notification was the following descriptive note:

Late C18 to early C19 cottage with later addition at each end. One storey. Stone rubble walls with plaster cladding; slate gabled roof with chimney and plaster cladding and brick capping at South-west end.

Cottage nucleus with central planked door with repaired sash window with glazing bars each side. Inside, fireplace with massive wood bressummer at South-west end; pegged roof timbers of roughly trimmed branches, some recently (1977-78) replaced.

Later chamber to South-west in domestic use (1978). Two casement windows with small panes have been inserted in front wall. At South-west end, service room, with chimney, and with front wall set back, retains C19 hearth. Addition at North-east end with two casement windows, with small panes inserted in front wall in 1977-78.

A cottage with roof timber of the 'archaic' type mentioned in P. Smith, 'Houses of the Welsh Country Side'. Included as an example of the C18-C19 single storey Welsh vernacular cottage-style.

The more ancient history speculations of my own were not of consequence to this report, nor did it mention the ancient rocks, but the last paragraph epitomizes all I had thought about the little farmhouse from the beginning. It could now hold up its head with the national buildings of the district, making all my continual letter writing worthwhile. Everything was significant now. I took out the little parcel of Deeds and read them. Their possession was to be the open sesame to years of discovery.

9 *The Deeds Tell their Story*

There was the Conveyance of Ty'n-y-Llidiart *in fee simple* from Trevor Roberts to myself and then of course from Annie Jones of Cefn Castell, Pandy Tudur, on 13 January 1973, for £1,800 to Trevor Roberts, 'builder and Contractor'. Then there was a record of mortgage transactions from 1927 up to 1967 indicative of the terrible difficulties under which the small Welsh farmers laboured; a bundle of Official Search Certificates showing the property's small financial usefulness had been bandied about through employed and unemployed folk all over the Midlands of England, through banks, financiers and moneylenders in some desperation to raise money and hold off debtors.

And there, as Part 4 of the Land Charges Register, was the grim note of the 'Undertaking' that was the critical 'Closing Order'.

Undertaking dated 12 December 1958 that Ty'n-y-Llidiart, Gwytherin, will not be used for human habitation until such time as it has been rendered fit for the purpose and the Council cancel the undertaking.

So, ever since 12 December 1958, the old house had been forsaken, deserted, waiting for someone to come along and make it habitable again!

There was the record also of how Mr T. Roberts and Mr Kenneth R. Phillips had come forward with those grandiose proposals for 'Extensions and improvements to existing cottage and construction of septic tank'! Against this was set out the definite reasons for rejection which must have dashed Trevor Roberts's hopes and convinced him his investment of £1,800 was doomed:

That permission be REFUSED for the Reason specified hereunder:
The proposal would result in the creation of a new dwelling in an upland part of the County, and would conflict with the Policy of

the Local Planning Authority to secure that, except in very special circumstances, new residential development should be located within existing settlements, in order to foster the growth of such settlements, to facilitate the economic provision of necessary services and to protect the attractive characteristics of the area generally.

There it was, but under the prosy and benevolent wording lay the flaws which neither Trevor Roberts nor his surveyor had operated, probably because mere conservation would not give the profit anticipated in their magnificent plan.

I had imagined that the deeds would trace back some extraordinary history towards medieval times instead of showing pathetic efforts to raise money on the security of the property, efforts designed probably only to buy more cattle and sheep in order to raise some profit and buy food after paying the interest on the mortgages. The big farms, Plas Mattw and Ty'n-y-Ddol on either side of the Cleddau river in the valley below, each had taken some financial interest at different times, but it was from Annie Jones, the mother of my neighbour Gwilym Jones who now farmed the adjacent Cefn Castell, that Trevor Jones had bought the property in 1973.

Looking back to the earlier records, Maggie Jones of Tyndol, Llangernyw, sold the little farm to John Hughes of Plas Mattw in fee simple for £190 on 4 May 1927, the property being described as:

All that farm called or known as Tyn Llidiart in the parish of Gwytherin in the County of Denbigh containing by estimation $7\frac{1}{2}$ acres or thereabouts together with the farmhouse and buildings standing thereon and formerly in the occupation of one Robert Parry and then of David Davies which sd farm formerly consisted of several encroachments on the common wastes of the Crown's Lordships of Denbigh numbered respectively 178 179 180 and 1030 on the plan of the said Lordship remaining in the office of the Commissioners of Her late Majesty's Woods and Forests and therein stated to contain in the aggregate 4 acres 1 rood 22 or therabs. only exempt all mines and minerals are reserved to the Crown in the several Conveyances of the sd parcels of land by the said Commissioners of Woods and Forests.

This jargon would appear to assert that the farmhouse existed by someone coming in and building on the 'common wastes' of the Crown Lordships, a highly improbable surmise in view of indications

that the site had always been inhabited and my own recent
discoveries. Such a description, however, was recited for every
subsequent probate or conveyance of the property and on went the
little farmstead being mortgaged and also willed to and fro along with
a piano and an oak chest, until, with the price having risen to £425, it
passed on 5 December 1958 to Annie Jones, widow, of Cefn Castell,
the adjacent farm where her son dwells today.

As I went through the documents, I congratulated myself I had
gone to a good Welsh solicitor who had thoroughly searched the title
and incorporated all the records on official documents attached to the
Deeds. So many local families seemed to have had a finger in this pie
that it would be dreadful if any impecunious descendant could come
forward and demand a slice. The larger field of Ty'n-y-Llidiart had
been parcelled away, some to Cefn Castell, the rest to Tyddyn Uchaf,
but almost an acre of land remained, as well as the wide lane, banked
and hedged, some 350 yards of it, leading between those fields right up
to the farmhouse from the road.

As I fold the Deeds and the detailed documents back into their
red-ribboned envelope, I cannot forbear thinking how romantic are the
stories told of Welsh peasants sneaking up to some location and
between sun-up and sundown or vice versa erecting a dwelling to
claim entitlement. Sheepwalks, moors and farmhouses are closely
watched by potential inheritors, each farmstead stands detached on its
rare site that provides water and shelter where it can crouch away
from the terrible winds, and this was so especially in the earlier times
when there were far more peasants on the hills.

I was beginning to understand something of the truth about the
contemporary Welsh social structure in contrast to the myths that are
reiterated over the years. Feudal survivals exist in memories only. The
big houses are there, in an architecture outliving the society that
created them, devoid of any far-flung authority. The Wynnes of
Llanrwst Gwydir have gone as repressive landlords, the more
benevolent Lloyds and Sandbachs have gone from Llangernyw; only
the Wynne Finch family has remained at Voelas on the far edge of the
moors. Though folk still talk of the Sandbach Estate, the mansion of
Hafodunas continues to change hands and stands empty and deserted,
its gardens reverting to the wildwood.

There were no English gentry hereabouts who held down the Welsh
in serfdom and lived on proceeds of rentals extorted from London.
When the weather changed and the crops failed, famine and
agricultural disasters struck nineteenth-century peasants just as hard

Ty'n-y-Llidiart before restoration, 1977

Builder and surveyor in the snow, making estimates

The former occupants, Ebenezer and Margaret Davies, and their daughter Mair

The famous Pandy Choir in 1930. Second from the left in the back row stands John Morris of Bryn Castell, tailor and renowned tenor. He was also the Clerk to the Parish Council

From the old tailor's notebook

Ty'n-y-Llidiart when discovered in 1977

The building team: John Davies, Trevor Roberts and Ken Phillips

Ty'n-y-Llidiart restored, 1978

Hearth and chimney piece with the massive bressummer

The ancient 'Knights' Causeway' past the cottage and down to the river

Gwydir, the burnt-out mansion, photographed by the Author in
1946

The Mayor of Aberconwy making his address at the re-opening of
Gwydir

Llanrwst, the old town hall, now demolished. Photograph by the Author

here as in Ireland but in Wales there was the chapel to explain such climatic changes as the work of the Almighty rather than the oppression of Westminster.

Those Title Deeds are a record of personal endurance rather than of national oppression, for shown there in mortgage and debt and legal action scattered from the County Courts of Bristol, Cardiff, Wolverhampton and Walsall to the High Court of Justice itself, claims and suits from moneylenders, banks and large farmers had battered against my little property of Ty'n-y-Llidiart from season to season. Money had been raised on it and repaid by the tight screw of the Law with the little peasants actually losing possession which had gone to the larger Welsh farmers.

On the occasion when I had been camping high above Pandy Tudur, I had stood on the top field with my friend the farmer and he had pointed out the panorama of farms stretching as far as the moors. He graded them by their size and wealth. I realized then how the size of the farm and its prosperity determined the respect of the community for each individual. Only in culture as expressed in poetry, singing or music could poverty be levelled in the majesty of appreciation that equates rich and poor alike.

As I tied the ribbon around the Deeds, my heart went out to those precursors of mine with their hard struggle on the tiny farm through the penurious winters of life in that cottage. I expect through it all they paid their dues to the chapel and kept a good suit of clothes for Sundays. I would like to have known them and hoped perhaps chance would bring some closer knowledge, acquaintance, even.

10   *The Closing Order*

Soon my euphoria of possession was to give way to a very real anxiety. I now had the problem of making sure that my builder's contract was carried out in such a way as to make the house 'fit in every respect for human habitation'. I emphasized this to Trevor Roberts, who reckoned the main difficulty was the great slabs of slate comprising the flooring. These had been laid in the old time upon a base of earth – not that this mattered then, for probably there would have been a changeable layer of straw, broom or sweet herbs covering them. Trevor Roberts insisted the Council's Health Department would never pass such a floor as damp-proof as he recommended concrete, sealed and laid on a plastic envelope.

I agreed but wanted the great slabs replaced above this. Unfortunately as they were shifted they had a tendency to break and would never fit, so this idea had to be abandoned. I felt sorry for him and his lads as they slaved to raise all that weight of stone to make it into a retaining wall instead, barrow-loading and stone walling.

I invited Mr Seth Roberts once again to visit from his Department of Environmental Health. Letters passed, but he did not come. I sought advice, but nobody from the Council came. I repeated more impersonal invitations to the Department of Environmental Health with no response. Of course they realized I had thwarthed another department. They were not going to be involved, certainly not to be implicated in a suspicion of co-operating in my venture. Moreover, I now suffered from that blight which shrivels Local Authority officials. I had had publicity in a big way. It was dangerous to have anything to do with such an enterprise in case that publicity should gyrate into unforeseen directions.

The Environmental Health Officer had formally eschewed any suspicion of giving encouragement to me by writing on 29 November 1977: 'I would therefore advise you that before you undertake any further work on your proposal for this property, you obtain the necessary planning permission from the Planning Department, Pentre Mawr, Abergele, and on receipt of same I will be willing to discuss with you the work necessary to revoke the Closing Order.' Of course, there could be no 'receipt of same'!

According to the latest modern treatises on Closing Orders, Ty'n-y-Llidiart would have to be made perfect 'with all mod. cons.'. Then, surely, bureaucratic indifference would melt, but if it did not and I had expert assurance to prove the habitable state of the building, I would have to bring the Colwyn Borough officials before a judge on the determination of the Closing Order to show cause why it should not be revoked. This would be troublesome, as in such matters it is not just a matter of a favourable legal decision but one of recovering costs. I therefore kept up a detailed and compliant correspondence to make it evident that if it were so, the Council could be proved overbearing.

Unfortunately the euphoria I had felt when the Welsh Office listed Ty'n-y-Llidiart as Grade II had communicated itself to Trevor Roberts who seemed to regard me as some sort of wizard who could do no wrong. Whenever I went down to see him, I muttered that phrase – 'made habitable in every respect'. This, every time he heard it, Ken Phillips sought to balance with his surveyor's valuation of the restored dwelling, remarking, '£25,000! That's what it is worth now. That's what Trevor Roberts has done for you!'

Such was as might be, for the Closing Order was not lifted. Nevertheless Trevor Roberts went furiously ahead. An articulated lorry came along from somewhere in South Wales, delivering the latest model of septic tank and drainage system, modern bathroom appointments were installed, electricity connected with power points for fires, refrigerator and mains water supplies, television, even an outside light to show the traveller up to the door. It all seemed rather a desecration of the old Long-House, especially considering that alcove in the end room where candles or lantern had been stood when the cows were once milked in the stalls there. But the Closing Order hovered about me, menacing failure!

Suddenly the correspondence from the Council became ominous. A letter came from the Director of Housing and Environmental Health, apologizing that he had not been able to reply sooner as he had been away from the office and stating, 'I must remind you that you will have to deal with the Director of Technical Services and his Building Control Section in regard to drainage, septic tank and other matters. For this purpose I have forwarded a copy of your letter to his department.'

Another department!

Naturally it did not take long before representatives of that department visited the site to find all the necessary work completed, whereupon a tangle of letters ensued threatening the direct consequences because that most appropriate department had not been consulted!

Other visits followed and it was not until 17 June 1978 that I felt confident enough to write and ask for the Closing Order (Hiraethog 1958) to be revoked. On the 29 November under the Housing Act 957 Section 16, the Chief Executive and Town Clerk of the Borough of Colwyn despatched a letter revoking the Closing Order.

At last the slur upon poor old Ty'n-y-Llidiart was removed! It had now been declared 'fit in every respect for human habitation'. No longer 'condemned', humans could legally pass through its front door and live therein.

Meanwhile, on 23 November another letter had come from that same Chief Executive and Town Clerk notifying me (obviously in routine from the Welsh Office) of the promotion of Ty'n-y-Llidiart, Gwytherin, as Grade II on the list of Buildings of Special Architectural or Historic Interest. The irony was that now, if I wished to make any improvement or alteration 'interior or exterior', I would have to seek Listed Building Consent from that same Council Planning Department.

Without delay I resolved to travel down to Gwytherin with equipment for camping. I would go through that front door and live legally within, if only for a few days!

11   *Fire upon the Hearth*

It was raining when we arrived on a dark November night. Trevor Roberts had cut away the brambles, brushwood and rubbish that blocked my lane and found, as he had predicted, the ancient roadway beneath was hard and firm. As I rounded the bend halfway down, a hare ran across my headlights, and then through windows there was the flickering light of a fire lit by Trevor Roberts's 'boys'. I had insisted on the two contemporary sash windows with their small panes being retained; soon, with the current craze for 'picture windows', they may be the only such ones in North Wales. The spasmodic flames sent a dancing light through them across the pathway and over the retaining wall to throw fleeting shadows everywhere. The light came and went with the changing shadows. The way between the long wall of the dwelling and the barn made an alley, dark like a portion of some street in an old town. Smoke poured from the ancient chimney.

I leapt out of my car and stood back to admire it all. Smoke was surely rising from the primeval hearthstone, passing the massive oak bressummer and going up out of the huge chimney through a red chimneypot to declare far and wide across the moorland that fire had come back to this hearth and life to the house!

I opened the door and switched on the light, the electric brightness brought to these walls at so much expense. The cottage interior lit up, dashing back the flickering firelight to bring the old cut tree trunks into stark relief where they leaned to meet at the roof-tree. The stonework around the chimney framed the hearth, and here a stone bench invited as in the seventeenth century. The effect was superb, astonishingly so as I roved within, delighted at how the 'mod cons' unobtrusively invited ease and luxury against the ancient structure. Beyond the outside windows it was pitch dark now but the farms along the valley had switched on their own electric lights that twinkled out brighter than the stars above in a wide panorama of lamplit happiness.

Then we found ourselves coughing, eyes began to smart. Smoke from the stove seemed to be collecting high above. Glancing again at the fireplace so casually described by the builder as antique and from an old farmhouse across the moors, I saw at once it was no more than a nineteenth-century kitchen range with oven attached which had been forced into and built above the old hearth. A wood fire was blazing in the grate from which, alas, fumes not disposed to ascend the open space and go up the chimney wandered about the living-room. Worse than that, sometimes in the very chimney they changed direction and changed their colour also, descended and were filling the whole cottage with blacker smoke. Either opening or shutting the door made no real difference. Enough smoke was rampaging now to cause us to rush outside to relieve smarting eyes and take deep breaths.

The great chimney was cold, full of damp air powerful enough to drive the warmer smoke downwards. No wonder, summer or winter in these hillside farms the fire on the hearth used never to be allowed to go out, an extinct fire being symbolic of tragedy, even of death. That huge old chimney might never agree with me unless we lived with it permanently and kept it warm. I stared at the old kitchen range with dislike. By the height of its grate the wood fire had been raised too close to the oak bressummer, which was now hot, so hot no hand could endure its heat. Smoke began to ooze out of cracks and joints, forcing its way around the entire massive oaken piece, making me fear it would take fire and blaze of its own accord. Whatever the retraction of the Closing Order might imply, the place was no longer 'habitable in every respect'!

Throwing the door wide open, I evacuated that fire with garden tools. Shovel and forks were better than hand-held tongs, so hot were the burning logs. With anything that came to use, I hurled the fire, piece by piece, into the dark of the night outside, where it crackled and spat under the rain, whining away under sparks to mere charcoal. For some time after the fire was gone, that great oak bressummer oozed out smoke which only just changed to steam as I bathed it from a bucket of water. At last, gradually, the air cleared and gave way to the bright electric light until I found myself free to gaze wistfully at the old kitchen range and its extinguished grate.

I like to think that Ty'n-y-Llidiart was at the least a seventeenth-century foundation and thatched no doubt from the rushes in the marshes below, for old thatching pegs had even been found rusting in its walls. No such oven had existed there in the old time. Smoke there had been in that old chimney without a doubt – the big hooks showed where bacon may have been hung from the oak beam – but baking and boiling were tasks done outside in the appropriate places. No, that kitchen range must come out and the hearth revert to my original wishes as expressed in the contract.

Trevor Roberts came upon the scene just as I was throwing the last embers outside. He was crestfallen and thoughtful. 'You can get these problems with the old farms,' he asserted. 'They were used to smoke in the old days. If you are going to have the fire often dying out like when you are away, it is best to brick up the chimney.'

'But I like the great chimney! I like to look up through the stonework and admire its strength.'

He gave me a strange look. He had not thought of that. 'Then the only thing to do is to pipe it,' he advised. 'Pipe it right from the fire to the top so that the smoke will have nowhere else to go. But that will be expensive.'

'Doesn't matter,' I declared most positively. 'I want a fire on the hearth! I want to sit by the original hearthstone like the old Welshmen did hundreds of years ago, with the peat from the hearth and the great chimney spreading its warmth to fill all the length of the long house.'

Together we settled on drawings to accomplish this. The original specification in the contract regarding a fire basket had also yet to be executed. This fire basket should be simple and made of undecorated iron bars. Yes, I insisted, it must be without ornament of any kind, 13 × 18 inches overall and set well back upon the hearthstone. A canopy of iron could be made by the local blacksmith to lead all smoke into the pipe taking it to the chimney top. Trevor Roberts shook his head doubtfully as I showered the details upon him. My wife stared ruefully at the bright electric fire and commented how warm it was; there were electric points everywhere in the house. Nevertheless the object of that exercise was to enjoy the pleasure of an antique hearth straight out of the olden time, and we ought to insist.

Whilst I resumed my work of drawing the canopy to specific measurements, my wife began to protest. The bedroom floors were covered with white dust! The vacuum cleaner picked it out of the cement so that it clogged the machine and filled the container bag. The brush and dustpan could sweep it up by the heap. How was this?

'Nothing at all,' Trevor Roberts consoled us. 'The floors only want sealing. I have yet to do the sealing. Indeed I have. The boys should have done it already, but they were lighting the stove.'

'Sealing floors?' exclaimed my wife incredulously. 'And with us installing all the bedroom furniture! How about our rugs and carpets?'

We made only a very short stay on that occasion. It was just a token visit to declare our right to live there now the Closing Order had been lifted and also of course to inspect the builder's work before making final settlements.

Next time we came in earnest to light a real fire upon our Welsh hearth. The chimney-pot stood straight above the chimney. The pipe had been installed and been duly fastened to the iron canopy below which rested the heavy iron fire basket. The old oven and stove had disappeared, spirited away without a trace remaining. As it was now at the end of November, and still raining, we unloaded more furniture before laying in fuel and putting a match to the grate.

Disaster of disasters! The smoke found easier ways to ascend than by going up through the canopy and into the chimneypipe. The vast chimney space welcomed its volume; smoke gathered there like a cloud and came down again to duck under the bressummer and darken all the beams of the living-room. Wood smoke stings the eyes, coal smoke chokes the lungs. I had been so sure of success I had used both wood and coal. The cottage once again had become uninhabitable and I had to set myself the task of shovelling away the fire and flinging it outside while my wife switched on all the electric fires and began to prepare a hearty meal. Fortunately all the electric gadgets in the kitchen worked. The refrigerator, oven, hot water supply, bathroom and lavatory – all the 'mod cons' were efficient in shiny, twentieth-century luxury.

It was only my obsession with the hearth, the desire to relax in an atmosphere of a bygone world, that had caused this misery. My wife said nothing, but I knew she was bound to realize this; indeed, I had even rejected Trevor Roberts's suggestion to have a cowl upon the chimney-pot. Ken Phillips, as surveyor, playing on my sentiment, had initially pointed out the anomaly of installing electricity in the cottage at all. It was a negation of the historical project, he had remarked, and instanced as witness the special alcove we had left in the end room, 'that receptacle for resting the candle while milking the cows'! Where would I have been as such a purist, with no light, no heat, only smoke.

There was no Trevor Roberts nor Ken Phillips to confront now. The floors were sealed, however, and effectively so. The horrible powdering of the cement had been stabilized. The furniture took its places, conventional, almost reverent. Bright bars of electric fires shone out, the bulb in the convector heater also glowed red, and the dark of night frowned ineffectively outside the little window panes.

After racking my brains on the matter, I came to understand I would have to act independently of my builder if there were to be found any solution to this snag of living with smoke. There were enough old bacon hooks and certainly more iron pegs on the bressummer by which to hang a pig or two, but I guessed the fire on that hearth would have been of glowing peat cut from the bog in the valley or from Denbigh moors, warming and rising heat through summer and winter to spread its gracious aroma through all the family.

How different from this noxious smoke that could hang about for days, acid and repugnant! After taking measurements from the iron canopy *in situ*, next morning I went down to discuss the problem with the blacksmith in the Nebo Road, Llanrwst, since he had supplied the canopy. He did not appear to be at the forge, but one of his sons came forward.

Were the measurements correct? If I required to have a larger spread to come right out beyond the fire, that would be very heavy. An entirely new canopy must be made, which would be most costly and no more likely to work than the present one. It would also be very ugly, like the apron over a factory forge. Could they not use copper? I suggested. But they did not work in this metal. Better have a coppersmith.

I came away concerned and disappointed. In this twentieth century small craftsmen able and willing to work on a specified task are hard to find. They, or their fathers before them, have probably been absorbed by garages as 'fitters' and recognize only vehicular work. Certainly I found no such a craftsman in the Conwy or Colwyn Bay districts. Only on my return to Essex did I succeed in tracking one down who proved as good as his estimate and in due course and prompt to time collected that canopy. Its bright, shining copper had been equipped with bolts and studded so as to be readily fastened on the iron relict below the chimney.

Once again in North Wales, I went to find that Nebo blacksmith. This time he was sitting in his chair, an old man in his late eighties, watching his sons work at the forge. His was a very old smithy, surviving now for agricultural machinery repairs rather than by shoeing the occasional horse. He had been told about my previous visit and had read about my cottage in the newspapers. It was clear his curiosity had been well aroused for he lapsed into reminiscence after reminiscence about the old times, his father's accounts and the history of their ancient smithy. He brought out some books of financial records, detailing old debts and interesting work done by his own grandparents. Somebody came out to say he had done enough talking. He must come indoors for a sleep.

His sons had been impressed with our conversation and as they came forward a date was fixed, for I could now assure them that the job was merely a matter of cutting away some of the old iron canopy and no work involving copper except tightening bolts. When the time came, sure enough they drove up to the cottage with oxyacetylene cylinders and apparatus to plough clean through that iron, after which the holes were drilled and the canopy bolted into place.

Who can imagine my breathless tension as I watched the smoke from the newly lighted fire on that hearth? The fumes rose in the wider canopy but spread down the sides again to be caught in the broad upturned, inward lip. They hovered, but were sent back by the main current of warmer air, up into the chimney-pipe and higher towards the sky above it. I ran outside to look at the red chimney-pot surmounted by its little cage. There was hardly any wind but the steady stream of smoke rose higher and higher.

Returning inside, we watched and waited. A little smoke did come out into the room, just enough to make one's eyes smart. I marked from whence it was emerging. There were tiny chinks in the cementing towards the chimney-pipe joints. Next day I sealed each place with fire-clay, and waited till evening when I lit a roaring fire and basked in the luxury of glowing coal and crackly wood, eyes were clear and there was no urge to cough away smoke.

I was really in residence at last!

12   *Colwyn Memories*

Now I was free of the hurly-burly of doubt and frustration, free to allow the charm of this beautiful land to work upon my spirit. Autumn had drifted into winter slowly, but that scarcely seemed to matter. My house was weather-proof and bureaucracy-proof, I thought. The postman came, driving down my lane to deliver his letter by Land-Rover, surprising me by his matter-of-fact entrance and exit.

I could have offered him refreshments, for his arrival had been a kind of declaration that I was an accepted resident, known to the Postal Service. Alas, his missive turned out to be a communication from the Rating Authority, and it was in earnest. Now I had intruded upon the borough of Colwyn, I must pay rates and contribute towards the upkeep of its services. Though so much energy had been devoted to prevent me being in the position to do this, now they proved ready and emphatic to take my money. Albeit I was on the far fringe of the borough, towards the very edge of the moorland, I had become a resident, an elector, but above all, a ratepayer. As I read the communication, any satisfaction for attaining these qualifications or entitlements vanished. The assessment was too high, incredibly so.

In my immediate letter of protest I demanded a review, declaring my intention of taking the whole matter through courts of appeal. I have always liked Colwyn and had actually the happiest memories of the town where it spreads along the margin of that northern sea between the green mountains and the shore. No matter whether the sea is stormy or silent, one can look over the waves there by the hour without tiring, for the eye travels down the light across the moving water, light that one can watch dancing on and on as far as the distant horizon while random shipping makes its steady way to Liverpool. None better understood the charm of this than David Cox, in whose seascapes called 'Rhyl Sands' one is looking for ever down the changing easy light across the sea.

Hardly will you ever find folk dozing or sleeping along the

promenades of these beaches that look northwards, not just because it is colder, but because the light itself has a waking charm within it. On southern coasts, Sussex for example by Brighton, Hove or Worthing, folk who rest by the shore find the light harsh throughout the day for they are bound to stare hard into it and looking seawards take it back upon themselves, the waves reflecting a steady fatigue from which slumber provides an easy escape. What a contrast this – the sleepy old folk of Hove on the council benches as painted by Sickert, to the donkey land of the North Wales coast beloved of David Cox!

I remember coming to Old Colwyn when I was to stay with my wife's Aunt Peggy in Meiriadog Road. In her lounge on the first floor one could take tea, the very finest Welsh tea I have ever tasted, and look right across the bay, for the house was so placed on the hillside that the curved windows projected and gave a wide maritime vision to the beholder. When a gale began, the white horses rode from wave to wave, from window to window, and the Little Orme spread like a theatre set while in the cold springtime there would be falls of snow gathering on the hills and capping far mountains.

In the quieter days of late summer one could walk by the promenade almost alone till far into the night. On the rarest occasions, at a certain time by the seashore as the crest of each wave paused to take its fall, just before it broke, right along its neck would run that magic phosphorescent gleam, the birth of infinitesimal beings from the microscopic water world, a phosphorescent spreading sparkle that would pause to display its glory and then ran the whole wave along before vanishing in foam. How many ever see this wonder of the bay that is worthy of the tropic nights of Hawaii? Ah, but in Colwyn they are civilized and safe, preferring to lounge comfortably within the trim houses with bright tiles that now go right up and into the Pwllycrochan Woods. Pwllycrochan could be translated as 'the pool by the cauldron'. They don't look for phosphorescent sparkles, nor pools with cauldrons up there today, but in those days Aunt Peggy had a maid whose sparse education had been enriched with a folklore inherited from the bygone centuries of these hills. The Crochan Man seemed to preside over her memories in a fancy brighter than realms of academe. I should have written them down, but in the lazy carelessness of the passing holidays I let them all go by me, though I did years later make one into verses:

Blodwen maid knew more than I
    Of happy things that be.
She'd dance the day's long hours by,

Her broom from sweeping glide and fly,
The laughter light each large dark eye,
    And much she told to me.

Her black hair twisted as she sprang,
    And caught her laughter too.
The 'Orange Girl' all day she sang
Till corners where old cobwebs hang,
The loft and both the chimneys rang
    To song and leaping shoe.

The crochan man at fall of night,
    O she could see him plain,
While I, stare hardest as I might,
Could scarce his flitting shadow sight
Or glimpse red flash of jacket bright
    Beyond the window pane.

When roses down their petals throw
    And days are twice as long,
Across the garden we would go
Before the colder breezes blow,
Before the sun was very low,
    Before the shadows throng.

Blodwen would plant one glassy jar,
    And I would upturn mine
To catch the glint of every star
Just where the taller grasses are.
With petals clear of speck or bar
    We either jar would line.

The largest petals all unfrayed
    The crochan man likes best
From off the uncut rose arrayed.
The fallen petals from the shade
To shine from out the glass we laid
    The crochan man to test.

O, easy for him 'cross the wall
    We'd lay the props to climb;
He might bring treasure for us all
But woe betide if he should fall,
Such height to walk and he so small
    At dark of evening time.

And I have kept these beads a-string
      The little crochan gave;
And Blodwen found a bright, bright ring
Which might be gold, or anything,
That loads of crochan luck would bring
      And life with petals pave.

O, easy for the crochan man
      To cross the wall today;
There is no need for prop to span,
The stones have crumbled where he ran:
But brambles all the roses ban
      And Blodwen's hair is gray!*

Though the house in Meiriadog Road faced the Bay, the road itself led away from the sea and on later summer mornings one could go into the fields beyond the old farmhouse there and find mushrooms in plenty. In those days either no one appeared to know or no one wanted them, most people of the seaside city being not countrywise having come mostly from Lancashire and the Midlands. Photographs taken as late as the end of the nineteenth century show field after field where, rivalling mushrooms, the red-tiled villas were to spring up to receive prosperous exiles from Liverpool or Manchester.

As a child my wife used to go up there to fetch buttermilk from Peulwys Farm. The farm labourers would be having a meal in that kitchen, taking their food not from plates or saucers but from dishes carved into the surface of the huge old table top! Such was labour-saving in those times; with one scrub-down all would be clean with no crockery to wash. I wonder where the massive table is today. Probably it backs some manger or even makes part of a chicken shed. Surely the folk museum of St Fagans would be glad to know.

Some fine August days I used to take rod and line to go across Mynydd Marion to fish the little Dulas river. A short cut once took me across the cliffs to Bryn Dulas where the slopes break into masses of shale. Clumsily going down the incline, I disturbed a family of merlins. Fully grown, the young had just decided to leave home and, being entirely without fear, behaved as if tame, for though well able to fly, they allowed me to pick them off the slates and handle them – to the terror of both parents who flew along the lower slopes, screaming panic and menacing advice. Those slopes were usually completely

* *The Mundane Tree*, Fortune Press, 1947

deserted despite the quarries nearby but whenever I took the same route, often hoping to make another rendezvous with those little pirates in grey, there was no sight of them, nor ever again did I get a glimpse of merlins flying over the slates.

It had been a hot summer that year, and drought had dried the stream almost to a trickle. The trout were hungry and congregated in the larger pools where they could be easily seen by peering over the bramble bushes. Worm fishing with a light fly rod was the only way to take them, and that by creeping upstream and casting under the brambles. The fish, though fat, were really ravenous, so ravenous that when I made a false cast, causing my cluster of wriggling worms to fall a foot away from the water upon dry shingle, a large trout plunged over the pebbles to seize the bait and there and then was hooked upon the dry land. But of course if ever, angler wise, I boast I once caught a trout 'when it came out of the river onto dry land', my tale is greeted with silent doubt rather than congratulation.

It is a fascinating little stream, the Dulas, coming through limestone, possessing all the charm its name implies, but no one bothers with it. Only a week or two before writing these lines, I went down to where it bubbles under the railway through sandbanks, over large and rocky pebbles to join the sea. Here the cold fresh water flows out and haughtily sweeps away the salty marine. There is coastal dereliction around which is annulled only by the strength of the water, and modern bungalows top the little cliffs. Stiff and stark, in a pool made by the larger pebbles, a long-dead salmon lay unnoticed. The attraction of fresh water causes all wandering marine life to check and linger as it moves along the sea-shore.

That day every pleasurable aspect was ruined by the stench of rotting fish carcases. As the tide had receded a green fishing net, tangled with a score of dead dogfish, had been exposed on the beach. A couple of sea anglers and I growled and protested with each other. This should be reported, they declared. A licence was required for laying such nets and traps along the coast, for not only dogfish but trout and salmon could be so taken. What were the Water Authorities and their bailiffs doing? It was certain, they alleged, that people in the bungalows laid the nets and sold the fish. Proof of this accusation I had not, but there below the hilltop bungalows several rows of floating petrol cans supporting nets seemed to vindicate the suspicion, especially as a couple of burly watchers lounged above the slope, gazing out to sea in pseudo-innocence.

The great seaside cities, Colwyn Bay and Rhyl, and the caravan towns by Prestatyn have left this valley of river and limestone alone and quite unpublicized though it was once a little paradise for Marchudd-y-Cynan, one of the fifteen ennobled tribes of North Wales of the time of Roderick the Great. His descendant, the brave Ednyved Ednyoed Vychan lived here at Bryn Fonige. A lofty and precipitous rock of limestone looks towards the sea and contains Cefn-yr-Ogof, one of the most magnificent and spacious natural caverns in Europe. Samuel Lewis, in 1833, excelled himself in his description:

> It has a bold front towards the sea, considerably elevated, and the entrance, which is many feet above the road, is under a lofty arch of comparatively fine proportions, forty-eight feet in height, within a very short distance of which, proceeding inward, rises a tall columnar rock, presenting the appearance of a rudely sculptured massive pillar, which divides the cavern into two compartments: the recess to the left soon terminates, but that to the right spreads into a spacious chamber, thirty feet in height, and extending to an unexplored depth into the interior of the mountain. The sides and roof of this surprising cavern are studded with beautiful pendant stalactites, many feet in length, ranged on each side with an appearance of perfect order, resembling the pipes of an organ, and reflecting the most brilliant diamond-like hues; and the floor is strewed with immense masses of stalagmite, uniformly of a deep orange colour, and of the most grotesque and fanciful forms.[*]

What has happened either to reality or to travellers' enthusiasm over the years? The latest edition of the *Blue Guide* drily remarks: 'Cefn-yr-Ogof (670 ft), ½m. N. of Penycorddyn, has a large, shallow cave.' The current *Ward Lock Guide* baldly says: 'A splendid viewpoint is the summit of Cefn-yr-Ogof, a hill containing (as the name denotes) several caverns'.

The meadows and the mountains seem tranquil enough to have been just as Lloyd H. Bamford Hesketh Esq saw them when, inspired by the dramas of history that had enacted themselves out around this green countryside by these blue seas, in true nineteenth-century fashion he built his own vast ornamental castle, Gwrych, stretching white ramparts above the hillside woods and raising a noble terrace 420 yards in length with a high arch flanked by two embattled towers. He aimed at and achieved one of the largest architectural efforts of this kind in Great Britain with eighteen lofty embattled towers, the

---

[*] Lewis's *Topographical Dictionary of Wales*, 1833

grandest, named after himself, being ninety-three feet high.

Years and years ago I had leaned my bicycle against the clean cut stone walls of the gateway by the roadside, had wiped the summer dust away from my face and read with horror the large statement carved in bold, clear characters. Solemnly it narrated the strength of the armies slain there between those peaceful mountains and the strand, declaring: 'On this spot more blood has been shed than on any other in the Principality.'

Here, in the eleventh century on the level ground between the mountain and the sea before the great cave, Harold met the Prince of North Wales, Grufydd-Ap-Llewelyn, and after the slaughter was driven out and back to Rhuddlan. Later Hugh Lupus marching on behalf of William the Conqueror, hoping to invade Anglesey, was attacked in the narrowest part of the defile by an armed band of Welshmen. Eleven hundred were left dead on the spot. Here also in Henry II's reign Owain Gwynedd, Prince of North Wales, made his stand. Having fortified the pass, he repulsed Henry's force with great slaughter and went off to Pen-y-Parc where he blocked further invasion. Finally, here occurred the celebrated incident where Percy of Northumberland lured Richard II out of Conwy Castle to betray him to be captured and handed over to his foes in this very place by the band of armed men appearing out of the hillside trees.

Today the grass grows greener, holiday traffic speeds along the highway and the bungalow town creeps steadily closer. And as for Gwrych Castle, that should have eternally glorified its rich new builders, a limited company today owns it and draws income from tableaux and spectacles, trading in imitation history, mock battles, jousts and tournaments, a miniature railway, exhibitions, and, of course, that money-spinner among cheap shows, a Chamber of Horrors. The painting and contents now are mostly third rate and copies, so different from those sold off at the comprehensive sale of the Earl of Dundonald in the Twenties.

Nearer Colwyn, quieter and away from all this, unvisited now and almost unchanged for centuries, is Llanelian hamlet at its own crossroads. The churchyard, set with tombstones and harsh walls, makes a small platform above the landscape where it is recorded that from 1666 a beacon was maintained. Out upon a summer walk long ago the dweller in Llan Farm, then known as Hen Siop (the Old Shop), asked me in to have a cup of tea. The thick and heavy thatch spreads over this old house like a massive, dark hood, giving little suggestion of the warmth inside where within those thick walls a glowing fire was burning as brightly as it used when ale would be served through the hatch into what is now the kitchen.

My hosts both shrugged their shoulders at mention of the infamous Cursing Well. Disreputable as it was, it has sunk into oblivion, out of memory altogether. They could point to a tree beside a hollow where it used to be in a field half a mile from the church, though not a stone remains, nor any sign of the spring. Once it was clearly marked and had a stone arch covering, being protected by a square wall seven feet high.

Both Pennant and Baring Gould wrote of it, but the enlightened mood of the nineteenth century soon hardened against such an ancient survival for invoking retribution of wrongs. The clergy united to make sure ceremony and superstition were suppressed, for, of course, both the old well and the yew trees in the churchyard were actual survivals of pre-Christian faith. The rite varied slightly in its efforts to secure results. The petitioner, to obtain his redress by cursing, was obliged to stand upon a particular spot while the owner of the well chanted verses from the sacred scriptures. The latter then provided three cupfuls of water. While drinking these the curser had to throw a portion of each cupful back over his head and utter imprecations against his foe. Sometimes the enemy's name could be entered in a book and the writing of it transfixed with a terrible pin, sometimes an inscribed pebble would be thrown into the well.

No doubt a fee would be charged, but there appears not to be any record of this. Baring Gould gives the date of the extinction of the well as 1829, but the Ancient Monuments Commission asserts that the local custodian survived until 1858. One suspects that some practices co-existed with him for there is evidence that the terror of the well triumphed across North Wales for many years and people travelled long distances to ease their injustices by invoking vengeance.

A stronger motive for erasing these pre-Christian sentiments was perhaps prowling in the background. At the beginning of the last century spa resorts were coming into notice. Tradition told that:

'A passing hermit passing through (? Elian the Pilgrim) fell ill at this spot ... and praying for a drink of water, a copious spring burst forth at his side, and he drank and got well. Whereupon he prayed that the spring might be the medium to grant to all who asked in faith anything that they might wish.'

Pennant indeed had taken note of the more benevolent powers of the well, declaring: 'The well of St Aelian, a parish not far from

Llandrillo in Carnarvonshire, has been in great repute for the cure of all diseases by means of the intercession of the Saint, who was first invoked by earnest prayers in the neighbouring chapel. He was also applied to on less worthy occasions and made the instrument of discovering thieves and of recovering stolen goods.'

So, in the more practical vein of his times, the man most prominent in closing down the heathenish well, the Reverend David Price, with his churchwardens and parishioners, 'ordered consented and agreed that a bathing place be made near Llanelian Well upon the land of John Holland, Esq.' The sum of 4s 6d was spent to advertise the attractions of the bathing place in a Cheshire newspaper, and the man who wrote out the advertisement received one shilling for his effort.

What positive optimism, I reflected, as I came down the steps one rainy day with the wind blowing hard over the hill; and, as for thirst, that hermit must have been passing by in such old times very long ago, when there was no welcome shining out from the windows of the White Lion to cure ailment and melancholy both together.

13 *A Valuation Officer. Ancient Stones*

I reflected with comfort and satisfaction on my own little farmhouse in its shapeless acre of land. The sunshine, the green glory of that mountain landscape was mine for a price that was minute in comparison with others. Such high land values, however, had set the District Valuer on his predatory path. I had appealed against the assessment, objecting to his incredible charges. I read with indignation the replies he had sent. Of course I must pay rates, calculated on something called 'rateable value', but it would be extortion to make me pay out of comparison with other dwellings in the locality.

A young woman had come down to Ty'n-y-Llidiart one very wet morning in March. She had taken out a tape-measure with which she had gone quickly round the exterior of the cottage and barn. She was disinclined to talk or discuss anything, but, the measurements taken, hardly giving me the time of day, off she went with a snap of her notebook!

The Valuation Notice referred to Tyn Llidiart, an urbanized abbreviation of the old Welsh name, the sort of disrespectful thing town dwellers did to these ancient mountain residences. Even more disrespect to Welsh tradition came in the District Valuer's styling of the cottage as a *'bungalow'*, a term which the Oxford Dictionary asserts is derived from 'bangla' = belonging to Bengal, and refers to a 'one-storeyed house, lightly built, with a tile or thatched roof, originating in the East'! However, in financial terms more respect was being shown, for the Gross Value was reckoned at £135, the Rateable Value as £86.

I could not tolerate this charge, not even for a Bengal bungalow, so I protested again on pages of indignation. It seemed the Colwyn Council did not want to argue with me any more, for they wrote immediately to say they had transmitted my appeal to the District Valuation Officer, but I must comment that ever after they have respected the Ancient Welsh name of the farmhouse.

Now it was an anomalous position in which I found myself. I had been extolling the merits of Ty'n-y-Llidiart to Colwyn Council so they could admire the place and lift their Closing Order, but now I had to point out its demerits, using the very description given me by Mr Bentley, their Planning Officer. 'The site is located in an isolated upland area at the end of a long length of unmade track etc, etc.'

On a fine June mid-morning, when that lane was full of leaves, bird-song and blossom, the Valuation Officer arrived to discuss my protest. I ruefully reflected it would have been better if he had come through a snowstorm or at least a drenching gale. At our elevation of 950 feet, the winds from Snowdon would have damped things down. But there he was, D.J. Eccles, in a neat brown suit, efficiently smiling as he shook hands and complimented me on the delightful aspect, charming this and that.

I groaned out a few disconsolations and demerits. I had the valuations of local farms and similar places taken from estate agents advertisements: Codau – rateable value £46, rates payable £26.21; Tan-y-Wal, Llansannan Road – rateable value £57, rates payable £32.48, to name just a couple.

I suggested a nominal £25 in my particular case.

Refused at once!

Mr Eccles, in his curt, official way, pleasantly scoffed at my arguments. Ty'n-y-Llidiart was as good as a new dwelling on the borders of Snowdonia, within reach, indeed, with a choice of the finest seaside resorts in North Wales. Valuation was not what a place was worth on sale but what income the property would produce if let. How ideal, he expounded, the very place for children – no stairs, away from main roads, in beautiful country, with every convenience, hot and cold water, electricity. And a listed building! That had doubled its value. Everyone would want to live in such a place and would pay hundreds weekly in season!

The morning wore on with the pendulum of pro and con. I became obstinate, he became tired, even, I suspected, bored, but certainly not as bored as myself. He reckoned the estimated £86 Rateable Value was generous.

Bit by bit we came down to £74, I agreed. Whereupon he said abruptly, 'Done!' and closed his book.

The abrupt shutting of that book, the brisk utterance, 'Done!', which closed the deal shattered me. Could I have brought him to a lower figure? Had I been the victim of flattery as he had gone on praising Ty'n-y-Llidiart? On the other hand, Trevor Roberts was always talking in the same way, that if I ever decided to let the cottage 'it could be a gold mine'.

I watched the Valuation Officer's car bump away along my lane. Maybe he was right, for property is property; at least the Rateable Value is a considerable guide, a testimony in fact, to its commercial value on the market, but Trevor Roberts was surprised when I told him and whistled, 'That's high! My word, that is high indeed.'

I had no such monetary interest in my farmhouse after that long struggle and only needed to relax and enjoy the surroundings. Those early Spring days gave just time enough to make the environment mellow again after so much building activity, and I had asked the builder to level the site with his heavy machinery. Already hired mechanical diggers had been used to make a slope with draining levels that would take away the winter rainwater. Over the years so much rubbish had been thrown behind the dwelling as to make the rear field appear to come right level with the roof slates, and the whole heap had to be cleared, the debris from hundreds of years.

Now, before Spring could race upon us, I resolved to sow the whole area with grass. I would dig the ground like a garden with fork and spade, make it level and sow by hand. It proved a back-breaking job, for the lower patch had once supported pigstyes and cowsheds on foundations of heavy boulders. These had now been bulldozed into the soil and had to be dug out. Some were huge. The wet earth bound them into the clay. It needed a crowbar even when using the trolley-truck as a lever to lift each out separately. I persevered, arranging them to make an extra wall bolstering earth away for the house. As I manoeuvred them into view, I comforted myself by reflecting how these were evidence of the ancient buildings once here, quarried and shapen stones of the old historic site.

Not all were building stones: bits and pieces of archaeological evidence rose before my fork, fragments of old, thick earthenware I then thought of no importance, along with precious, thin dark red snatches of real samian which I put carefully by. Smooth, round stones came up, like those I had seen on the walls of two local farmhouses.

'What are those?' I had asked.

'Round stones. They are round stones, indeed,' was all the reply I ever had.

But on showing one or two of mine at the Victoria and Albert Museum, South Kensington, for an opinion: 'They are quern stones,' came the decisive reply, 'as used for grinding corn.'

For my mind there were too many of them, and they seemed to have been naturally made by swirling pebble pools in the original slate formations much like pearls in oyster shells. I speculated that they might have been used by the Roman siege catapults when making an assault upon some old semi-wooden native *castell*. Other stones, polished and shiny black were indications of some more domestic use. A fine large axe, chipped and polished appeared to date from more primitive times, coming as it did from the bottom of a deeper ditch. Three pieces of metal intrigued me: a bronze rod with cast and gilded top as if for reins of some chariot, an old eighteenth-century pewter ink-pot, and a pewter cylindrical can, crushed and completely out of shape.

Once again I made the pilgrimage to the V & A Museum on their appointed day and showed the pewter can.

'That is a Roman vessel used as a receptacle for weighing,' I was delighted to be told.

Two large rocks that lie on their sides in the lane are marked both on the Ordnance maps and on the Deeds of Ty'n-y-Llidiart. Perhaps if they were stood erect one would know if anything lay underneath, or maybe an inscription on that hidden side, yet no one to whom I made this suggestion welcomes my invitation to erect them to find out. One smaller stone nearby had peculiar marks running in lines like the runes on ancient stones in Anglesey; this I thought too interesting to be left at large in the lane, and I have locked it away hoping to find some mystic sage who will unweave the magic of such an incised message, or indeed pronounce it as nothing more than arrow sharpenings or duller still tractor grazes!

When the nephews of the farmer who now rented these fields decided to drain, plough and sow the larger meadow opposite, called because of its shape Cae Delyn (Field of the Harp), they found in line with the spring where the well lies, huge blocks of stone that must once have belonged to ancient buildings. Modern earth-moving equipment has little time for these and I found all the sets of boulder foundations dumped on my precious, monumental rocks. I protested and made my sermon of woe as archaeological as possible. The farmer was pleasantly apologetic. I could have the lot of them, every stone. They were not to stay on my land in any case, for he had intended to move them. No, they had found no metal objects on that field except a brass circular sort of tray. Yes, round, quite thick. All brass. I described how very ancient, dirty gold can look like brass. No, they replied, it was not green at all. I explained how old gold has no patina and might scratch like brass. It was probably brass, I suggested, and quoted a few such finds and estimated values. But on the other hand, who knows? The farmer and his two sons said nothing, but their long faces expressed volumes. I saw them talking together as I went away. Suddenly all three hurried off, possibly to make a search for that 'brass tray'.

Next day I came up to the field to see them and was quick to raise the conversation by offering to buy that tray at a good price if they chanced to find it. But no, it could not be found. It had been thrown away. In the dustbin? They could not remember. It must have been an old piece of wagon, old machinery or something like. The discussion seemed to make us all sad, so I left the subject and never raised it again. Before the crop was showing there and on a Sunday when everyone was at chapel, I went over Cae Delyn with a metal-detector and found nothing, nothing at all. The old wells had been obliterated and the field levelled, so deep goes the twentieth-century plough. The snipe, I feared, would not come there now, nor the curlews.

'No, no, no,' said a neighbouring farmer. 'You can't clear a mountain like that. The land takes it own water level and the sown grass will go to rushes as it always does hereabouts and before five years have run away.'

I took the ploughman at his word and accepted that heap of dumped well stones and boulders, trucking them to stand behind the cottage, making a great wall to keep back the field slope from the concrete path there, giving myself assurance I had preserved evidence of earlier buildings and also protected my cottage from damp.

14   *Tyddyn Uchaf – The Valley Farm*

The farm of which Cae Delyn is a part was owned by the brothers
Aneurin and Goronwy Owen. They had written me a most kind and
congratulatory letter when they learned from the newspapers of that
Council meeting and its satisfactory outcome, and, as they came over
the fields in their Land Rover, they would often pause to pass a word
or two on the weather or discuss the sheep their dogs were driving.

Sometimes I would cross their fields and stroll down the lane to take
tea with them in Tyddyn Uchaf. One passes the well which still
supplies their water and then by a square of tumbled boulders, once a
peasant cottage they still call Tyddyn Uchaf Bach, then down
alongside a little pine-wood where the sparrowhawk sometimes flies.
The path becomes an ancient lane so walled in by ramparted banks
that one almost seems walking underground. A steeper descent takes
one over a stream where lies a sheltered hollow that might be an
alcove of fairyland. The streams come out of the meadow here to unite
over pebbles that throw the sunlight back from their glazed and
rippling surfaces. An old ruined quarry hides a little pool and suddenly
reveals the still water reflecting motionless shadows, trees and bushes.
The wind is held back there, and everything thrives in the shelter.

Tyddyn Uchaf farmhouse rests on a small south-facing shelf,
isolated from the weathers and out of this world. Walls protect only a
few yards of flower garden which shines with the brightest colours
planted to illuminate almost every season. The two brothers and both
their sisters lived with splendid old Welsh furniture in their stone-built
house that seemed as old as the hills from which it hid.

I recall Dilys and Nellie Owen marvelling at my enthusiasm for
rocks and stones as they poured the tea. They knew of the rocks on
my land but did not seem to appreciate the two standing rocks in line
with them at the bottom of their own field. Mine were horizontal but
theirs were upstanding; sometimes I had wandered over to see them,
two rounded pillars, half sunk, but still rising four feet above ground,

possibly in a north-to-south line with my two. They stood significantly above a little precipice where below a semicircle of cliff, a spring rose to feed a deserted and overgrown pool. This was more than an ancient abandoned quarry. Surely those pillars marked the holiness of some mysterious rite, magic ceremonies of old time, dance, oblation or sacrifice, all out of memory and unknown.

Neither Dilys nor Nellie seemed to think it any great matter and promised to show me later a rock really worth seeing.

Now, as I remember Gwytherin, should I not more appropriately put down my pen and leave that village to the sheep-walks above its clustered loneliness, never to say anything, never whisper the medieval memories of nuns and recluses? Were it not better to turn away from St Winefride in silent respect? For the Chapel is strong here. The preacher's uplifted band is against all well-saints, the convent is levelled, the Catholics driven out centuries ago and any wealth they had, man knows not of it. Desolation has befallen this last refuge of the holy saint. Isolated in the hills, its population, so far from any modern public services, has aged, dwindled and declined. Almost every dwelling was said to need a twentieth-century refabrication. The village stores-cum-post office often changes hands and is sold to optimistic folk from the Midlands who tend to move away in despair. The church is neglected, almost unattended.

It is as if, after Winefride had died here and after they allowed her bones to be carried away, when they drove out the Catholic holy men and the devoted women, when they tore down the convent and carted off the stones for cattle byres, a sadness came down like a long enduring raincloud, and the village has hovered gradually sinking in a time capsule, undisturbed. There is a discreet curtain the chapel has drawn in case aliens make their pilgrimage here; neither memory nor veneration of Winefride is required, for was she not Catholic or something Roman?

Yet, despite the sad peace that should prevail, the trumpets of the Press have blared aloud, discordant, amused or intolerant and disapproving, leaving no reason why I should halt my pen.

The attractive village hostelry, The Lion Inn, had been once again for sale. Lined with black its white walls face the church and look towards that levelled convent where the nuns once moved their rosaries in prayer. Welcoming windows with notices offering 'Morning Coffee', or 'Hot and Cold Snacks always available' were of no avail because no one ever came by. After all, that road narrowed and only led tortuously 'over the mountain'.

Into the quiet of all this had come as licensee South-Wales-born Ron Bailey. If only he had read the local newspapers that are as detailed and accurate as any English parish magazine, he would have known how everyone in this valley is a related North Welshman.

The ill-fated licensee should have made acquaintance with the families of the present time, august celebrities, such as of Councillor Evan Roberts, School House, for forty years Elder and Secretary of Siloh Presbyterian Chapel, organist there for forty years, the former Chairman of the old Hiraethog Council and Chairman of the managers of both Gwytherin and Pandy Tudur Schools. There was also in Gwytherin Mr David Evans who farmed for forty years with his sons, also farmed at Plas Mattw and Foel Cathau along the valley and who for twenty years was respected as Chairman of the Llanrwst Show. Semi-deserted the village cottages may be but the hillside farms and their farmers are powerful and influential. Mrs Evans herself, for example, was President of the W.I. and had eleven children and two grandchildren.

No such celebrities came to cheer up the bars and parlours at the Lion. The South Wales accent is quite different from the dialect hereabouts and the spirit thereof also. Mr Ron Bailey wandered about his empty hostelry and shone his electric light across the little deserted street. Nobody came. The electric light he wasted only lit the rain outside. Folk arriving just parked their cars to use the public telephone booth and went away. With so much water everywhere, how could one expect people to be thirsty? Perhaps also these villagers were not the drinking types?

He decided to set things going in a theatrical blaze. He engaged two striptease artistes from an agency and advertised their promised Sunday performance, taking care not to advertise in Gwytherin. Private parties were collected by coach from Llanrwst and further afield. Such was the interest that extra clients had to be brought by car. The Lion became surrounded by vehicles. Although it was on Sunday night when all good folk should have been at home, and in any case nobody went to the Lion, no one from Gwytherin, that is, all the population knew about it. The trouble was, however, nobody would admit to knowing in case he might be suspected of attending. Most of them declared vociferously that, had they known, they would have gone to make a protest.

The local reporter was quick on the scene but Monday morning was too late for the action. When questioning the licensee, 'I have no comment to make,' was all he got in reply. Appeal was made to the local police. Such a dreadful thing to happen to such a village needed immediate recourse to the arm of the Law. From far Abergele Police Inspector Albert Roberts cautiously asserted: 'We have had no official complaint about the show, but we have heard about it. We have looked into the matter and have spoken to the licensee about it!' To the ministers of religion for the district it seemed as if the very gates of Hell had been opened in that village. Speaking in a haze of innocence, the Gwytherin Community Council Chairman, Mr Cemlyn Williams grumbled: 'We had heard that this show had been held and we were unanimously against such a thing when we discussed it at the council meeting. But we did not make a protest because we did not know what the facts were. I do not believe any local people attended the show. If we heard that another show was to be held in the village the council would protest against it.'

Of course, the Lion Inn soon became vacant. Another and more conventional licensee came quietly upon the scene.

It seemed sacrilegious to contemplate the holy places in association with such primitive reversions, so on our promised excursion we did not stop at the churchyard, but drove on to the end of the valley as far as the lower road would allow. There we left the car at a point where track and river come very near as the hills come closer and the valley levels into a more classic beauty. By Ty-hwnt-yr-afon there was a ford over the pebbles and a weir above, mills and millstream, old springs and wells, ancient farmhouses and friendly people who all appeared to have some purpose that brought them out upon the path where we must encounter them. Each lingered to pass the time of day with Nellie and Dilys Owen. Maybe they learned as well what my wife and I were about, but I knew not the language and my wife did not stir herself to intrude into the conversation. So we walked on and on, meeting folk who emerged like friendly sentinels to make us feel welcome. Dilys and Nellie Owen, being related to most of them, gave and took remembrances and regards to every one and to the families each represented.

On we went and climbed until we could see up into the two valleys, the Afon Cledwen below and a shorter, steeper valley that would lead almost into the sky, up and onto the Hiraethog moorlands. There are great rocks up there by the place named Llys Dymper, lines of them widely spaced and mysterious mounds in that cloudy landscape, but I only know them from the marks on the Ordnance Maps, nor can I do aught but guess whether the name once signified 'Palace of Desire', 'Pleasant Palace', or, more practically, since everyone says there is nothing on that site but barren marsh, *Overthrown Palace.* Some day, I resolved, I would go up to the middle of the high moors and search for this ancient memory that was now nothing but letters on a map.

We paused as the track climbed more steeply, and before a ravine we all stopped. Wooded banks along the cliffs hid the stream deep below but, like a colossal giant was Carreg-y-Cawr, the 'Giant Rock' itself standing there, left in some bygone millennium to bear witness to the might in those glaciers of the departed Ice Age. Nothing was beside it, just the huge rock balanced on the cliff above a stream that might one day eat away and undermine its stability or some tremor or lightning stroke descend to start it rolling down the valley.

The Rock was known today but the Giant was not, nor could we learn about him, or her as might be, yet I came away feeling we had perhaps omitted something essential; maybe a flower should have been placed before its base, or a small stone been laid upon another there. Some unanswered question had been suggested, prompting a call to return like an implication of neglected duty as if a power within the stone demanded performance akin to the ancient promptings for sacrifice.

For the rocks and stones men have moved, and the mounds they have made with only the ancient power of human hands, all the Hiraethog moors are extraordinary, but this rock, Carreg-y-Cawr, has stood from the beginning of things in its massive integrity. The great primitive urge of early man to move rocks, to handle stones, must have come upon the tribes of Hiraethog time and again but before Carreg-y-Cawr they had been foiled, glacial erratic as it was.

15   Gwytherin, Winefride's Town

Rain, snow and sleet, and now the early summer sunshine had made
the old stones I had salvaged appears if they had always been where
I had placed them. They gave me joy whenever I walked by, these
boulders that had been ancient foundations and then mere farm
buildings, and with them later on the great stones from the Cae Delyn
field, stones that had surrounded the old wells that the bulldozers had
pushed chaotically out of their mysterious groupings. The largest of
all, some six feet or more in length, the ploughman had said he wanted
for his friend to use along the river, and the three of these I was not
myself capable of handling. All the others I had stacked behind my
dwelling and daily I would go and admire them, wondering on the
building they had once supported, the Roman slaves who had hauled
them up the hill, and the wooden palace that must in the days of the
Legions have rested upon them where they stood around the clear
springs that came out of the hilltop above.

I resolved on another bright afternoon to go down again to
Gwytherin, to waste time and linger there. It is one thing by the
fireside to read of such histories in old books, it is something
incredibly more intense to stand on a site and let relic and topography
work their will upon the imagination. The Lion Inn was again empty
now, the post office also was forsaken and closed and had long been
advertised as 'For Sale'. Two or three children played in the road that
went on towards Llansannan but their very game, forlorn, slow and
querulous, seemed a symptom of desolation.

The only way into the churchyard was by steps over iron railings
above the wall. There was the church, its porch unwelcoming and
bare, covered with birds' droppings and the broken old nests of
departed swallows. Creeping away from the walls hung out-of-date
notices, implying that rarely, rarely came the pastor to unlock that

door, for he shared ecclesiastical duties between various other parishes. It must be far out of living memory that the bell was tolling here for daily matins or evensong. Through a dirty glass window I could just perceive the stripped walls within, as barren and uninviting as the exterior.

The silent church, the staring terraced houses opposite the empty pub and the vacant post office: if ever there was a lost village, it was here. The latest *Blue Guide* has no mention, neither has the *Shell Guide*. One or two of the houses had the look of rentable holiday homes. The Council had actually stirred itself to making special rescue grants to these homes in the hope of stemming utter desertion. As I had climbed to the other side of the wall and into the churchyard, those children had stared, unbelieving. Someone also watched me from a lonely upstairs window, but the high green hills made a frowning circle all around.

North of the church stood the four famous upright stones, the inscription on the eastern one VINNEMAGLI FIL SENEMAGLI plain to see and thought by scholars to date from the sixth or seventh century. They crested the bank that frowns above the road going down to the school. I associate them in my memory with the other stones in Llangernyw churchyard with their crude, incised crosses and with the tumuli close by that village – the one at Hendre Isaf, I believe as yet unopened and the other at Hendre Du where 'until about the middle of the last century stood a tumulus in opening with several tombs, "cistfeini", sepulchral urns, and fragments of Roman pottery were discovered.'* Such stones, scraps and fragments I incline to associate with my site around Ty'n-y Llidiart, for on these hilltops, where the moving of stones has been practised from earliest time it was routine to bring masonry downhill to either of the two villages, Gwytherin on the south or Llangernyw on the north. With the attrition of centuries, wooden upper walls and roofs would disappear till shapen stones or assorted boulders found themselves in other foundations. When they took down the old church in Penmachno, they found the ancient blocks known as the inscribed ORIA and CARAUSIUS stones. Today in Gwytherin the monastery, the convent, the nunnery with all its cells and associated architecture have vanished utterly, but cemented into the sturdy farmhouse walls on those mountain sides, who knows what ancient symbols, heathen or divine, lie hidden?

* *The Heart of Northern Wales*, W. Bezant Lowe, MA, FCS

What has happened, I wondered, to Winefride's memory hereabouts? She did come here after the crime against her and here she died peacefully the second time; it was only the first time that she died at Holywell on that hill, but here she came into a peace, almost an anonymity of oblivion.

The great mounds in Gwytherin churchyard sleep silently, but the mighty old yew trees stand like grim druidic sentinels to forbid speculation of the prehistoric rites they personify, only by the dark green shadows of their presence spelling a pre-Christian ordinance of forgotten ceremonial. Among them, almost modern but ageing slowly, stand the wealthy tombs of prosperous German farmers, men who came here in World War I as prisoners of war, married and thrived in more Teutonic style.

Something strange must have happened in Gwytherin to cause this obliteration of Winefride's memory. And so it did, a shame concerned with the neglect to retain and venerate her sacred remains, here, in her chosen resting place; for 500 years from her seventh-century death they allowed her remains to be removed to Shrewsbury. Winefride had died the first time at Holywell on that hill looking northward across the Dee Estuary to the sea. In those old times respect for the saints would multiply as they went about seeking opportunities of acquiring land so as to build churches, sometimes by blessing, sometimes by fear of malediction. St Beuno seems to have been very much of a property developer in this direction and he had also a reputation for aiding people who had been decapitated, though this is said to refer to his skill in ministering to the demented. On his travels the saint came upon his niece and only child, Winefride, and, in return for a grant of land, agreed to undertake her education so that she could become a nun. While she was alone and her father and mother at church, Caradog, a chief of Hawarden, came to their cottage and attempted to seduce her. As she fled to the church, Caradog drew his sword and severed her head. As the legend recounts, the head fell inside that holy place and the body outside.

Hearing the commotion, Beuno came to the church door, whereupon under his glance Caradog 'immediately melted in his sight as wax before a fire'. Beuno took Winefride's head and replaced it perfectly so that all remaining to indicate the disaster was 'a small line on the neck'. Michael Drayton has the story in his *Polyolbion*, describing the holy well that sprang up where the saint fell:

The liveless tears shee shed into a fountaine turne,

And, that for her alone, the water should not mourne,
The pure vermillion blood that issued from her veines
Unto this very day the pearly gravel staines;
As erst the red and white were mixed in her cheeke,
And that one part of her might be the other like,
Her hair was turned to mosse, whose sweetness doth declare
In liveliness of youth the natural sweets she bare.*

How account for modern ecclesiastical sophistication? The miracle is now explained to our rational minds as describing how Winefride 'lost her head' overwrought with hysterical fear from which Beuno rescued her while Caradog melted away and fled before the dire imprecations of her saviour.

Where the head had stopped after rolling down the hill a powerful fountain burst from the rocks. Moss beside the spring diffused a fragrant odour and, on each anniversary of her decollation, the very stones that had been discoloured with her blood were wont once again to change colour to carmine.

Slanderers say the story was invented by the monks of the near-by Cistercian abbey of Basingwerk, but all prospered in the vicinity, and still do, both from miraculous cures and from miracles. The Roman pontiffs encouraged and promoted such a holy place. Pope Martin V furnished the abbey with pardons and indulgences to sell to devotees. Before the Battle of Agincourt in 1415, Henry V prayed for St Winefride's aid and came in person to make his visit of gratitude after the battle. Even today there is a hospice for poor pilgrims who continue to arrive in their piety. Eventually, however, commercial undertakings grabbed this wonderful water supply, mining it to themselves. Their mines and tunnels affected the flow of that holy spring which ceased altogether in 1917. Since then a reservoir has been arranged to ensure continuance of the supply.

I could not resist my own impulse for pilgrimage and there, between the parish church of St James and the ugly textile mills lower down, found myself walking round the deep crypt over which stands the chapel built by Margaret, mother of Henry VII, with slender arches of late Perpendicular work. Once a little gem of architecture and of sculpture, this is now weathered and water worn, but the water glistens, ripples and moves across from the well into the pool. Stone faces grin sardonically down, the outlines of figures and animals graven below arches and upon pillars have been dissolved so they

* Polyolbion, Michael Drayton, (published 1613) page 160

appear more like distorted, modern sculpture than medieval dreams.

A notice gave the times for men and women to bathe. Three times through the pool is the routine and then to kneel at last on the submerged Stone of St Beuno. There were canvas booths in the chapel for undressing. I shivered. 'Surely no one bathes on a cold day like this,' I commented to the lady attendant.

'Yes, indeed,' she replied. 'This morning we had four or five visitors in the pool.'

I glanced at the graffiti proclaiming cures of the past century, deepest, boldest of all the great square letters cut on behalf of 'PATRICK MURPHY, MEATH. CURED 1823'. Faith can endure, but hope can surely drive a mortal to his own conclusion!

Outside on the high road traffic clatters by at speed, articulated lorries, omnibuses and fast cars, but the slowly moving water seems to catch the noise away into its own silence. In these days there would not be the evidential pile of crutches thrown away by the disabled; only the devout women praying before St Winefride's statue, the old records carved into the stones and the quantity of religious books, cards, and tokens on sale bore witness.

It was a cold March day when I next came to Gwytherin, and that March wind had begun to blow coldly as I sat beside the stones in Gwytherin churchyard. After St Beuno passed away, the lonely Winefride had sought a safer and more remote place for her devotions. Her wanderings brought her into this sequestered valley where another of the multitude of Welsh saints, St Elerius, dwelt beside the convent. To this nunnery, apparently then flourishing under the superintendence of Theonia, she was admitted and took the veil. Here in quiet seclusion she lived to become abbess herself and died her second death in peace on a June day in AD 660.

Some tales declare that her grave was under the four inscribed stones, but there is another ancient gravestone in the churchyard 'ornamented with a cross fleury and chalice and bearing an inscription which is now almost illegible'. Tradition declares that the mortal remains of Theonia and Winefride were actually deposited in this very church. Poor Theonia's body may lie there even today, but 500 years later was the time of the Crusades, of relics and of miracle-working body-snatching so it is no wonder St Winefride's body was seized and taken to Shrewsbury. Such a relic was too valuable to be allowed to remain at Gwytherin. It is said that wherever the cortège halted a holly tree sprang up in protest and the route is so marked to this day. Lewis, writing in 1833 declares of her remains at Gwytherin, 'the wooden chest in which these were preserved is still kept'.

No search will reveal any trace of the holy splendour that once moved through the Gwytherin village: the monks renewing the weir and clearing the mill-race for corn to be ground at the main watermill below the bridge, and the silent nuns passing to and fro with rosary and psalter. The very site of the convent shows only pebbles and a few humps and hollows in the level meadow. Only the Ordnance Maps have preserved a hint of what used to be by the surviving place-names that spring up from the print on their paper, throwing a medieval charm, a dark glitter from the Christian Dark Ages naming the ancient woodlands along the stream: Coed Sophia, Coed Jocelyn, Coed John Strange, Coed Salusbury, Coed Robert, Coed Eriviat, Coed Helena, Coed Cecilia and higher up the valley Llwyn Saint ('holy grove') and Bryn-y-clochydd ('the bellman's hill').

Some archaeologist may elucidate the history behind this sequence of ancient, mostly un-Welsh names grouped here, a medieval island in such a Celtic topography. I have questioned everywhere to no avail. As for the people of Gwytherin, the names no longer exist for them; though the gentlemen of Her Majesty's Ordnance have discovered and printed them in the larger style of type, this generation knows them not. Their mystery enhances their fascination for me, though I must cease from asking more locally for such curiosity about names is not understood, even if they do represent holy women. As it is, old farmers tell the story of Taipellaf with disbelief, relating with lips turning down in deprecation, how once folk tried to build up a grand palace there, above where the weir is, beside the mill. Day after day the villagers laboured to put the stones together, but by dawn each morning the work had been undone and not one stone left upon another. Astonishment overcame their disbelief when I vouched for the tale's veracity. Why, were not the stones from the Holy Convent that had sheltered the Saint herself? How could such be laid together for a secular building? Steal the stones from the nunnery as they might, how should it profit them? But today every building block has gone from where the ancient convent stood and the place is green and level as any meadow.

My interest in the legend and associations of St Winefride did not go unnoticed by my friends who planned an exciting excursion along the other side of the River Clwyd where the hills of Flintshire guard the river landscape on the one side and the long shore line lies, beautiful in its distance, on the other. Offa's Dyke ranges along the crest of these Clwydian Hills and its track is clearly marked all the way to Prestatyn, but it was not these historical associations my friends had in mind. Looking back sometimes I wonder had not they taken my interest in the Holy Saints too seriously, for, after a gratifying meal in the roadside restaurant known as 'The Teapot', off we went to the Jesuit Spiritual Exercises Centre of St Beuno's, near Tremeirchon.

Our whole journey there made a sequence of wonderful green landscapes and far-away vistas until we came to the Jesuit College of which Gerald Manley Hopkins wrote: 'Away in the loveable west, on a pastoral forehead of Wales, I was under a roof here, I was at rest ...'

In beside the square that fronts the College façade stands a notable column surmounted by an ancient sculpture which was once purchased for a comparatively small sum from the parish authorities at Tremeirchion and brought here to command at last real appreciation. The College contains one of the finest libraries in North Wales, a fitting place for that poet to seek refuge and impersonal inspiration, especially as it was at Holy Trinity Church, Tremeirchon, that Dafydd Du, 'The Black of Hiraddug', was incumbent in the middle of the fourteenth century when he translated the Psalms in Welsh metres and assisted in regulating the complicated system of Welsh prosody. His figure in ecclesiastical robes lies in Holy Trinity Church under an ornamental arch, but his work must have lent encouragement to the Jesuit poet all these centuries later.

The College was in Retreat when I entered, but the well-illustrated exhibition of Hopkins's work was open, carefully arranged and supervised by helpful attendants. The tortuous twisting of words and meanings into English by the style of the old Welsh metres so characteristic of Hopkins is not to my own taste, however much it comes into fashion in this century when it has been the mainspring of so much that makes the inspiration of Dylan Thomas and the poets of so-called 'sprung rhythm'. By steadily working through the exhibition, however, I came to a new understanding of this poet who shut himself away from life in order to meditate here. The attendant, noticing my interest, went to the trouble of photo-copying *Two Mediaeval Welsh Poems* (text & translation) for me: *Ffynnon Wenfrewi (St Winefride's Well)*, doubtfully attributed to Iolo Goch, and the other, *Stori Gwenfrewi a'i Ffynnon (The Story of St Winefride and her Well)* by Tudur Aled (1480-1526). The latter poem was of particular interest as written by the best known of those poets who flourished in my neighbouring village of Llansannan. Among extravagant simile and metaphor culled from the Orient, he praises the beneficence of the Saint:

'Look at a hundred people, light candles,
I saw senses recovered there:
The blind man sees, let him go to her church,
And the cripple, if he came by crawling;
Let them come there with the fool,
From there he comes a wise man.'*

Here at St Beuno's I learned of another, almost secret, holy well. Before the passing of next summer I went to seek it, and what a search it proved! Cefn Church is easy to find and admire, where it stands upon its own hill to overlook the whole valley, solitary in the grace of its Early English architecture, witnessing to St Mary across wide panoramas. But the well is far away beside Wigfair, which translates as Mary's Wood. I traced my way round by the Cefn Caves, now, by order of their proprietors, closed despite the attractive descriptions in the old guidebooks. I crossed the majestic bridge, Pont yr allt Goch, that traverses the Elwy River by one majestic arch, eighty-five feet in span. Then after many enquiries, some quite fruitless, and needless diversions, I found that one goes down a small lane towards a long walk across meadows to the wooded hill, all the while wondering how this beautiful phase of wild country is so little known and what conspires to keep it from public knowledge.

The path goes somewhere else and one must tramp over tall meadow grass to where, out of the utter depths below, rises suddenly a small river and flows 'discharging about one hundred gallons of water every minute and strongly impregnated with lime' over wild watercresses. Out of its polygonal basin, once beautifully and elaborately sculptured it comes, before the ivy-covered walls and arches of its own ruined and roofless chapel, cruciform in shape and once in the later Decorated English style. The pillared canopy above the water has gone. Thieves have been here and stolen away the holy stones from the sacred Ffynnon Fair† that was said to rival Holywell in beauty, but now surpasses it in the sublime splendour of its poetic ruin and the charm of its enchanted dingle. The well was used for baptismal purposes as much as for blessed cures, but because of its secret location the chapel became noted for clandestine run-away marriages, held in defiance of parental approval. Then in the times when Catholics were persecuted it became a venue for their

* Translated T.M. Charles-Edwards, MA, D.Phil Gwasg Gomer, Llandysul, 1971
† St Mary's Well

ceremonies and devotions. Now it stands as a witness to the hatred of the Chapel Nonconformists against the menace of 'well saints'.

Yet what these ruins evoke is the antithesis of hatred for their dilapidated remains seem to come alive with sentiment as they linger, ghosts as they might be, or creations from Gothic illustrations in the old poetry books of Sir Walter Scott.

16 Making a Mountain Garden

That spring had been planting time for me. Planting, sowing or setting hope into the soil, is something that always appeals to the optimism of the spirit. The Owens had presented me with some clumps of snowdrops and I had added to these a few surplus groups brought from my own garden in Essex. Now, as cheaply as I could, I bought bulbs by the sackful, daffodils – the huge and glaring 'King Alfred' for one prominent place, mixed bulbs for lacing the lane and surrounding the lawns that had already been sown with grass seed. These levels I planted with yellow crocuses and topped the stone banks with purple and white varieties. The chance came to buy some sacks of jonquils more cheaply, and I packed hundreds of them into the grass in good weather and bad, hurrying to race against the changing seasons and remembering ruefully the heavy labour and the summer days spent on digging and levelling that ground. Once I had unearthed there an iron bedstead which Trevor Roberts's bulldozer had consigned to an oblivion some twelve inches deep.

I would work on and on in spite of that fine mountain rain and the heavy mist that came to prove it was late afternoon. At 965 feet, the clouds could take possession of the cottage, although sometimes they would be just threatening with their thick, water-logged air hovering thirty feet or so up, leaving visible only the hedges and down to the lower field.

One afternoon I heard the strong, low-flying sound of wings and along the lower range of visibility, almost beating against the hanging cloud, came a big swan crying plaintively as if for direction. I knew it for a Bewick's swan searching for the Hiraethog lakes, for Brenig or for Aled above Gwytherin, perhaps travelling off course from the Conwy Valley or the coast. The great frame of the flying bird vanished into the mountain mist as heavily as it came, seeming to leave the world empty again and desolate. Desolation! That is the sentiment of such a day in these hills, when the mist comes down and insulates the world, cloaking the whole and providing isolation, surroundings so invisible they seem not to exist, not only depriving the landscape of its wild creatures but blotting out the reality of humans in a weird, maddening silence of cold unreality.

I worked through those planting days, dreaming of sunshine and flowers. Bluebells I planted in the lane, large-leaved primrose clumps I dug in, pulled out of Essex gardens. Four standard red-may trees I found favoured places for, and a long line of little box bushes was arranged to mark the northern hedge.

So close to the 1,000 feet contour appeared an adventurous situation in which to plant my fruit trees, and more so when with vivid memories of the hedges that make lanes of County Kerry so red with wild fuchsia, I planted a dozen or so bushes of that most hardy variety Ricartonii. Unfortunately my fears were justified, for, after just one winter, they had come to nothing, as did the violets, whether white or blue; all disappeared after the frosts with scarcely a sign of their departure. Even the box bushes shed their leaves and took a year or two to consider the climate. Luckily I left them undisturbed, surrounded by weeds as they became, left them standing bare and bleak until three years later I found them nearly all in leaf and strong, wrestling with rampant weeds around them. By this time I had learnt how sheep have their own ways of enjoying the countryside and wander everywhere taking samples of every menu nature provides. There were also slugs and snails, huge slimy and omnivorous, that had been bred beneath and between those ancient stones. I would not lay pellets nor poisons for fear of harming the birds but, whenever possible, picked them off the concrete in the bright moonlight, and put them away into tins, cold glutinous animals that ate and expired in their oozy silence.

There was another marauder who could not be immediately identified. A large biter he, selective, but leaving no traces except fragments from his feasting. Glancing through the window one spring morning, I saw him come lolloping up from the field below – a fine hare, seeming, as he slowly sprang across the bitten grass, like a young deer. He took no notice of me as I watched from the window, but I wished I could have told him he was welcome to dine at my table any day and wondered whether to plant choice lettuce or other succulent vegetables for his delectation. Later that summer I changed my mind, realizing how difficult it is to protect or interfere with any balance of nature, for on two occasions I found large hares prostrate on my land: the first where it had leapt high upon the bank behind the cottage to expire as it finished that leap, and the second dead behind the bluebells in my lane. Where they had come from I knew not, but it was as if they had sought out Ty'n-y-Llidiart as a refuge, in some sort of appeal for safety here from some shooting party, and I was sad. Still more did I grieve when I found a young leveret in the ditch Trevor Roberts had made for me. It ran to the end and hid in the pipe there, so I left it, hoping it might grow up as a resident and become a friend. Alas, weeks later, cautiously creeping along that ditch, I found only the skin of its back lying like a torn glove, as if a fox or pine marten had torn it clean away.

Eventually I finished my planting, setting a walnut tree grown from a nut the squirrels had buried in my Essex garden years ago. I dug it in as a defiant gesture against this climate, and also, in memory of my older garden bombed in World War II, the pear Margarite Marillac. Of course I realized I would have to plant others also, as Marillac has no good pollen, so I placed Doyenne du Comice and Conference somewhere nearby to comfort her and cased them all in rusty barbed wire with bits and pieces of old metal scrap as armour against vegetarian predators tame or feral.

By these visits, as springtime came along, I had made a wonderland. First, snowdrops painted white patches here and there. All the daffodils danced into bloom, following the crocus in the grasses; the bluebells made a carpet of colour upon the slopes beside the lane while the jonquils last of all blew waves of perfume under the avenue of mountain ash, perfume which lingered and wandered slowly here and there as if unwilling to associate with anything on this earth.

The word went into the village and I was told local people were walking up from there to see the display. I was delighted. The avenue of mountain ash imprisoned the perfume of jonquils, refining the visual experience. This year was no more than the beginning. Next year, when the sown grass had matured upon my landscape, next year would be twice as good, for bulbs multiply from year to year.

Two old flowering currant trees came out in a show of red blossom against opening leaf sprays fresh and green. Underneath them, search as I might, only one yellow aconite from all the dozens planted stood up to show itself, but searching below the old pair of flowering shrubs, I found a very large iron key with a neat stone above it. Of course, the currant trees were once either side of a gate. Here below the stone was the key to the cottage, placed there for late comers after curfew! Naturally it would not fit my new lock, but I treasured it for it held a hundred years of secrets, tales of love and tales of death, of all that had passed through the doorway and along the lane.

One flowering currant was being strangled by a terrific hawthorn. This I cut away and pruned both trees together. Each must be fifty years of age or more. Local people did not recognize them as *ribes* but in former times folk had come from as far as Llanrwst to take cuttings from them. Somehow, as guardians of the key, they took on a new importance, more than as mere specimens of the common garden flowering currant, and I cared for their survival, although in view of the demise their age foretold I planted scented yellow azaleas with jasmine and honeysuckle to take their stand and leave no empty place at the old gateway in some future time.

The grass I had sown grew, the snowdrops and crocus flowered. Great swathes of daffodils followed, but I was to learn how ruthlessly giant slugs wandered at night, snails crawled from under my revered stones, hares showed preference for shoots from raspberry canes and my little curtilage where I had so admired myriads of butterflies – tortoiseshells, peacocks, painted ladies, in fact every possible variety – became a crowded nursery for caterpillars that very soon stripped foliage from almost every planted tree and shrub. I was being taught the great lesson learned by every hill-dweller: to accept those powerful scales of nature that bring everything, human and animate, into equilibrium. I planted, I watched and accepted the inevitable, welcoming success when it occasioned, but without bothering with sprays, insecticides or fertilizers. How could I, arriving for a week or a fortnight at a time, expect to drive away intruding sheep or protect precious alpine plants from galloping weeds? Again, how could one estimate what would survive at this thousand-foot contour? I reconciled myself to take planting as a gambling venture each time, for I was unwilling, as my neighbours did, to make a sheltered garden, close hedged and walled from the wind. I needed to sit and watch the distant moors, or go to the top of my mound to stare at the Glyders or the Carneddau Mountains.

'Tundra!' remarked a friend grimly. 'That's what you have got up there, arctic land. Tundra! And grass is all you'll grow in the end!'

Grass certainly grew, and my first summers were spent in the suburban labour of lawnmowing. In season the grass raced me and grew so long as to be difficult to cut. I once mowed a nest of fieldmice who jumped about and startled me with their metallic crick-cracks of protest though all had safely survived the mower. That same time I found a pheasant had chosen the far corner to lay her full clutch of eggs so that quite half the patch had to be left the summer long, happy indeed for the crop of grasshoppers that were breeding there and for the wild pansies too. It was then I decided I liked the grass long quite as much as short. After all, the bulbs needed to have considerable time after flowering to mature their foliage. They were an underground asset that went on multiplying regardless of predators or winter reverses.

Long grass makes a real nature reserve and has its own abundant variety of blossom and seeding. I came to admire it for the diversity of its shadows that waved in each wind and planned to plant hyacinths and even tulips within its safety.

One of my requests to Trevor Roberts the builder had been to make an 'owl hole' in the barn. The distant look in his eyes as I described what I required made me wonder whether he took me seriously. He did eventually make a hole in that thick stone wall just under the apex of the roof, but it was an awkward hole, lopsided and far from round. However often I was assured that owls would not bother about geometry and would probably never come anyway, I could not tolerate the sight of it. Swallows would come and I had them in mind particularly. They would not bother either, I was promised; a hole was a hole to them.

But not to me! I must have a perfect circle there. It would be no fun watching my birds flying through such crumbling stonework. After several attempts by the builder's men by rule of thumb rather than Euclid, I resolved to do the job myself, at once and that very spring, before the swallows came up from the southern lands. After one or two efforts I used the metal door from a discarded washing machine. The cement around it set well, and the chromium plated alloy gave shape and character to the barn wall.

Would it be too slick and too modern to attract feathered friends? Not at all. Through the years the number of nesting swallows has amounted to and now averages a whole dozen. I can sit at the cottage door and see them flying in and out any time of the summer. The marsh meadows down towards the river must provide a gourmet's delight for them, and my long mountain ash avenue offers a dessert of larger insects along its leafy shades. Only the pied wagtails that used to perch at the old crumbling entrance seem to have a dislike of the shiny metal and are not now to be seen. Once one could have counted seven of them sitting in a row, although that was when a shallow pool remained beside the hard-standing and the pebbles below.

Now today I can defy all those who have scoffed or glanced in deprecation at my 'owl hole', for inside the barn I find the old tin bath under the tie-beam full of owl pellets, every one of them neatly dropped into the bath as, after digestion, the remains of each meal were rejected. What a triumph! A white barn owl in residence! Have I also the only 'house-trained' owl known to science? I have yet to catch sight of my welcome new tenant, but a nesting box is being made from an old tea-chest and so much care given for seclusion and comfort that I can now enter my barn only with timid hesitation and almost on tiptoe.

Compiling a list of birds that come by Ty'n-y-Llidiart would only enumerate the residents and the passengers that are to be found on most British mountainsides, but there are a few more vivid impressions that will always stay with me, and foremost in delight, returning real as memory, is that of the curlews. They come to nest in these hilltops when the fields are still wet, and here they find a quiet refuge away from the shore at the very time tourists begin to infest the coastal beaches. They like my little place, taking possession and loudly protesting each time I come up from Essex. Flying low across the grasses, they call to their nesting mates. Sometimes the air becomes full of anxious vibrations as they scream to protect or teach their wandering fledglings. Oftener, stalking like poultry, they would be seen running silently through the damper places where the green plovers stand. When the hilltop fields dry out as summer comes, they tend to find their way, all families together, back to the sea-shore again, so I could meet them searching for seafood along the west shore at Llandudno or by those stonier beaches at Rhos.

Listening on my higher ground, I would become one of the first to hear the cuckoo. Like some cry of a disembodied spirit from medieval times, the call would come out of the woods above St Winefride's old convent, travelling down the bushy riverside through the old monastic copses to Coed Robert, and then from oak tree to oak tree and hedge to hedge to that little dell below Gwilym Jones's farm at Cefn Castell and up to my small meadow sometimes to land, especially in the early morning, upon my very roof.

The tunnelled avenue of trees, ivy-covered oak, mountain ash and wild cherry, that shelters my lane, supplies a diet of summer fruit and autumn berries. All the companies of tits and finches loved to feed along it, blackbirds and thrushes were always there, while at the changes of seasons passing migrants would take shelter in flocks as they made a diversion, choosing to avoid the bleaker Hiraethog moorlands – indeed, I have seen the ground before the cottage suddenly become a uniform green as a multitude of chaffinches alighted.

In the warmth of early summer, no doubt there were many nesting sites when the warblers and the whitethroats arrived, but I always left the search for them to the cuckoo, knowing that, especially in the case of robins, any discovery by humans is too often followed by total abandonment. As some reward, last year I was privileged to watch two grasshopper warblers toiling to feed their overgrown cuckoo progeny which squatted on the earth, opening a beak wide enough to swallow either of them.

One bird I seldom fail to note as he goes on his rounds is the buzzard. Each pair has its particular territory and one soon knows where to find the patrolling flight. Some are as regular as clockwork as they come along their valley, signalling approach by a querulous, plaintive mewing. They appear to know when I am in residence and fly so high, disappearing with white undersides stacked against the light of sky or cloud, that I can sometimes miss them even when they are calling directly above. At other times, especially in midsummer when they have young to feed, they fly low along hedges and stone walls and are gone almost as soon as one sees them. To have such a large bird flying free through the hills is like an emblem of old freedoms, more than a mere bird-watcher's joy.

Not to miss any renewal of this experience, I sometimes travel the back road beyond Gwytherin over to Oerfa: there is usually one to be seen thereabouts, perhaps perched upon a sheep fence searching for rodents; otherwise to the hills along the Conwy river and around Bodnant Gardens, above the deeper clefts and ravines exercising that magnificent perception of aerial vision. High in the heavens these birds are safe, but elsewhere only the quick, ghost-like flitting by wall and hedgetop saves them from the wandering shot.

Imagine my dismay when I found the stiff corpse of one of my pair beside the barn wall. Not a shot was to be seen upon its feathers nor any sign of a wound, nor could I tell how long it had lain there. Dutifully I enclosed it in sealed plastic suitably parcelled in brown paper so as not to insult Post Office handlers and posted it away to the laboratories of the Royal Society for the Protection of Birds. The bird had been dead too long for diagnosis, came the prompt reply, but they assured me it had not, so far as could be noticed, been shot. I had suggested that perhaps the electricity connections had injured the bird, but they found no sign of singeing by electric contact. I was left to make my own surmise, perhaps death by consuming some creature poisoned by insecticide or agricultural fertilizer. I could not think of it without gloom, for the sky seemed bare, the delight of watching those great hawks fly into the clouds above my world had gone. Next season, however, there they were, high and triumphant as ever, even when they flew lower mobbed in turn by crows, magpies or the screams of green plovers.

There are places down by the River Elwy where the nightingale can be regularly heard, places on the way to Llanfair Talhaiarn, and this is delightful because I used to be given to understand she never came to sing in Wales, either from climatic reasons or being ousted by the volume of Welsh song from the chapels. Along this river also can be seen the darting, straight line of the dipper's flight. On one of my recent walks, after watching a television programme lamenting the diminishing range of this one-time ubiquitous marvel, I was thrilled to hear its sharp call above the rush of the river. It sped towards me, making that straight line of flight above the pebbles as if hurled from a catapult towards the Cledwen Bridge they call Pont-y-Garreg-newydd or, in English, 'New stone Bridge'.

There is a memory made of many evenings summer and winter, blended into a composite picture as the brain makes the grandest spectacle out of many happenings or a painter his masterpiece from many superb images that fuse into unity of their own accord. This is of the times I have gone out at dusk to stand at the field gate and look down the valley. The moon hangs over the Hiraethog moors, silent and hardly moving. The car lights spark out, crawling along the far criss-cross laid out above the valley towards Denbigh, and, as if to discover whether it is going to be dark at all, a wandering bat flits down the shadows of the lane, flying between the rowan trees.

Above the expanse of the huge Cae Delyn meadow, the larks are flying and, as day darkens their song increases, louder and louder, forbidding night, demanding the light of the sun, for there they see it still as it sets in the west in that reddening sky over and beyond the Glyder ranges, demanding the sun shall stay his setting, with every crescendo of outpouring song demanding day and life and the glory of being. Higher they sing and higher they fly, defying the night till the last beam from the Celtic twilight sinks below the far horizon, escaping the vision of even the highest lark. Yet, though the sun may disappear, on they fly undaunted for, even as he goes down, shines that great moon hanging over Hiraethog and they sing him up against the night, loudly, boldly flying until the chill wind brings a mountain cold into the air, and life itself dwindles and the farmhouse lights blink out on the higher hills. No longer would any extra effort of song and wingbeat raise ascent a few feet to keep the day in sight. From the boldest, highest lark, the sun had vanished where the bright red clouds glowed about the shadow line of the Glyders. Slowly the dark had come down, and the cold, and the dew. Every aged, lonely crow had winged away to shelter now. Only a curlew sometimes plaintively cried from a distant marsh.

17 *Of Sheep, Sheep Men and their Dogs*

White broken wisps of mist would gather to steal under the moon across the lower valley, almost in advance of evening, leading one to speculate on the ancient times when with the night fear swept over the Hiraethog moors. Instead of unfaltering electric lamps declaring each farmstead and townland, then beacons burned across those far heaths and bogs. University excavating teams have explored the prehistoric enclosures and the grave mounds of Brenig, where they found the ashes of those ancient fires and among them the ear-bones of sacrificial children burned to earn blessings from the dreadful gods of the primeval life. The blessings never came, the winters froze and froze, and today those moorlands have become even more bleak and barren than in the early times. We know the climate has changed and grown much colder, too cold to live happily throughout this century's seasons when the snows seal roads to as great a depth as anywhere in Britain. By the time the Romans had come, these high moors were empty and all the legions could do was to build straight roads and hill-forts to safeguard the ways along the outer edges.

The declining population ceased to preserve the tracks across the heather in their frozen winters. Only the sheep-walks prevailed, as they do now when the flockmasters of Gwytherin mark up their books and records. In this twentieth century there are swifter robbers on the prowl when lorries and cattle trucks can transport livestock so quickly for immediate disposal. Sheep-rustlers are able to find their ready markets in the Midlands and the over-populated South. Quick money and high prices can follow a nightly clandestine expedition and leave the Welsh farmer re-counting his flocks with disquiet.

The mountain shepherd has to make sure that his own flocks are on the sheep-walks for lambing time. Incredible as it may seem to the townsman, sheep are intelligent animals and, however they may probe for greener pastures, must seek even in mature age to drop their lambs where their own parents placed them, and here will be the roots they know and recognize. Many have been the quarrels because some farmer has seized sheep off another's sheep-walk to claim the lambs for his own. Not so long ago, a Gwytherin farmer found his flock had increased by several hundred and penned them in, though most were unmarked, so causing local consternation.

In these hill districts, though one may see the farm work from a distance only – the quick passing of cars along a highway – the bleating of sheep – it always turns out that everyone knows his neighbour's business. The flockmasters of Gwytherin took it upon themselves to put matters to rights as if in the old days when *cymmorth* could be levied – *cymmorth* means 'assistance' and has long been abolished, as being a cloak to cover unlawful assemblies called together for cattle-stealing, for avenging some wrong done to a neighbour or indeed for organizing a raid. Raid there certainly was. The sheep were seized. The *cymmorth* neighbours in the raid threatened to throw the offending farmers in the river. Matters in enthusiastic Welsh rode high; barns and dwellings, lives even, were in verbal peril and sought security in the Police Court as well as in the pages of the local newspapers. But, after all, what can local policemen do if called out to count and identify unmarked sheep?

Today, particularly among farmers who are located along the A5, the old Welsh droving road to London, cattle-rustling and sheep-stealing are anticipated risks. One farmer, as he strengthened his new wire fence, complained to me that he had lost altogether 300 sheep and that not very far from Gwytherin.

At sundown around lambing time there was never any question of listening to the singing of the larks. At the coming of spring all the air used to be full of fretful bleating that would last as far into the night as one could keep awake. From the Clwydian range to Hiraethog and Denbigh, from Wenlli mountain and across the Conwy to all Snowdonia, this was sheep-land, and all the sheep declared it so in no uncertain voices. And the farmers are shepherds, shepherds without a shadow of doubt, but not the Arcadian folk who wander dreaming with 'Pelion's shadow outvying The light of the dying day'. Hard-headed they are, with centuries of patrimony and tradition behind them, an inheritance possessed likewise by their sheep.

The miner in terraced streets along the Glamorgan valleys may lament his lot without a thought of the old-time peasant and without a thought that he would come back to a crumbling one-roomed cottage to dry out by a peat fire after a day on the wind-swept mountain. Such shepherds would look to the lights of the town where miners with money in pockets and bellies full of beer could fill their chapels with song and throw good humour and jokes around in the social clubs. Little wonder they tended to drift to the industrial centres, and not only in Victorian days but right until now when urban comfort continues to lure away old-time loyalties and paternal habits. Even in May 1980 T. Myrrdin Evans, President of the Farmers' Union of Wales, told his Annual General Meeting: 'I want to emphasize the effect of the recession in our rural areas. During the seventies the number of agricultural holdings in Wales fell by ten per cent. The number of small farms, those under twenty hectares, fell during the same period by over eighteen per cent.'

'Do you think I would be a small farmer in Clwyd?' said a schoolmaster to me a year or two ago. 'To make a living wage I would have to leave my wife all day to watch the sheep and feed the chickens, while I went to get work in Dolgarrog Aluminium Co or Llandudno. No one understands how bad it can be when a severe winter like 1979 can finish you, can ruin your flocks and you must starve yourself to feed them.'

Standing at my gateway, listening to the clamour of the sheep, I could pick out with my binoculars almost a dozen little ruined farmsteads, deserted, now swallowed up by larger farms, all indicative of the sharp penury I had once understood when describing a long deserted *hafod*.

> O, lift no hand, but let it all decay,
> No thatching peg shall pull these rushes tight,
> The wearing wind may carry walls away,
> Ice on the ingle show the cold starlight
> And every timber whiten day by day.
> Let piercing nettles leap across the sill,
> Old mosses level out the pitchèd floor,
> Neglected damsons down the crannies spill,
> For we will set another hearthstone up
> And look upon this place no more, no more:
> The very walls abrim gray sorrow's cup.
> O, let them break, and gather rushes green,
> Below a newer roof-tree set your store
> By brighter windows than the past have been!*

Taking my usual walk to the end of my lane, I met Penry Williams who farms the opposite hillside. He had congratulated me on my

* *Sonnets, They Say*, Walpole Press, 1949

struggle to restore Ty'n-y-Llidiart. He himself owned a ruined *hafod* attached to his farm and was thinking of repairing it. He spoke angrily of a councillor based in Colwyn who had urged the destruction by neglect of the small Welsh farms condemning them all as 'tuberculosis breeders'. To him the population of the mountainside was the lifeblood of Wales, just as the health of the people was the obligation of each council. It was a council's duty to make each dwelling healthy and habitable, not to encourage their neglect and ruin.

Now another pattern had gradually developed. Sheep farmers would rent these deserted parcels of land as they came up for auction or directly from estate agents. They would stock them with sheep purchased to graze for re-sale, by no means good insurance for the welfare of the land, meadows being used to exhaustion. But this practice allowed them to live within the villages, travelling by Land Rover to tend sheep, waiting opportunity to accumulate land and transform themselves into large farmers ready to swallow smaller fry. A man might live in a close community now to enjoy suburban life with all its amenities and yet farm sheep across the hilltops.

Of course this energy to purchase sheep and cast them upon the sheep-walks did lead to much trouble. Such sheep are not exactly 'bread upon the waters'. They do not always 'return after many days', and sometimes farmers themselves become inordinately rapacious.

As long ago as 1951, over in distant Nantmor on the other side of Snowdon a dispute over pasturing rights on Moel Dynewyd had divided neighbour from neighbour in bitter hostility. Thomas Askin of Cwm Caeth suddenly found a neighbour, Miss Owen, arriving with a letter denying his right to wash his sheep in the stream. Notwithstanding he claimed the right to do this and also to graze 175 sheep on the adjoining mountainside. For forty years these rights had been enjoyed, as his neighbours could witness.

After close argument, Miss Owen agreed that she would not object, providing he gave notice of any sheep-washing. However, after giving this notice, he found the wall built across the stream for that purpose was smashed down, and it cost him two hours labour to rebuild it. He sought out Miss Owen at Gelli'r Ynn and told her he would come next day to wash his sheep. She denied his right to do this.

Next day he went up to the sheep pens and was in the middle of gathering the sheep when John Jones arrived, flourishing his pitchfork. Shouting and threatening he began to pull down the dam. Askin stood his ground and persuaded Jones to come to his farm and consult the deeds, one of which stipulated that he had the right to graze 175 sheep on the mountain. In response Jones declared that the deeds were mistaken, producing maps to prove his side of the argument. As in many such arguments 'proofs' only served to exacerbate both parties and the issue was unresolved, so that later Thomas Askin found all his sheep turned out upon the mountain where two gates in the wall were wide open.

Thomas Askin confronted Mrs Emily Jones at her farmhouse door and she was alleged to have gloried in the fact that John Jones had been up the mountain to turn the sheep down. Next time, she declared, the sheep would be impounded.

The matter was to drag on endlessly while day after day farmers left their work to testify in a civil action at Carnarvonshire Assizes with witnesses testifying that on the one side such rights had never been challenged before, and on the other that they did not exist and so could not be challenged, while all this time the sheep, whether free or impounded, were bleating on those hillsides all through mid-March.

The problem of the tens of thousands of sheep grazing on unfenced mountains since World War II became more and more serious. When, particularly on the Conwy mountains, the sheep were gathered for shearing or clipping, some sheep in each flock would be found not readily identifiable, and there were always strays who had ambled up from the roadsides. In March 1964, the High Sheriff of Carnarvonshire licensed eleven members of the National Farmers' Union to act as 'stray sheep bailiffs'. This was a revival of the duties of the *setiwyr* and recognizing an individual, trusted by the flockmasters, as knowledgeable in the identification of sheep earmarks. There was no present-day legal basis for the appointment of these, but it was thought to date traditionally from the old Welsh institution sanctioned by the Sheriff after the Norman Conquest not being actually carried into English law.

In Denbighshire the manorial custom of 'strays courts' was followed, twenty such 'strays bailiffs' being appointed by the Chief Constable and the National Farmers' Union in collaboration. They had to control areas defined largely according to long established sheep-walks, to deal with strays and when necessary continue the old custom of public displays of the animals unclaimed. Sometimes the county patrol shepherd would determine the ownership of an unmarked lamb at a mountain gathering by applying the test of 'mothering' to the ewe belonging to the claimant farmer. Sheep do not readily adopt orphans, so acceptance of the lamb would substantiate the claim without doubt.

Intensive cultivation, the spread of sheep across the moors and the increase in their value coinciding with fear of sheep-stealing, made recording sheepmarks and sheep-walks an increasingly complicated but necessary matter. As long ago as 1964, Mrs Esmé Kirby of Dyffryn Mymbyr, the now well-known Snowdonia conservationist, was offering a reward of £100 for information leading to the arrest and conviction of thieves besetting her flocks along the A5 highway. She estimated her losses as 250 sheep worth about £2,000 in revenue at that time. Other farmers were complaining of well-planned night raids that used vans and trucks and sped back to the Midland cities. However active the police may be, at night the sheep are alone and unwatched on the mountains. In these recent years it appears that thieves come in to stock up their freezers, actually butchering the animals as they drive home. Sheep entrails, etc, from illegally slaughtered animals have been found along roadside quarries at Bylchau, and above Dolgarrog, and even as far towards England as by the Horseshoe Pass.

Nothing illustrates the striving of sheep farmers to get more sheep and more grazing than the dispute at Dwygyfylchi. The *North Wales Weekly News* first exposed the problem which still re-echoes along the lower Conwy. In the old days the landowner would be usually the magistrate as well as the proprietor of most of his surrounding farms. His marauding acts of enclosure went unchallenged. Today the local newspapers act as guardians of public rights when infringements are perceived. So when great mountain fences topped by barbed wire suddenly went up to enclose seventy acres of Foel Lus, Ffrith Fawr, for sheep men, the North Wales Press recorded the event.*

The local historian, Mr Ivor E. Davies, became eloquent. 'The area enclosed,' he declared, 'is the choicest portion of the Common nearest to the Upper Conway Road and the most accessible. The land overlooks the village and the Sychnant Pass. The variegated colouring of its bilberry, heather and bracken covering provided a feast to the onlooker. It also includes favoured haunts of bilberry pickers in season and has been for generations of small farmers, quarrymen and others, the grazing ground of their flocks.'

He concluded hopefully and almost like a prayer, 'The public will look to Penmaenmawr Council and to the County Council whose function it is to guard long established rights and privileges attached to our common land.'

---

* *North Wales Weekly News*, 26 March 1964

I take an important note about this case for the trusting appeal of the local historian to his local Council and to the County Council 'to guard the long established privileges attached to our common land'. Nobody made the observation that these two bodies did precisely nothing. If the Hughes family had not been well represented in Court such an encroachment could have succeeded. As I drive through Clwyd, everywhere I see fences springing up enclosing the moorlands. All the Denbigh moors, the heather-clad open spaces, are now fenced, ostensibly to keep sheep off the roads, certainly to protect both sheep and automobiles, but I doubt whether it is to guard those aforementioned 'rights and privileges attached to our common land'.

As I would stand looking across the farmsteads, surveying my grand panorama from Moel Fammau to the Denbigh moors littered with white-walled farms, I rejoiced at how the scene remained intact. From Pandy Tudur and Gwytherin to Llansannan they seemed confirmed in their own individuality, each surrounded by husbandry without the levelling out of fields and intrusion of commercial animal farming by outsiders. Nevertheless, this was sheep-land, with the clamour of sheep reverberating across the landscape, sounding far into the night in the months when lambs were weaned or strange newcomers arrived.

One morning Mr and Mrs Owen from Tyddyn Dafydd lower down the valley came up to my gate, searching for a heifer that had strayed. As we talked of sheep matters, Mr Owen produced skilfully carved shepherd's crooks he had made during winter evenings, each with his own imaginative design interesting me more than the antique shapes I had bought years ago in Athens.

They had their sheepdogs coming along with them, of course, for here the sheepdog shares everything with his master and tries hard to prove himself just as intelligent. They declared that in the matter of sheepdog training and testing North Wales could easily hold its own in the world. The best-known champion for many years was Norman Davies of Ysbytty Ifan, whose dogs have represented Wales at the International Shows at Ayr in Scotland, though not all his dogs have been bred by him. When he won the championship Rose Bowl in the Welsh National Trials with Ken and Gwen, it was known that Ken had been obtained in part exchange for another sheepdog, although he had trained his Gwen as a pup, an indication of his own testing and handling skills. In general the shepherd shares his whole reputation with that of his dog and at the right season week after week is devoted to bringing attainment to a standard of perfection that can be tested in and out of local trials to the objective of the National. To succeed in this, great stress is laid on showing not any fancy or circus tricks by one's dog, but integrity in the type of work which is done during daily routines on hill or farm, exercising a dog's ability to gather, drive, shed and pen the sheep.

Alas for the sheep when there is a new dog or grown puppy to be trained! My neighbour Gwilym Jones has a high reputation for the quality of his training combined with a natural sympathy for the wellbeing of his flock, and he too continues to collect his share of cups and trophies in open competition. One day I was marvelling at his tutelage, for throughout the morning his sheep were being driven out of the lower field into the smaller meadow, then herded back through the open gate, driven around the lower field and back to the meadow. Puzzled, I watched this happening, for it seemed overdoing the exercise. Suddenly I realized there was no shepherd, no Gwilym Jones. His dog, so well trained, had taken over, confident in his prowess he could work unsupervised!

I hastened to tell his master, who listened incredulously and then bolted across his fields to rescue the flock from their merciless sergeant-major.

Dogs take the relationship between their master and his sheep more seriously than we understand. *The Times** reported the case of the Surrey farmer who, having paid £65 for a sheepdog trained by a Welsh-speaking farmer, complained to the Surrey County Council Trading Standards Department. The dog could not understand a word of English! The Council decided to take no action. Presumably if the dog were incapable of learning English, the farmer was just as incapable of learning Welsh – only a few words would have been necessary, as surely the Welsh Language Society would agree. How stubborn! For the poor animal was only doing his best, and kept barking in his own real language, trying so hard that he had to be put down!

One trouble in the hills is sheep-worrying by semi-urban dogs. Not everyone is as open as was Robert Tudur Thomas of Pont Sylltu, Llangernyw, just below my hill. When his case came up before Llanrwst magistrates he openly admitted being the owner of a dog which worried sheep. Two dogs were seen jumping and snapping at a sheep on the farm at Pentre Wern. Though they made off, one of them lingered and was later found tearing at an old sheep's carcase. The

---

* *The Times* 5 March 1975

dog that got away was never found, but Mr Thomas's dog, though no live sheep had been injured, was destroyed and Mr Thomas fined £3. His letter to the court reads as sadly as the loss of a domestic animal can, expressing surprise, as the dog had never shown any inclination to chase sheep during the time he was training it: 'The dog had not been a good worker and was regarded as a family pet.'

An advertisement in the *Cambrian News* expresses the indignation one particular farmer felt:

PUBLIC NOTICE
ANY DOGS FOUND STRAYING ON THE LAND OF PANDY BENTLY HALL, LLANGEITHO, WILL BE SHOT ON SIGHT
SIGNED

H. DAVIES

But the notice is in English. One would have thought, for the sake of the dogs and the Welsh Language Society, it should have been in Welsh.

Sometimes it happens that even trained dogs cast their eyes on a neighbouring farm and resolve to enjoy driving sheep there, with other canine allies. Mr Jones at Carneddau Farm, Llanrwst, suffered from such a nuisance in the winter of 1969. He had sixty sheep grazing in his field and one morning found they had been worried, some having had their tails bitten off and some with blood staining their flanks. Though at that time there were no dogs to be seen, later, on one December night when he heard dogs barking he ran to the fields carrying his torch and found three dogs worrying the sheep, one of them having apparently only three legs. A fortnight later when in the early hours of morning he was attending a cow in his barn, he heard that familiar sound of the excited dogs and found the same two dogs and another with them driving his sheep. A day or two after that another farmer, Lloyd Williams of Ty Gwyn Farm, had the same trouble. He saw four dogs, including the one with no more than three legs, chasing his sheep, all 200 of them. Seven or eight had their tails bitten away while some had bites on their necks. Of course the police were called upon to visit the owner of the three-legged dog who proved to be Mr William Mostyn Owen, councillor of Llanrwst Urban and Denbigh County Councils.

Although the complaining farmers, Messrs Jones and Williams, identified and named the two as Del and Shagw, both animals were provided with witnesses and alibis. Wives, daughters and employees of the owners, and caravan dwellers also, came into court to offer evidence of their innocence. Mr E.C. Marshall Hughes, defending, protested on behalf of both dogs that it was a case of mistaken identity. He really represented the three-legged dog and, though reluctantly agreeing that there were two dogs on the rampage, he asserted that they were not owned by Mostyn Jones. 'I would go so far as to say that the three-legged dog could not possibly chase sheep!' he declared.

In spite of all this accumulated effort, Mr Mostyn Jones was found guilty of being the owner of the offending dog and fined £9 and it was directed that Shagw and Del be kept under proper control.

Of course the question of identification is the difficulty. Not many owners are as neighbourly as Tudur Thomas of Llangernyw. Sometimes only the full force of the constabulary can determine this problem, as on one March day when a Mr Goodband noticed a dog standing over a lamb in Hindhead Field, Upper Colwyn Bay, the rest of the flock having fled into a corner. As he himself could not manage to catch the culprit, he hurried to Pen-y-Bryn Farm to warn the owner, who was aghast to find thirteen lambs had been attacked, six of them badly injured. The dog was still there and he actually saw it jump upon a lamb; and it was there even when more police arrived.

Identification now became essential. If they caught the animal, it might never be claimed. Who would readily admit to such a responsibility? So the police officers formed a posse, and there they were, Inspector Morris and his two officers, stealthily following and tracking that dog. He might have led them anywhere 'over the hills and far away', but they kept him in sight, pausing when he paused, the policemen running when the dog ran, until eventually after some miles of tracking they came to Lawson Road, Colwyn Bay, where the owner, Robert Watkin, began to explain. He usually kept his dog tied to a stake, but after giving him a meal that night, he must have left the door ajar. As soon as it was noticed the dog had gone, both he and his son went outside and roamed around looking for him. They had no idea the animal had gone to the farms.

So much harassment, so much effort on the part of the police, demanded adequate retribution. The whole legal canine book was thrown at the unfortunate owner who found himself charged with 'being in charge of a dog found worrying sheep, being the owner of a dog found straying at night, being the owner of a dog not wearing a collar, and with keeping a dog without a licence.' The magistrates, however, seemed to give thought to Mr Watkin's explanations as a town resident and fined him only a total of £8 on all the charges.

The Colwyn Police were good at following animals in those days. I remember well how my wife's aunt came to her door in Old Colwyn to be suddenly confronted with a severe constable in blue equipped with pencil and notebook, a dead chicken and its owner from the field opposite the Queen's Hotel. They had followed her cat, followed it quietly and stealthily all up the main road and home into Meiriadog Road. Aunt Peggy was very fond of that cat and paid the alleged charge of £1 damage without hesitation, glad to see the chicken-keeper depart with that dead fowl and the constable. She should have taken possession of the chicken, but when the story was told, she looked sick at the very suggestion.

18   Old Times in Denbighshire

There were days one likes to remember when folk living by the sea had more contact with the hill farms of their hinterland. Aunty Peggy would have Mrs Jones, a farmer's wife, come down from Llysfaen to take her little party to Dolwen and Dawn. She brought a trap drawn by her white pony that appeared a great deal older than them all on these picnic trips since everyone had to get out and walk the gravelly roads up those steep hills. Mrs Jones had a daughter who seemed to be eternally stewing mushrooms through the late summer days; maybe she sold them along the coast. Across the bridge at Dawn lived Mrs Owen, who came around Old Colwyn to sell her butter and eggs, all neatly displayed in huge, shallow wicker baskets. She would always offer hospitality at her farm where none enjoyed the rest more than that white pony.

The box trees are just as large, as luxuriant and as fragrant with perfume as ever, though the roads are metalled now. The heronry is there still, but the name Coed Coch (Red Wood) is not so permanent on all the gates since the estate began to be broken up after Miss Brodrick's death. I can recall her even today as she would stand, tall and grey, by the great door that opens on the portico of the five fluted columns of Penrhyn slate stone, and a commanding and graceful figure she made, standing before her splendid mansion. Many changes have come upon the house since, the pictures and treasures having been sold in the London auction rooms, the mansion changed to Heronwater Private School and now today owned by what seems a transatlantic religious foundation with all the empty atmosphere of solitude around it, so transformed from the day when, on some ramble over those hills, I heard the very earth shake with the thunder of the famous Coed Coch ponies and, side-stepping to the wall for shelter, watched a hundred or more gallop by and away over the incline, leaving a cloud of dust and the echoes behind them.

The famous Welsh Pony Stud was broken up at a dispersal sale in

1978, long after Miss Brodrick died in 1962. Of the two outstanding stallions Coed Coch Bari reached the price of 21,000 guineas and the older, Coed Coch Salad, 14,000 guineas. As late as 1983, though some ponies were shown at Plas Llewelyn, Dolwen, by Mrs Fetherstonhaugh who continued to run Coed Coch Stables, only six mares with foals were on show, a fragment of the famous enterprise which had once shipped stock to some twelve countries, including the USA and Australia, although the tradition of horse breeding lived on, not only of Welsh mountain ponies but, for use on valley land, of the heavier Welsh cob of fourteen hands minimum in dozens of small studs run by farming families.

There used to be more than 2,000 prize rosettes at Coed Coch, but more satisfying than mere show results was the joy of the mountain ponies, the work of Miss Brodrick and her old retainer John Jones of Cambwll, Dolwen, which gave such delight to children and riding schools everywhere and made the lives of the ponies themselves comfortable and easy. John Jones was attached to Coed Coch as a boy. His genius had been the driving force in building up the stud and maintaining its reputation. He never retired but preserved an active interest until the age of eighty-nine years, being known at every showground in Britain.

Other farmers, such as Hugh Evans of Garth Hebog, Melin-y-Coed, could narrate far different recollections of the Welsh pony trade. He spoke out at one late summer show up at Nebo, where he was exhibiting the Fronwen Stud of pedigree riding ponies established by his father William.

'Up to about thirty years ago,' he explained, 'we sent the stallions away to the collieries around Newcastle, where they worked underground hauling the coal trucks. I remember in my father's time about forty ponies going away twice a year in railway wagons from Llanrwst Station, some of them bred at our own stud, but mainly those he bought and sold as a dealer. Only the stallions, which had to be at least four years old, went down the mines, while the mares were kept for breeding.'

It was not until the demand from the pits ceased, due to the underground tramways being changed to electrical working, that the Evans family, like the other North Wales breeders, resorted to specializing in pedigree riding ponies. One would like to think such changes came about for altruistic reasons – the contrast between the wild Welsh moorlands so green and free, against the 'wretched, blind pit ponies' in Hodgson's poem, but this result was purely for technological and commercial reasons and not, as Hodgson begged for the ringing of 'The Bells of Heaven'.

Perhaps I am a townsman at heart and never would I rear animals either as slaves or for slaughter, yet I am certainly not such a townsman as Mr Barlow. Long after the white pony and trap, and the gravel roads also, had vanished, Aunt Peggy would hire him and his Rolls Royce from the garage below Meiriadog Road, Old Colwyn and we would all go for a picnic and drive around the Denbigh moors. As the proprietor of his garage and owner of the Rolls Royce, he felt an obligation to join in our conversation, but he had only one phrase with which to manage this: 'Plenty of land for building hereabouts!' was his contribution with which he punctuated the drive and the intervals of silence in the picnic, managing evey permutation of words and intonation his Lancashire accent provided – 'No shortage here, building land everywhere. Don't have to look for it. Vacancies everywhere!'

The vast Clocaenog Forest plantation had not been thought of when we would drive over those immense, empty spaces. The tall heathers caught the sunlight then and shone red against the blue sky as we motored around past the Sportsman's Arms towards Bryn Trillyn. Even these days in summer I can never pass that lonely inn without recollecting that its vicinity occupies its own place in the *Guinness Book of Records* as having the deepest recorded snowfall in Britain, and, also, with an altitude of over 1,500 feet, makes claim to be the highest inn in Wales.

Just within sight of the famous Hunting Lodge we would make tea among the heather and winberries, through the lazy afternoon speculating on that ostentatious, empty mansion which Mr Barlow dismissed with the comment as he went back to his Rolls, 'Funny place to build that there!' As he sat smoking I remember leaving the roadside picnic to scramble through the rough heather right up to that house on the summit. There it stood in the wild open world with bracken and grass and heather growing right up to its walls, without any garden at all, never a trace of flowers or fruit except briars creeping into chinks of its mortar.

We could stand beside it, this place Aunt Peggy always referred to with such reverence as 'the Hunting Lodge', stand as if we owned it, right on top of the moors at 1,627 feet, the summit of Bryn Trillyn itself. Commanding a view of everywhere, even to the door where my cottage looks out, it stands there today as untenanted as then, glancing at all the mountains at Gwynedd and the breadth of the Irish

Sea. Black and foreign ridges of forest conifers blot away the old lines of landscape and the blue distances of Clocaenog horizons today, but one hopes a wiser generation will plant the beautiful Welsh oaks in years to come.

There was no more prospect of immediate cash for the owners of that mansion than for the Forestry Commission in planting oaks. Sheep, ignoring as I did that notice forbidding trespassers to enter the open doorways, found shelter there and roamed within, defiling floors where royalty had once walked. Splendid plasterwork and plaques moulded in a nineteenth-century classical style were tumbling from ceilings and out of the walls, even the paint was peeling away. Though the exterior presented the rugged face of survival, all the interior shivered with desolation.

No one could stay there long and be happy, for it was no old ruin. The blight was that of yesterday, of only our fathers' time, of neglect, folly and the ensuing poverty. There, over the imposing half-tower of the entrance door, stared the arms, carved in stone, of Lord Devonport. He had chosen this point at Bryn Trillyn, 1,627 feet, rivalled only by its neighbours, Eithin, 1,742 feet, and Bron-banog, 1,644 feet, from which to command his grouse and their keepers right across the moors.

The first house had been a mere shooting-box built of Norwegian timber with two Norwegian craftsmen imported to superintend its erection. They gave it security by fastenings to the rocky foundation. Nobody realized how those dreadful winds around the mountains can dry out timbers and fan flames. When the building caught fire, it blazed like a beacon to all the corners of the compass. Though everyone from Denbigh to the coast saw the conflagration, nothing could be done, for apart from wells there was no water, none at all, on that summit. The supply had to be pumped up by manpower from the brook beside the inn.

In 1913 there was no shortage of money, and John Jones, a local builder from Pentrevoelas, erected the traditional mansion in plastered stone with big windows from which not only the keepers could be seen on their rounds but even the grouse themselves which came right up to the steps and fed, sheltering beside the walls. Famous visitors came as guests of the Devonports, including Edward VIII when Prince of Wales, and Lloyd George who himself suggested the name *Gwylfa Hiraethog* (Hiraethog Watchtower).

While money flowed, the splendour of Gwylfa Hiraethog shone. A two-horse wagonette brought guests from Denbigh railway station. A regular service was maintained. Servants had their rhubarb pies and eggs at the Crown Inn, Denbigh, where they travelled every day to fetch coal, newspapers and books along with other necessities. But the winds at changes of season were hard to bear. It was said that the cook was once blown across the yard with the wind in her skirts, lifted clear from the ground like a balloon. There was employment for the staff and money paid for their work, but else there was nothing for them to do. Today it needs a great stretch of imagination to understand the complete isolation of those mountain locations. When the winds ceased, the mist would come down, the fine upland rain with it, and stay, and of course for five months of the year snow was always threatening. Though all the local shepherds used the Sportsman's Arms they were mountain men, Welsh-speaking all, who found themselves abashed, muzzled and speechless in the company of the Gwylfa's pretty imported housemaids and other staff. Suddenly they would become conscious of their limited English and remain glum and ill at ease. Dull as it was for the staff, the mansion provided money when work was otherwise not to be had. Five keepers were employed just to protect and rear the grouse, and by late summer farmers' lads could count on wages for each day beating the heather, and a good lunch as well. Always these birds came under Lord Devonport's eye. His reputation depended upon their numbers. He would ride across the moors like a keeper himself. Mountain walkers or tourists after winberries experienced the sharp edge of his tongue.

One of the first signs of impending disaster came when he had an altercation with an under-keeper and the staff noticed that he was not replaced. In earlier days the game-keeping side was never allowed to suffer reduction. Yet even in those times the young housemaids would not stay; the lonely edifice was so often in the clouds with winds howling and screaming around. Guests themselves came only for brief shooting excursions. For a few days it might be pleasant to see the frost shiny on the heather and the grouse feeding by the windows, but for a few days only. It was too isolated even to hold balls or social events. The Devonports sold out in 1925, but no one came to live there. In 1940 once again the property changed hands. They said that the brewery owners of the nearby inn were the purchasers, and rumours spread of hotel speculation, of flat-sharing holidays and such like. But the wind howls round that empty building without providing so much as a ghost story, and it is too isolated even for vandals to steal the fabric for building-materials.

As we packed away the teacups from that summer picnic, the

weather seemed faultless, too pleasant by far to leave the heather and stroll back to the road. I noticed Mr Barlow there, polishing his Rolls Royce and stroking it with the greatest affection. For a moment I wondered, had his faded conveyance survived those years, once having existed in glory as that resplendent vehicle round which the locals would crowd to gaze, astonished by its uniformed chauffeur guarding the bright brass lamps, the polish and the elaborate cushions on which would sit the lords and ladies from the palaces of London when they descended from trains in Denbigh?

We took narrow roads back to Old Colwyn and Mr Barlow, driving with greater caution, ceased his comments on property speculation, no doubt thinking more about the width of the lanes in relation to his driving. Whether it would be complimentary or a denigration to enquire about the antecedents of that Rolls, perhaps the only one in North Wales that fitted the period, I could not tell for his conversation refused to expand and I let the chance slip by.

Pobdy Mawr, one-time hearth of Robert Roberts

The Roman standing stones, Gwytherin

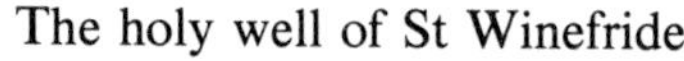

Gwytherin church and the druidic yew trees

The holy well of St Winefride

St Mary's Well, a favourite location for clandestine
marriages

Neglected gardens at Hafodunas, once Squire Sandbach's mansion

My neighbour Gwilym Jones, Cefn Castell, and his prizewinning
sheepdog

Llanrwst Show, 1946. Photograph by the Author

Llanrwst Bridge: 'homage to Inigo Jones'

Judging sheep at Llanrwst Show, 1946

Doctor Samuel Johnson's cottage as it was (note the spelling in the old postcard). *Below:* All that now remains of the sage's fireside hearth

The high moorlands above the Conwy Valley

Llanelian: the one-time hostelry near the 'Cursing Well'. (The roof of
Ty'n-y-Llidiart would have resembled this one which the Author
photographed in 1932)

Dolwyddelen: 'Roman Bridge' and the slopes of Siabod

Cartref Sir Henry Jones. The old cobbler's house is the birthplace of the boy Henry who became a Glasgow University Professor and a founding father of University College, North Wales

19   Grander Houses from Tudor Times till Today

Transfer of human necessities from past to present, especially building materials, quarried stones, timber, slates or lead, has been the activity of the generations across the centuries, and not just from the old castles but from those old mansions of the Tudor times, once a glory in Wales. As I stood at my own gate looking across the moors towards Gwylfa, I thought of the mansions built in the more splendid Renaissance times when so many anglicized Welshmen came to London or Oxford to learn the humanities and brought back English heiresses with a Saxon entourage that would try to become more Welsh than the Welsh themselves. Now in these industrialized later centuries they too have vanished.

Looking towards the Vale of Clwyd I could see the far valleys by Henllan and Denbigh, the land of mysterious place-names that indicate the track of the Roman road from Varis (Bod-vari), names such as Holborn, Eriviat, Constantin, or Moel Cathau (Hill of the Battalions), and I linked them with the exotic names of the Gwytherin woods in my own valley, names also associated with the palace of Lleweni, for the lords of Lleweni owned estates along the river down below, by Gwytherin.

I myself had gathered up the quarried stones bulldozed and ploughed away from round the two wells on Cae Delyn opposite. I had stacked them around my cottage garden, all that remains of the old Roman villa fort and its Welsh successor, so that I could gloat over them. But the walls of that further Lleweni are scarcely a memory, for all its Renaissance wonder.

It was my great pleasure any time of day to stand by the gate and look across all the valleys, over Llansannan towards the Vale of Clwyd with Denbigh almost in a line. All along the edge of the moors in a high contour as if marking the edge of primitive habitation and worship stand the ancient, unexcavated funeral mounds each shown on the map as a 'tumulus', in the tawny moorland colour up to which the green grass creeps as if supplicating the heather, the bogs and the peat wilderness, especially the mound visible upon my eastern horizon behind which the sun rises.

In the days of the Tudors, sheep represented wealth. Then the anglicized families of Denbigh grew rich and aristocratic, and they stayed so right up to the days of Cromwell. Denbigh Castle came to be the last castle in Britain holding out for King Charles, obstinately defended by Sir William Salusbury, of the Lleweni family, whose reputation was such that he was allowed to march out from that castle with drums beating and colours flying as if he had been the victor. Tradition narrates that the 'Blue Stocking Hero', as he was known, mounted the Great Goblin Tower and rhetorically demanded whether the Parliamentarians had any further claims. On hearing the shout for the key of the castle, he threw it down amongst them as he retorted, in a coarser Welsh than the English version gives, 'The world is yours! Make it your dunghill!'

Crueller than most has been the treatment of this structure, so useful for the grasping hands of stonemason and builder without regard for its brave history, but as for the palace of Lleweni, only whispers of its glory in the neighbouring township remain, as Bradley wrote in 1898: 'Some miles of crumbling park wall and a couple of farmhouses made from part of the ruins of the great mansion that once stood there.' Though some make quite a show of 'Lleweni' being a Welsh corruption of the Latin *Leoni* (lions) it is obviously an English version of the Welsh *llwyni* (smiling groves) − appropriate enough, for nowhere smiles the River Clwyd more than here as it flows by the old park and the ancient wood beside those buried foundations.

The first Salusbury died in 1089, having established himself under William the Conqueror, and in later years another Sir John returned from the Crusades to find the abbey at Denbigh and die in 1289. Despite its antiquity, the original mansion was demolished in more recent times to build Kinmel Hall, Edward Hughes having bought Lleweni for £209,000 in 1813 and being more interested in developing the great Kinmel estate by land purchase and enclosures of common land. Everything of this home of the Salusbury family, so carefully gathered by the Norman founders by lawful marriage with rich Welsh heiresses, so manfully increased by siding with that Earl of Richmond who became Henry VII, all came to be scattered, the great library of rare books and manuscripts, the collection of old master paintings dispersed and perhaps lost.

The family had its occasional reverses. When the Earl of Leicester enclosed Denbigh Common, two sons of Lleweni joined the mob of the town's burgesses in a protest riot and levelled the Earl's new fences. The omnipotent earl, close favourite of Queen Elizabeth, had them both executed, construing opposition to himself as high treason. Possibly in revenge for this, Thomas Salusbury became involved in the Babington Plot to replace the Queen by Mary, Queen of Scots. Thus his brother Sir John the Strong (after whom is named another Gwytherin wood below my cottage) succeeded to the estate. He was renowned doubly strong, having two thumbs on each hand! Legends grew around him as a lion-slayer, giant-thrower and tree-hurler. After him came Sir Henry, the first baronet, whose eldest son, Sir Thomas, was among the many North Wales gentlemen who began their education at the Welsh foundation of Jesus College, Oxford. Pennant mentions him as having 'a natural geny to poetry and romance exercised in those juvenile studies produced from his pen, the *History of Joseph* in English verse, in thirteen chapters.'

By far the most famous literary figure of the family was the learned William Salusbury of Cae du, a house even in Pennant's time no more than a deserted ruin with, remaining on the chimney, 'a massive stack of masonry in which is a small secret closet, with a loop-hole window, where the Reformer is said to have executed his sacred task.' He too received his education at Oxford, afterwards studying law at London. Though reputed to be conversant with eleven languages he chose to write almost exclusively in Welsh, being a literary pioneer in that language with the first Welsh almanac ever printed in 1546, followed next year by an English and Welsh Dictionary dedicated by permission to Henry VIII. His translation of the New Testament, not from the Latin Vulgate but from the Greek, was published in 1567, years before Bishop Morgan's entire Bible was published by the royal press in 1588.

Those times were violent indeed, and dangerous even for the administration of justice. On one occasion David ap Jenkin of Nant Conway slew the Red Judge on the Bench at Denbigh with a dagger. The assassin escaped unpunished and gloried in the deed. Long after, he publicly exhibited that fatal weapon corroded with the blood of his victim. In the records of the Old Town Hall was found a letter with the concluding wording: '... requiring us, in the King's Majesty's name, to deliver unto you the bodies of certain malefactors now remaining in the Town Gaol of Denbigh, for the murdering of Robert Salusbury, gent., late Alderman and justice of the peace; and one David ap Edward, xxiii Jany., 1616'.

The male line of the Lleweni Salusburys became extinct in the sixteenth century. Some idea of the accumulation of their estates is given by the career of Catherine of Berain, the great granddaughter of Henry VIII, in female descent. She was actually Catherine Tudor and a near relative of Queen Elizabeth. Already the daughter and heiress of the Tudors of Berain, she had married John Salusbury, heir of Lleweni, and on his death, Sir Richard Clough who when he led her to her husband's funeral, proposed marriage. As she left that church, she was intercepted by another suitor, Morris Wynne of Gwydir. Though obliged to refuse him, she promised with great civility, he should be her next spouse as soon as the new husband departed this life. She proved as good as her word when death soon provided the opportunity for remarriage. Morris Wynne also did not outlast her and, as soon as could be, again she married, this time to Edward Thellwall. Repute accorded her seven husbands in all, as if to keep up with the more renowned Tudor Henry VIII. So her properties had multiplied. At the Great Sessions held at Denbigh in the eighth year of Elizabeth's reign, she had appeared to enumerate all her lands, mills and hereditaments before the jury, for the great estates from all around Denbigh had passed into the Salusbury possession, from Henblas to Gwytherin and Bryn Barcut in the valley below my cottage, from Rug to Bachymbyd.

Bachymbyd! What memories that name brings me! House of that learned Sir William, it stands today almost unnoticed beside the Denbigh Road. There I was in the peaceful times between the Wars, driving along that Denbigh Road one rainy afternoon in springtime.

There was little traffic on the roads then, but I was proud of my careful driving and still more proud of my car, an ex-RAC patrol car, made by the defunct company of Clyno.

The hood was up, in spite of the rain the brass headlamps and the polished metal shone brightly; the dickie seat was folded back, my passengers and I sat in the dry in that comfortable car on cushions stuffed with real horsehair. We needed take little notice of the rain on that easy straight highway as the clouds opened and the storm broke loose.

Directly in the centre of the road I could see a cyclist. Cowering from the rain, he pedalled furiously as he came down, keeping to the centre. Afraid lest if I swerved to right or to left, I would collide if he so moved on seeing me, I came to a halt and sounded my horn by pressing the great rubber bulb. That proud ornamental horn that made such a polite request! But this was no time for politeness. Faster he pedalled and crouched lower, never looking up. Onward he came to the music of the horn as to a rising trumpet charge, onward faster and faster, hard into the very centre of my radiator. The shock was incredible to him, to myself, to my passengers. For he stood there, upside down, with his chin on the bonnet of the car. His legs and large boots beat a tattoo in the air, to the left, to the right, swaying violently, indecisive which way to fall. For half a second he balanced on the perpendicular; then down he went in a clutching, grovelling scramble down below the very radiator. Only Aunt Peggy spoke, asking the unwanted question, 'What did you do that for, Stowers?'

Almost before I could open the car door, five or six brawny lads had come out of the cottages and carried him away. Out came the resident of Bachymbyd, a huge, massively built farmer in leather. He arranged for police and for garage attendance and service. Alas, my Clyno manufacturers had long gone out of production. The rebuilt radiator was to take weeks to obtain and install. As it was, hours passed while we waited beside Bachymbyd's splendid ivy-clad façade, which gleamed with shiny wine-coloured masonry and the falling raindrops. Our host brought cups of tea and lent information to our appreciation of his dwelling, becoming so sensitive to our enthusiasm that he found a photograph for us.

As for the cyclist acrobat, I never set eyes on him again, though I am sure my insurance company dealt with his bill, which included charges for a new cycle, taxi fares to and from work, dental charges and new teeth, lost wages and so on – an assessment many times the actual value of my automobile.

Was the new acquaintance who emerged from Bachymbyd to proffer assistance some remote and lineal descendant of those Salusburys of Tudor times whose names still survive along those woodlands in the Cledwen valley below Ty'n-y-Llidiart? That I never knew, but now I have learned the significance of that Norman Anglo-Welsh family, the whole landscape takes on a deeper importance and meaning whenever I look across to Denbigh from my cottage windows.

Not so neglected as Lleweni, but with luck giving survival to their haphazard existence, are the walls of Gwydir at Llanrwst, once the home of that old tyrant and historian, Sir John Wynne. In the lush green meadows between the Conwy River and the forested hills, the old Elizabethan mansion stands erected on an older site where the poet-prince Llywarch Hen fought in AD 610, and where Prince Iago battled with Ievan in the tenth century, and years later Traherne ap Caradoc was to fight against Griffith ap Cynan. Not for nothing did these riverside meadows earn the name of 'Gwaed dir' ('land of blood'). In those days the shallow barges could be drawn right up to the great slabs of forgotten stone where the old oak tree roots now shelter only fresh run salmon.

Stronger men afterwards came upon the scene, notably the warrior Goch. The English called him Sir Howel Pole Axe when, as leader of a hundred Denbighshire men at Poitiers, he struck off the head of the French king's charger with one sweep of his axe and took the royal rider prisoner. He himself met a hero's death in Flanders in 1388.

There were terrible days to come with war at home as well as abroad as the old Welsh rhyme declares of the rivalry between the Red and the White Rose, in which the Yorkist Herbert, Earl of Pembroke, laid waste North Wales:

> 'In Harlech and Denbigh every door flaming,
> The Vale of Conway reduced to embers.'

Sir John Wynne records 'The whole country was reduced to cold coals.' And he goes on to narrate: 'In 1466 Thomas ap Robin of Cochwillan was beheaded, near the castle, by Lord Pembroke's order, on account of his staunch adherence to the Lancastrians; and his wife (Gwenhwyfar) is reported to have carried away his head in her apron, prophesying to the Earl that his own pitiless head should soon be severed in like manner. Not long after this the earl was taken prisoner at the battle of Danesmoor, and was beheaded.'*

The lifestyle and tradition acquired in such wars lived on beyond them. In the valleys of North Wales robber bands in military formation terrorized the villages until John Wynne of Gwydir and Lewis Owen of Dolgellau joined forces on an expedition to comb them out of the mountains. From the numerous bands they arrested, eighty were condemned and executed by hanging. At this execution the mother of two condemned men, berserk at finding her pleas unavailing, tore open her garments to bare her breasts, screaming, 'These yellow breasts have given suck to those who will wash their hands in your blood!'†

As surely as the similar prophecy of that lady of Cochwillan, the doom this mother invoked came to pass. Not all the outlaws had been caught, and Lewis Owen of Dolgellau was coming back from Montgomery Assizes when he ran into an ambush which was laid

---

* *Gwydir History, p.46*
† Bezant Lowe, p.208

where the road dips to cross the river, midway between the crest of
Bwlch-y-Fedwen and Mallwyd. There, in 1555, his escort was
overwhelmed almost before they reached the bridge, and Lewis Owen
fell, slain it is said by thirty-four counted wounds. John Wynne,
however, continued the task of subjugating the mountains. His family
prospered, travelling to London, exercising the law from chambers in
the Inns of Court like so many men from these parts, multiplying
lands and properties by avaricious marriages – landlords whose
influence weaves like a powerful thread through the history of North
Wales but who were remembered by their tenants as severe and
exacting.

I first saw Gwydir when it stood forgotten and neglected soon after
the war and remembered that Welsh rhyme of the older wars:

> In fourteen hundred sixty eight
> When basely flamed the fire,
> When our Nant Conway suffered more
> For there the flames burned higher.

When Sir John Wynne was writing, he declared the stones of his
earlier ruined mansion still carried the marks of those fires, but he had
replaced the older building with a fine Tudor palace with oriel
windows, turreted chimneystacks and formal Italian style gardens
hedged with box and planted with cypress, cedar and yew, arranged
with sundials and walls mathematically spaced and neatly paved with
flagstones. The Earl of Leicester came to stay here, and Queen
Elizabeth and also Charles I. A.G. Bradley, writing his *Highways and
Byways* in the last decade of the nineteenth century, could comment as
he went by, 'Not a great deal of the original mansion of 1555 is left,
but it is still a beautiful and ancient house, full of carved oak, and
tapestry and Spanish leather and treasures and relics of great people
innumerable.' It had passed away from the Wynne family by then
and in the second edition of Ward Lock's Guide is noted: 'Open when
the Earl of Carrington is not in residence. 12-5 daily, Sundays
excepted. (*fee optional*)'

There was no need to look for traces of fire when in 1946 I climbed
the curtilage to take a photograph The walls were smoke blackened,
windows empty and bare and the chimneys over the ruin stark against
the blue sky. A disastrous conflagration in 1922 had gutted the whole
residential 'castle' and there it had stood all through those inter-war
years in the pessimism and depression until Arthur Clegg, on his

retirement from bank managing, chose for himself the occupation of chatelain and began in 1944 preparing to restore the ruin. He financed the work himself and slowly, using contemporary materials, brought the fabric back into a semblance of its former splendour.

For several years the air of dereliction hung about, despite the peacocks and the gardens. I well remember the tawny owls of a summer evening. They would be returning to feed their young, carrying young rabbits that swarmed around in those days. Sometimes the weight of the prey they clutched would bear them down till they could hardly surmount the ivy-clad walls, but they always did, by inches only.

As happens in the passing of time, Clegg Senior grew old in removing the dilapidation and in 1962 aged eighty-three, died, leaving the task to his son. His work had been a splendid example in private conservation for he had laboured to obtain antiques and period furniture with which he conjured back the Elizabethan atmosphere. Gwydir became classified as a historic monument. Visitors flocked to pay the entrance fee for which the display of fifty peacocks provided an assurance of good value. His son Richard gave up work as a solicitor and came back from Lancashire to maintain his father's property. An appreciative and reliable staff of guides was employed so that there were few in Llanrwst who did not come to know a great deal about the Wynne family history. When in 1982 he chose to retire, leaving Gwydir, to reside at Conwy, the little town of Llanrwst was shaken to find the old mansion advertised for sale and all the carefully gathered contents exposed to an auction view.

So it was, however. Messrs Jackson Stops & Staff put the entire contents under the hammer in the second week of May 1982. Local councils and local patriotic groups did nothing. Words and sentiments come so easily upon the tongue, but not so readily does the pen run along a cheque book. The famous Wynne full tester bedstead, dated 1570, was sold for £5,600, another, later and described as seventeenth century, made £2,000, while the grand dining-table fetched £2,700. All the contents, so carefully gathered by the Cleggs for their Wynne associations, went far and wide away from Wales, dispersed among the thousand folk who gathered about that marquee upon the great lawn. They could gape at the spectacle of Mrs Maggie Williams who paraded each day of the sale in her own traditional national costume. Now aged eighty years, in her day she had been a noted pennillion singer and remembered better times and evenings there, when handclaps of applause made a more pleasing sound than the fall of the auctioneer's hammer.

As the wind came down to chill the chattering groups dispersing after the sale, it was rumoured that the house itself, advertised widely at the asking price of £150,000 had been sold to 'a South of England couple' for a figure 'approaching that sum'. The contents themselves had realized just over £75,000.

Richard Clegg, not in the best of health, survived hardly two years in his retirement at Conwy, whereas the new owners, Mr and Mrs Redmond, braced themselves to make a twentieth-century success as castle-owners, for the coming year was the United Nations Year of the Castle. The local Press, the tourist agencies and the local authorities applauded them as conservation patrons doing the work for which they themselves were unwilling to find either effort or money.

There was a splendid celebratory Opening Day. Gwydir Castle had been saved! And saved in time, before deterioration, neglect or even further fires could spoil the achievement of the Clegg family. That opening day was a brave effort, like the sparkle of happy colour, of sunshine that precedes the thunder of tragedy in the theatre, recognized only by those who have read the play.

The castle lawns had been mowed and rolled flat and the box hedges trimmed. A bright array of stalls ringed the central pavilion where marquees enticed the wandering Llanrwst folk to view demonstrations of Welsh crafts. When the folkdancers were not displaying in the courtyard, the Deiniole Silver Band, as smart as their neat uniforms, played throughout the afternoon and there was a *frisson* of excitement going through the whole gathering.

It was not that Michael and Jackie Redmond, the new owners were present, but a television film was being made. Opex Films were on location with television actors. Mrs Redmond and her son were featuring and wearing medieval costumes. Scenes from the film, an over-wise spectator whispered, might be enacted at any moment, recreating the fabled time of Owen Glendower. The Film Director, James Hill, had said, 'I have read quite a lot about Owen Glendower during my preparations and as far as one can tell from the historical sources, he seems to have been a very wise and just man.' The words conveyed little in that most Welsh of all Welsh towns but suddenly there was a clash from the Silver Band!

Into the centre stepped the neat, dark-suited figure of Councillor Rhys Hughes, wearing the golden chain of the Mayor of Aberconwy upon his broad shoulders. His introductory speech showed the wisdom and the learning of the schoolmaster he had been, invoking Lloyd George and the notables who had inspired North Wales.

Without use of microphone, his voice came over clearly to that crowd in those pleasant tones and rolling vowels by which English is spoken in North Wales, mellow, refined and full of generosity as opposed to the linguistic harshness sometimes usual in the southern valleys. His words bespoke success for the Redmonds, which the challenge of costumes moving through the crowds, the pennillion singing within the mansion and the proud, parading peacocks, some fifty of them guarding the walls, all seemed to endorse.

Certainly neither time nor energy was wasted in putting Gwydir into 'The Year of the Castles'. The Redmonds sought out associative antiques and contemporary furnishings, projects were developed to encourage namesakes of the Wynne family to come from the USA as tourists. The oak trees planted by the future King George V and Queen Mary in 1899 were celebrated. Research was done and overdone to produce suggestions of a ghost, a theme which seems to increase interest for some in this computerized century of ours; the private Wynne Chapel was furbished, and down in the cellar, to show where the tyrannical Sir John, himself his own gaoler, policeman and magistrate for all that area, confined prisoners at his pleasure, dungeons were excavated.

Alas for the irony which invades our lives! I find myself looking at a photograph in the local newspaper.* There is a grille shown with its ropes and chains and the caption below the picture reads: 'At the entrance to Gwydir Castle's dungeons, helper Tony Brown poses as a prisoner secured by Mrs Jacqueline Redmond.'

Three months later, 23 June 1983, and only a year after taking possession of Gwydir, both the Redmonds were found guilty of fraud and each gaoled for eighteen months for the conduct of three companies in the Isle of Wight, criminal bankruptcy and disqualification orders being made against them. They had been accused of deliberately setting out to defraud customers with unpaid bills and bounced cheques. The judge declared when sentencing, 'You were engaged for two years in very dishonest trading as a result of which a large number of traders have lost tens of thousands of pounds.' Mrs Redmond, who had walked those Gwydir lawns in medieval costume with such charm and grace, Judge Martin Tucker, QC described as 'a clever, scheming wife who to a certain extent had bullied her husband into it.'

At Winchester Crown Court where the case was heard, it was

---

* *North Wales Weekly News,* 24 March 1983

stated that they had been living at 'Gwydir Cottage, Gwydir Castle', said to be owned by Stealth Investments with a registered office in Jersey, but a detective reported he had been unable to trace the nominee directors of this company because of Jersey laws. After the jury's verdict was given, Michael Redmond's record was read out in the usual dull police voice which disclosed, one after the other, his previous convictions for dishonesty, conspiracy to defraud, burglary, and handling stolen goods!

How remote is Llanrwst! How naïve and trusting! Here, on credit, though heavily, criminally in debt, the couple had seemed worthy successors of the Wynnes of old. (Perhaps they were!) At least, their pseudo-affluence won the admiration of the little town and their downfall shocked everyone. It may be the Redmonds even from prison relied on Stealth Investments who apparently owned the property. Though criminal bankrupts are stripped of their assets to clear their debts, the complexities of the Jersey laws made determining the identity of the company's board difficult. As it was, Mrs Redmond's mother took control of Gwydir and managed it with a skeleton staff. 'It is a sad business,' she observed, 'but it has not had any effect on the numbers of people visiting.' In fact the numbers increased, and the peacocks flourished, fed by sympathizers, determined they should not suffer.

Events did not drift for long, however. Coutts Bank of London were the mortgagees and lost no time in putting the old mansion up for auction. In November, 1983, it was sold for a price much lower than the Redmonds had given. Some 150 local folk came to the auction, most of them mere spectators crowding into the stone-flagged lower hall. Bidding started at £80,000 and in a very few minutes was sold to John Jackson for £121,000. John Jackson, they said, was 'in the property business', having moved to North Wales from the Warrington district in Lancashire, but I knew the family as keeping the interesting little antique shop on the northward road out of Llangernyw, Tan yr Onnen, just down the road from my little farmhouse.

'The castle will be primarily my family home,' said Mr Jackson, 'with tourist attractions for all ages. It will not become an amusement park,' he promised, 'but maybe a children's zoo, a few donkey rides, possible film shows both educational and interesting. We want to make it a castle for everyone, where youngsters can come to enjoy themselves and the ladies can see the furnishings.'

Despite the low price, superstitious folk thought the venture rash, regarding the old house of the Wynnes as an investment in ill fortune. But the ghost trade began with a flourish. Thirty-four American tourists paid £1,500 each for their ghost hunting trip and were keen enough on the excitement Gwydir provided. Through various rooms of the castle the party slept, or perhaps rather, woke through the night in their sleeping-bags. Though Mr and Mrs Jackson have never actually seen either of their two proprietary ghosts, tradition defines them as a medieval monk who died in the escape tunnel below and now haunts the gardens from which he never emerged alive, and the sixteen-year-old maiden supposed to have been seduced and murdered by Sir John Wynne.

The tourist guests were not to be disappointed for according to the *Sunday Telegraph*, on 2 September 1984, 'Mrs Buchanan, her husband, 44, a Seattle business man, Mrs Fran Owen were in the upstairs dining hall when the figure appeared. "It was six feet tall ... It made no sound whatever but there were occasional flashes of white light," said Mrs Buchanan. "It flitted between the Queen's Room and the Main Dining Hall." '

20 Llanrwst, 'A Most Welsh Town'

One often had cause to wonder at the timidity of the local authority for Llanrwst. How stupid to let such an asset as Gwydir slip away unless they felt incapable of managing it.

The town has a pitiful record in this regard, having savaged away its compact architectural plan of narrow little streets, of ancient houses built from huge stone blocks, terrace grouped in friendship against the rain and all the elements of harsh winter yet preserving a cool comfort in hot summers. Square and firm in medieval sociability were those houses where neighbour could smile to neighbour. Now they are all torn down and destroyed for little housing estates more suitable to Slough or Norwich. And the one fragment of grandeur the council possessed, its town hall – for years regarded as a nuisance, then as a public toilet and market store, gradually reduced, libelled and denigrated into demolition – has now gone for ever, to the applause of the shopkeepers in Ancaster Square, ignorant that they have promoted Nemesis in the shape of more market stalls there. For the Council fills the ancient square with booths each market day, charging rents to stallkeepers crushed as close as London's Petticoat Lane and most competitive to all those shopkeepers who without foresight sped on the departure of their ancient town hall with its surmounted Eagle of Gwydir, clock, black stone work and its comely arches.

What a story is revealed by linking the records of those Council meetings which contemplated its destruction! The councillors seem like bad boys plotting some guilty action, their sententious remarks like the wisdom of Toy Town. The tradesmen, led by Councillor Llew Phillips, sponsored the agitation which the local Press reported without taking sides, there being no Welsh Hampden to come forward rallying opposition. 'Demolish Repulsive Town Hall, say Shop-keepers!' and 'Protest Petition to Llanrwst Council' read the headlines in the *Weekly News.**

* *North Wales Weekly News*, 12 July 1962

Councillors prodded forward their Clerk and their Architect. The latter procrastinated and then proposed to fix 'tell-tale' glass against the building to indicate any movement and prove the structure dangerous. But no defect in the structure could be found; any slight movement was normal and not excessive. Pressed by some councillors, the Architect agreed that something would eventually have to be done with regard to the building. Councillor Phillips then said that the Architect had received a fee for his previous report and he should have another one for the present report.* They had already taken down the cupola and its market bell, almost a footstep on the road to ruin a year ago.

It was then suggested that the Council wrote to the Historic Buildings Committee pointing out extensive repairs were necessary, though no details of these were yet manifest, and asking for a substantial grant to cover such work. Of course the foreseen reply arrived, recalling that in 1953 an application had been made by Llanrwst for a grant, when it was decided that the town hall did not fall within the very limited category of buildings which could be regarded as having quite outstanding historical and architectural interest, though it was accepted as having some merit. In refusing a grant, the letter added there was little point in again raising the matter.

Such a letter was as good as saying: 'Pull the place down. It is not worth our money!' And the councillors fell into step behind their shopkeepers, only haggling as to who could demolish it most cheaply.

Speed was essential before opposition rallied. Councillor Phillips declared action should be taken immediately. Actually Aelwyd (the Welsh Youth) were becoming restive for they used the hall for their meetings. And patriotic Welsh national feeling would put a stop to demolition for ever. Councillor Phillips promised to provide them a room himself until they found satisfactory accommodation. 'I can guarantee this,' he promised.*

The Council Architect in rather equivocating style had murmured: 'It is great in character and we should be very sorry to see it disappear'.* Also, someone had been looking into the past and found the historic old building described in Lewis's *Topographical Dictionary*:

The market place is a spacious square area, in the centre of which stands the town hall, a plain substantial structure, erected at the

* *North Wales Weekly News*, 4 October 1962

expense of Maurice Wynne, Esq, of Caer Melwr, as appears from a stone over the principal entrance, bearing the arms of the Wynnes, and the initials of the founder, with the date 1661: above this is a clock, with a cupola containing the market bell, and surmounted by a large gilt eagle. The general quarter sessions for the county were formerly held in this hall, which practice has been discontinued since the removal of the assizes from Denbigh to Ruthin. The petty sessions for the Uchdulas division of the hundred of Isdulas are held here.

If only some Welsh patriot had been tried in that building! As it was, only the cause of the Youth Club (Aelwyd) was presented by a letter in Welsh from Mrs Goodwin which the newspaper translated: 'We feel that to demolish the building at such a stage with no building available to replace it would indeed be a sad blow to the young people and indeed to the Welsh culture of the town.'

Part of the town hall had probably been an Aelwyd clubroom for longer than many of these shopkeepers had been in business. Old folk now remembered how sixty years ago the Welsh poet Gwilym Cowlyd had successfully led opposition against a campaign to demolish that very building!

It was not, however, until April 1964 that the building which Councillor Phillips had begun on 2 July 1962 to denounce as 'a meaningless relic' came crashing down. The Council had agreed on 27 February to pay £650 for the demolition.

Builders' labourers levered out the massive blocks, hurling them down into Ancaster Square from the parapets, and the great stones of walls some two and a half feet thick were shifted away, leaving the crowds who stopped to watch in a lost state of dismay and shock. After all, the town hall had stood there beyond the memory of grandfathers and then beyond into the beginning of time in Llanrwst. Richard Clegg of Gwydir wrote to the Council asking for the clock. Suddenly folk realized how Llanrwst had once been famous for clock-making. The museum then at Rapallo, Llandudno, also wrote offering to give the timepiece a good home. The Council's Rate Collector, Ifor Jones, began reading and discovered in Iorwerth C. Peate's work *Clock and Watch Makers in North Wales* an entry listing amongst a number of Llanrwst clockmakers the name of John Owen, working in the mid eighteenth century 'who was the maker of the old town clock at Llanrwst'. Alas, as reported on 17 February 1964, the Council Surveyor, E.E. Jones, had blandly stated that he 'did not consider that the clock had any historic value.' Fortunately another Mr Jones and Mr Hugh Humphries came upon the scene to give up their whole Saturday to taking the clock down before demolition began.

'Much credit is due to Mr Humphries for this operation,' asserted Mr Jones, 'and also for the care he has taken with the clock all through the years. And quite apart from my official interest in council property, I wanted to help because, being a local man, I've also got a lot to say to the old clock.'

Now reference back averted reference back, hindering Council discussions on town hall matters. After all, there was now no town hall and even to this time of writing there is none. The Council Architect seemed shocked at the rambling townscape he had exposed as he stated: 'The demolition of the town hall had revealed a very motley crowd of buildings but I believe that the business people would agree to tidying up their premises on the principle of a Civic Trust Scheme.' The Clerk brought forward a letter which was anonymous. The production of it caused consternation but its anonymity ensured that all agreed it must not be read. Nevertheless it gave a mysterious aroma of suspicion. Somebody suggested building a tower to take the clock!

On 26 March 1964 readers of the local newspaper must have been surprised to read that the Council were having second thoughts about arranging for a commemorative tablet to be set in the walls for the councillor who led the campaign for the demolition of the building. Clock and stone and weathercock had all captured attention, for this Councillor Phillips had asked for possession of the ornamental foundation stone that had been above the principal door bearing the founder's name and his coat of arms with the date 1661. That Councillor's Committee had recommended that no objection be made to his applying to the demolition contractors for possession of the stone. At this the General Council did suffer a tremor and, during a debate in which Councillor Phillips withdrew from the Council Chamber, decided by the Chairman's casting vote to refer the matter back for further discussion.

Mr Clegg from Gwydir had also asked for the stone. Councillor William Thomas said that at the Committee he had thought little of the stone because at the time he was not quite sure of its historical value. He now considered they ought not to take any step that would lose the stone and the clock to the neighbourhood, but Councillor Norman Roberts said he would like to stick to the recommendation to hand the stone over to Councillor Phillips. He proposed that the minute be confirmed. Councillor William Thomas proposed reference back and so it was. Councillor Phillips, when asked afterwards the intriguing question as to why he wanted that stone, declined to say, 'because his request was still under consideration by the Council'.

I record these events in detail not merely because my own little peasant farmhouse, the grand mansion of Gwydir and the historic town hall make a threesome of contrasts, but because here in the heartland of North Wales, where the effort to preserve language and song is strongest of all, the Welsh Nationalists appear to be letting the tangible monuments of their heritage slip away from them. Even Gwydir has now been saved by a man from Lancashire. Only one patriotic letter did I read that expressed indignation at the Council's attitude. On 2 April 1964 H. Parry Jones sent letters to the newspapers demanding that these relics should not be lost to the town. And where are they today? And who can see them? I notice another letter, twenty years later, from Gwyn Jones of Bettws Road, Llanrwst: 'Whatever became of a once much-publicized Llanrwst tourist attraction, the delightfully attractive Grey Mare's Tail waterfall?'

Of course it lies just below the crossing of a stream on the way to Llewelyn's Old Church at Llanrhychwyn, but in these days tourists going around Llanrwst seeking it would be suspected of undue facetiousness, such is local apathy. Llanrwst has abandoned its real heritage, relying only on its bridge and the contentious name of Inigo Jones. Let us hope some publican, thirsty for trade, will not start a similar demolition campaign for a new bridge, modern style, by a new twentieth-century architect who would open out the landscape to let the town grow with such arguments as: Why should not Llanrwst have a Left Bank? Paris has one! Of course suggestions for change do arise, as when someone in the Council Chamber proposed that it be widened. He was met with a stony silence. The bridge was built for wagons and packhorses, and in 1636. There is no room for men to stand and talk, nor for couples to court, hardly enough space for one glance of the eye between a man and maiden.

The North Wales topographical writer Norman Tucker dared to propose it be set in a park across a lake as a museum piece bearing the royal coat of arms. This would suit the mooted project to divert the Conwy river and enable a bypass to be constructed. Nobody applauded. Bypass Llanrwst? Another bridge, another crossing, with no traffic for folk in the square to watch? Already there was no clock to glance at. Soon not only would there be no town hall but only council offices, a chainstore and pens for cattle.

Obviously it was time to call a halt, to stop denigrating the town bridge by suggesting no one could prove Inigo Jones did not come to supervise its building. Was not Richard Wynne of Gwydir, Groom of the Bedchamber, then Treasurer to the Queen, while Inigo Jones was the Surveyor General. No genuine Llanrwst man would require any further proof than what his forebears had said. The town hall might go, Gwydir Castle might be sold away, even the old Jesus Hospital Almshouses be converted, but the bridge – not a stone to be moved, not for coaches, nor articulated lorries, not for anything whatsoever; the spirit of that brilliant Welshman with the grand name protected it, rising above its narrow humped back like a challenge. Of course strangers never could nor would understand.

On one occasion Richard Hughes of Cae Person, Llanrwst, was driving an Electricity Generating Board lorry and had just got over the brow of the bridge. Cae Person Estate was only a stone's throw from the bridge so as a local man he knew it well. He realized he had several other vehicles following him. As he passed the hump of the bridge, a company director named David Mills from far away Congleton in Cheshire was negotiating the corner of the bridge on the Llanrwst side. Mills swept on in his twenty-five-foot heavily laden van with all the independence and assertion of a company director, disinclined to give way to a mere lorry-driver and his three-ton lorry, albeit there were five other local workmen within it.

The two vehicles stopped and then pressed forward, threatening each other until they were nose to nose. And there the arguments began. Should these six Welshmen give way to this English company director, obviously not even a union man? The long queues of traffic began building up while the driver from Cae Person, declaring he was first on the bridge, refused to give way, and his opponent likewise. The latter now demanded to know where was the police station and, on being told it was half a mile off, abandoned his van and ran all the way through all the bends and corners of Llanrwst. Alas, there was nobody there! Desperate and still more furious, he ran back between all the accumulating traffic to resume the argument in more forceful though not more persuasive style. Four lines of vehicles as it seemed from the four points of the compass were converging there, from Abergele, from Llandudno and Conwy, from the A5 and from Snowdonia.

Upon the scene eventually came also, emerging through the compression of traffic, Police Constable Catherall, whose pacifying remark, 'You're acting like a couple of kids!', failed to move either vehicle but exasperated Mills the company director who declared, 'This man is a lunatic! I know what the Highway Code says about reversing onto the main road!'

This was the signal for the constable's notebook to come out, for slow and deliberate writing of particulars of names and addresses, of details from driving licences. By the time the cautionary statement warnings were being given to either driver, not only was the congestion extraordinary but the population of Llanrwst had begun to assemble as if for some celebration. Friends from Cae Person Estate shouted encouragement to the electricity lorry, encouragement in broad Welsh which fell upon the deaf ears of the driver from Congleton. The traffic jams had reached right back through the town. Never had the old bridge been so loaded.

But the constable slowly closed his notebook. The bridge must be cleared. Both vehicles must move back off the bridge as they had entered it. He had the duty to disentangle the traffic. Then, as they waited on either side the bridge, and the exasperated traffic trickled away, neither driver realized the full import of the constable's words after the explanations had been written down. They were both to be reported for causing an obstruction!

So on the Friday, in the cold and humourless atmosphere of the Nant Conwy Magistrate's Court, the drivers met again, both pleading Not Guilty.

It was local policy, declared the local man, Richard Emlyn Hughes of Cae Person, that whoever reached the top of the bridge first had right of way. To which, a trifle unwisely, but of course in ignorance of Llanrwst sentiment, the company director retorted, 'I wouldn't have thought that Llanrwst policy overrules the law of the land.' Hughes declared he was on the bridge first, to which Mills replied that he would have been committing an offence by reversing into a main road.

The magistrates coldly found the charges proved and fined both men £5, which left the Welshman indignant as he left the court room declaring that he was thinking of appealing against such a conviction.

This incident was far from unique among traffic happenings upon the famous bridge, but it served as a signal to hasten the provision of traffic lights which in 1984 were installed in such a way as not to intrude across the picture postcard scenery. The publicity also revealed that the Aluminium Corporation of Dolgarrog despatches a weekly average of ten heavy lorries across the bridge, each lorry weighing about twenty-eight tonnes, and this merely to save a detour to the lower Tal-y-Cafn crossing. That company began to object to a limit of $16\frac{1}{2}$ tonnes being imposed.* Once again a Llanrwst councillor urged, 'The Council should start pressing for a new bridge, despite plans for a local bypass.'

Poor Llanrwst! One day it may have only for glory its ancient church with the Gwydir Chapel and the Nonconformist buildings with their classic façades. I feel so strongly for Llanrwst for it defines itself to me as the most Welsh, and I mean ancient Welsh, of all the towns hereabouts. Whether the rain comes down and folk crowd in doorways, or whether they come out into the sunshine of the square, or in winter when the narrower streets keep the cruel mountain winds at bay, or in the nights when doors are shut and rain gleams on those black walls and deserted pavements, even when the moon shines and the flying clouds speed in loneliness across from the Glyder Mountains, the town holds a spirit of friendly kindness within it so compact and quintessential, perhaps not possessed by the wealthier shopkeepers and stallholders who have nothing of such local loyalty, not being dwellers, but a real inheritance shared by the more ordinary people who group in Cae Person or in such house-rows as Conwy Terrace or Station Road. Tourists come and go, passing on without a glimmer of knowing, but those who stay in the town or find themselves in trouble, they learn of it from the true citizens of Llanrwst.

* *North Wales Weekly News, 25 October 1984*

21   Heroes of the Valley

Often it happened among shops and shopping in Llanrwst that Pandy Tudur came to be mentioned. Not only did the shop assistants know it well, but most had relatives dwelling therein while some had attended the old British School just beyond the village. Eyes would brighten at its mention. A plain enough building that school, tacked on to the house like as an afterthought, though inside the schoolhouse itself was so cramped as to appear added accidentally. Years ago it was closed during those reorganizations that saw staggering blows dealt to village life when the schoolmaster and his older children in the smaller villages were drafted away to some far-away centre where amalgamation of mere numbers was thought to improve quality. I well remember the pleasant evening meals taken in that Pandy Tudur schoolhouse where I came to appreciate the happy life Headmaster Trevor Jones was spending in his village. Often the name of the school crops up in the pages of the local Welsh language newspaper *Gadlas* as events in the Youth Centre are reported amongst other transient human affairs of the district, but specially the name 'British School' still survives upon the cast-iron post box built into the wall and painted red, thereby stamping a strong claim for historical recognition.

A television team has captured this well by selecting the Pandy British School as the location of *W.16* a delightful reconstruction of school life for which they had the advice of its former Headmaster, Trevor Jones, who provided the Victorian copperplate handwriting upon the blackboards, an ancient pedagogic craft now defunct. Some Pandy children were mortified that the child actors came from Penmachno village rather than Pandy. They were certainly brilliant and faultless. Perhaps one can reconcile Pandy's disappointment by suggesting that Penmachno boys and girls are more naïve and old-fashioned and had more battered period clothes ready to wear!

It proved a remarkable production, especially to myself intrigued and mesmerized to see how it blended that intense seriousness with satirical humour and good nature so typical of North Wales today.

It was surely time, I thought one spring morning, to call on John Hughes where he lived at *Y Craig* ('The Rock'), a pleasant residence overlooking Llangernyw and that lovely valley. Not only had he expressed a wish for us to meet, but I was grateful for his interest in preserving my old cottage. Since his retirement from the life of an educational and social worker, he had devoted all his energies to the welfare of his own village, reaching beyond to the promotion of Welsh affairs and Welsh culture in particular. He had become active in the Eisteddfodau, local and national and had been made a member of the Gorsedd. For years he had been an elected Councillor of the Borough of Colwyn. At first regarded only as 'the man from the mountains', his innate shrewdness coupled with his sense of history gained him the respect of all. He had become the first representative from Llangernyw ever to become Mayor of Colwyn but could more truly be regarded as a plebeian patron of Welsh plebeian literature and the culture of the Hiraethog Hills.

He was as fond of making speeches as any elected representative and he welcomed me in his cheerful drawing-room where books and papers evidenced energetic involvement. Like all those associated with Llangernyw, he was obsessed with admiration for the life story of Sir Henry Jones, the poor cobbler's son from the village who rose from being a lad tramping daily to the British School at Pandy Tudur to the glory of Professor of Moral Philosophy in the University of Glasgow. He had been the first Professor of Philosophy at the University College of North Wales and one of its founding fathers.

His *Life and Letters*, bound in a thick octavo volume* are to me as boring as can be expected, but the little green book which preceded them, also published posthumously, as *Old Memories* depicting his youthful struggle to eminence, is fascinating.† He tells of his early days at that British School in Pandy, of his two brothers working for four shillings a week as gardeners at the squire's house, 'Hafodunas', of the cradled baby hoisted ceilingwards and rocked to sleep by a string. These childhood memories he wrote freely in the last few months of his life during his last illness with death staring him directly in the face.

He had bitter memories of the schoolmaster at the Llangernyw School of that day and mentions the penalizing of Welsh-speaking

---

* Hodder & Stoughton, 1924
† *Ibid*, 1922

pupils who, if they were caught using Welsh, were caned and made to wear the block of wood known as the 'Welsh stick' until they could report another pupil for the same offence and pass on the punishment. The favouritism of squire, parson and schoolmaster for the orthodox church-goers is described in a way which makes it easy to understand how the fervour, almost hysteria, of the Nonconformist Revival suited the Welsh temperament as contrasted to the cold, indifferent Church of those days.

Henry Jones's mother met the schoolmaster of the British School at Pandy and here, transferred to an upbringing opposed to the 'Church of England', he prospered, working as a shoemaker's boy, waking to study from 4.30 am, sometimes reading in the quiet and warmth by the heating boilers under Hafodunas Hall. As he writes: 'I was to go to school at Pandy where there was a bunch of grown-up lads when work on the farms was slack, and I was to stay there for three months and see whether "something would not turn up" '.

Education was a sort of surviving medieval charity thereabouts, with donations of books and promises for the future. The squire's wife, Mrs Sandbach, resolved to be his patron and came from Hafodunas to sit on a chair outside his father's workshop, opposite the door. She promised him admission to a preparatory class for the Caernarvon C. of E. Teacher's College and offered to contribute to his maintenance. This would mean reverting to the aegis of Llangernyw Church and becoming a member of the Church of England. Imbued with the British School spirit of Mr Price, he declined, however tempted, and belittled the Church of England Training College. Nevertheless Mrs Sandbach persevered. She invited him to Hafodunas to pursue what Henry Jones later termed proselytizing until she was driven to sneer at 'something concerned with the Chapel'. Hereupon he bridled and walked out. Not even the peace offering sent from Hafodunas in the shape of an old overcoat could win him over.

Stubbornly he persevered and won his place at Bangor Teacher Training College. Today he is still honoured in this Welsh village almost as much for his rejection of Church in favour of Chapel as for his academic successes.

Perhaps it was the invasion of that valley by Scottish tenant farmers which directed him towards his northward future. As he mentions, 'The squire had taken to letting his larger farms to Scotch tenants till he learnt his lesson.' They were peaceful but energetic invaders of the neighbourhood and arrived with their domestic servants, shepherds and other dependants and I suspect, just like the English in Ireland, who became '*hibernioribus ipsis hibernis*', were soon submerged.

John Hughes glowed over this immigration aspect as he took me to see Sir Henry's boyhood home, of which he was the proud curator. Arranged as a museum with its contemporary furnishings, the old cobbler's house of Elias Jones is faithfully preserved. Signposts along the village direct one to it. I signed the visitor's book, placed the anticipated donation and afterwards was conducted perforce to the old chapel also kept as a faithful exhibit of the olden time.

John Hughes was devoted and sincere. The penetrating damp of old mortar was brushed aside by his enthusiasm, an enthusiasm which has only recently flowered and inspired the musical folk drama *Harry of the Valley* (Harri'r Cwm). The local acting society has dramatized the biography of their village hero, arranging to give performances throughout North Wales in a sequence in which the locals, chiefly male, re-enact rustic scenes in a huge cast against a backdrop representing the *Cartref* (home). Of course, locally it was a delight for friends and neighbours to see acquaintances playing these parts. The 'Singing Shepherd', Tom Davies, had the leading role, and a succession of youngsters pursued the autobiographical parts. Even I pricked up my ears at the mention of Henry Jones visiting Wombwell's Circus when the famous menagerie called at Llanrwst, for George Wombwell, a distant Tollesbury relative of my mother, had been fabulous in my young days, and I myself had visited the menagerie, by then in its decline.

Harri'r Cwm's success was repeated over and over again, stirring local patriotism and chapel enthusiasm wherever it went. The prosy, boring portions of the tedious *Life and Letters* were skilfully eliminated by placard-bearing players who presented their large notices that skipped the years in one sentence and linked more interesting events into a progression of scenes.

As I walked back toward 'Y Craig' with John Hughes, he told me about Robert Roberts. From his study shelves he lent me the monograph by T.O. Phillips* and showed his copy of *Robert Roberts. A Wandering Scholar as told by Himself*, now a rare book.

What a tale it presents of pathos, frustration and the futility of mere learning in this ruthless world! Such a tragic contrast to the progress of Sir Henry. No old miracle play could show more distinctive opposites with so allegorical an illustration as these: 'Harry the Valley' progressing through life from righteousness to righteousness,

---

* *Robert Roberts (Y Sgolor Mawr)*, Univ of Wales Press, 1957

honoured with the stamp of academic certification everywhere, reverenced with the ritual perfection religious performance requires to become a knighted Professor of Glasgow University, replete with the learning contemporary fashion of his time expected: the 'Wandering Scholar', on the other hand, fit subject for Hogarth himself, was shunned because he could not acquire University documentation or academic recognition in certified papers. He went wandering across his world seeking relief both in alcohol and in self-improvement through his book-learning by wide and promiscuous reading, yet except among his own people, who know him even today as '*Y Sgolor Mawr*' ('The Great Scholar'), unrecognized, rejected and imbued with the bitterness unrecognition brings.

I did not ask John Hughes, a highly respectable, most conventional, a real Chapel man, which of the two he preferred, for I did not wish to embarrass him, but grateful I am for his enlightening me with that character of old Wales. It could be that his inner feelings are not very far from my own.

I was staggered, moreover, weeks later to read how Robert Roberts had emigrated to Melbourne in Australia where he had written his book in which descriptions of the outback are as vivid as those of his old Welsh home at Hafod Bach. In the Melbourne hotel out there he had made the acquaintance of a wealthy squatter who invited him to act as tutor to his younger son. He also kept the station books and he gives the name of the squatter as Johnson, the name of my grandfather's brother who went out to Melbourne before the mid-nineteenth century and prospered sheep-farming on stations just that distance north of Melbourne and named one settlement 'Brentwood' after the home town where I myself live. He describes Johnson's entourage as: 'The family consisted of Mrs Johnson, a kind motherly woman, sufficiently refined for the bush, two fine youths, cheerful lighthearted fellows, with little book-lore, and not much love for the same, but good riders and well versed in all appertaining to flocks and herds, as Dandie Dinmont is described by Domine Sampson. Two lively girls, and a younger lad, my special charge, completed the family.'*

'If I had known of this connection,' said David Hughes, the Llandudno bookseller who had obtained the book for me, wryly smiling when I afterwards told him, 'I should have charged you double!'

* *The life and opinions of Robert Roberts, a Wandering Scholar as told by Himself,* William Lewis Ltd, Cardiff, 1923

Poor Robert Roberts did not stay in any Australian situation for long, whether as tutor or employed writing for Melbourne newspapers. In the latter occupation he received fine testimonials from the editors and proprietors. In 1875 he ceased writing his autobiography and brought it back to England, thinking that by now the episode of his inebriated sermon from the pulpit at Corwen would be forgotten. Fourteen years had elapsed since it had come to the notice of the Bishops of Bangor and St Asaph just before he left for Australia and he dared to hope it would no longer be held against him. He was offered three curacies, but the implacable Bishop of Bangor refused to license him and would not say why.

He wandered through temporary teaching posts with growing despair, losing through a lapse into drunkenness his last permanent post at a grammar school in Wolverhampton in 1881, then living at his parents' old home for four more years, unable to obtain either pupils or a place, drinking heavily though in dire poverty. He died in 1885 and was buried in Llangernyw churchyard. His facility in acquiring both language and learning gave him a reputation which even today astonishes the folk of his valley. Unfortunately it was all misdirected. He had neither the advantages the University gives nor the literary expertise London can bestow and his lexicography was only exploited in the saddest fashion.

When he had returned from Australia and was as short of money as of recognition for his literary labours, he wrote to Chancellor Silvan Evans who was known to be engaging in the compilation of a new Welsh Dictionary. Robert Roberts was most critical of previous Welsh linguistic approaches, for the compilers tended to regard Welsh words patriotically as of some divine origin, whereas his own studies of languages showed all words as a human method of communication, all linked and allied in traceable associations. He had 120,000 examples from Welsh literature in his two-volume collection of materials, and in 1879, after a letter from Chancellor Silvan Evans, sent his two precious volumes by rail to Machynlleth. The correspondence which ensued can only be interpreted as brain-picking on the part of Evans for he was allowed to pay Roberts whatever price he chose and sent him a Post Office Order in 1881. As the biographer writes: 'From this it would appear that the Chancellor bought poor Roberts' labour of six years for a trifle.'*

---

* *Life and Opinions of Robert Roberts*, Introduction by J.H. Davies, Principal of the University College of Wales, Aberystwyth, 1923

Evans published his Dictionary in 1886, a year after Roberts's death. Comparative research indicated that Roberts had almost as many quotations as the Chancellor, but, so great is the Welsh tendency to respect academic office and the status of Academia, even of pedantry, that to this day Welsh writers gloss greatly over the story.

For myself, reading the Wandering Scholar's account of those times in this valley that I have grown to love, and remembering how the struggles and adversities of this rainful dale were recalled and written by him in the desert outback of Australia where the sun glares unchallenged by clouds, I think of his life as a tragic epic lived out by a genius to whom helping hand seldom reached out and whose talent wandered and went out like will o' the wisps over his Hiraethog moorlands.

Except for that piece of old iron covering the well head half way up the hill, there is nothing antique in Pandy Tudur. The topographical travellers and their guidebooks know it not except for a couple of words on the extinct Llandewi. Latest Ordnance maps give the misspelling Twdwr. The real interest worthy of record lies in the dramatic contrast of the two Victorian personalities, a contrast preserved as vividly today in the individualities of the two living custodians of their nineteenth-century habitations, one of whom, Councillor John Hughes, conservator of the historical associations of all that valley up to Llangernyw, carefully guards the old *Cartref,* the cobbler's house where Sir Henry Jones, the university professor, was born. Lloyd George once came to make a politico-cultural speech on that doorstep, his rhetoric in the native language rolling over the heads of the villagers as far as the roadside. John Hughes, overlooking the valley from his modern bungalow Y Craig, takes care that the little place with its three outer doorways facing south, not to mention the little chapel along the road, not only stands as a monument but is advertised as such.

But the birthplace of the Wandering Scholar no one celebrates. How can that reprobate be held for example to follow? Church, chapel, or eisteddfod can scarcely undertake his commemoration except as an example of the misfortunes that follow constant inebriation.

I was warned not to go to 'Hafod Bach', the birthplace of their Robert Roberts, *Y Sgolor Mawr*. A solitary farmer lived there now, completely alone, and he did not welcome strangers. I was told he had a gun. The villagers had often heard it go off and that showed such a farm was better to avoid. Naturally these exaggerated admonitions only stimulated my curiosity, and very soon, after some particularly gloomy forebodings, I made my way along the Llanrwst road, and, reading from the one inch Ordnance map, drove up a metalled track to the crest of the southward hill. This farmhouse was deserted, but, neatly kept, stood opposite a medley of farm buildings making a square. Amongst the old barns was the decay of an older long-house, ruined and now neglected. Suddenly a car arrived and I found myself talking to Mrs Roberts, the farmer's wife.

'No,' she declared, 'Robert Roberts never lived here.' That building across the farmyard had been a farmhouse, it was true, and she had lived in it as a child, but this was *Foel Fawr*, not *Hafod Bach*. Like most places hereabouts, the old farm had reverted to use as a barn when prosperity enabled the farmer to build a pleasant, newer house. For all that, they relied on the old place with its great stone walls to keep away the noise of the great winds. The newer farm, bright as it was, became so noisy with winds that one could hardly sleep when a storm blew. Winds were just the same at the newer *Hafod Bach*. She pointed the farm out where a gleaming, brick-faced house caught the sun lower down the hill. Its slates were shining up towards the hedges. That was not the dwelling of Robert Roberts either, for his old cottage had fallen down and been replaced.

Mr Evans, she warned, did not like being disturbed. A lot would depend on his mood for he never welcomed strangers. No postman would take letters there. His mail had to be collected at Llanrwst.

I left my car on the road below and at once saw why postmen could deliver no mail there. A notice vertically painted on the front of a tree announced 'UNSUITABLE ROAD'. Unsuitable it surely was, some six inches deep in cow-dung, going up the hill between tangled and overgrown hedges, and not only impassable because of this but by all kinds of old, rusty, and bright new barbed wire entanglements that blocked the gate and prevented entry through the hedges.

Managing cautiously to find a little space to penetrate, I began to pick my way up the hill, sometimes up to the ankles in muck. At last I rounded the bend at the top only to find myself confronted with an absolute No Entry, the path being closed as if by a barricade of wire screens. Through these I caught a glimpse of David Evans. A beam of sunlight lit up where he stood wielding a massive mallet made from old lead piping. He was beating some object upon the wall. I remembered the words of my adviser at *Foel Fawr*. 'I hope you will find him in a good mood. He never welcomes strangers!'

It would never do to try squeezing through those embattled

defences, let alone risk being impaled upon them, so I pushed through the hawthorns despite the bruising and the scratches and found myself in the wide, open field.

The house stood up, bold and clear in the sunshine, a fine house it must have been, indeed, and was so now, for all its desolation. The red brick cornering the masonry and framing the windows gave dignity and seemed to double the area of the façade. Nettles and thistles grew three to four feet high. The windows, dusty and dark, glared down, but with an ominous emptiness, for I knew as I strode through the nettles, no one was within, and I came round to the back of the house unannounced face to face with that solitary dweller to wish him 'Good morning'.

He did not return any smile of mine but went on hitting the object on the wall with that lead mallet while I announced the purpose of my visit. I had already stolen the opportunity to take a couple of photographic views of the house. Though he continued to stare coldly, it was only when I mentioned my Australian connection with Robert Roberts, my father's relatives there, and my own brother's life in New South Wales and outside Sydney, that his eyes lit up and I saw he granted me some right to stand there, yes, and more than that, he slowly began to respond to my interest.

'No. Robert Roberts was not born in this newer house at *Hafod Bach*. There was the old cottage, his real birthplace, just there!'

He pointed to a pile of stones around crumbling walls where nettles grew and old weather beams, stark as ribs, protruded. He would not have let it get into such a condition but where was the money coming from to build it up? He himself was disabled. Nobody helped him, nobody at all. Taking up his stick, he limped over the yard.

'This is all,' he asserted. 'This was the *pobdy mawr*.*' He tapped on the ancient beam. 'I used to see the dates, May 5, and the figures 1844 on the wood once. Can you see anything now?' But I did not venture to clamber and stagger over those broken rocks, timbers and nettles.

'No,' he continued. 'They are worn away, all of them. Everything is gone. Things were not with me once as they are today. If you had told me you were coming, I would have put a suit on and made a room ready. Nobody ever comes here. I keep them away. I value my independence. I may be disabled but that's the one thing I have. Nobody will give me a grant to do anything.'

I shuddered involuntarily. There was refinement in his voice and the

---

* Great oven.

proud and reticent self-reliance of the gentleman that rises above hardship, a quality from a bygone world.

'They get grants, these farmers and grow rich,' he continued, 'but I won't take charity, and I don't like forms. Disabled I may be, but I am independent. So the place stays as it is.'

Emboldened by his confidence, I suggested, as he went on, that he took advice and had his share of improvement money that was coming to some people. The suggestion made him angry. It depended on whom one knew, he declared. As for him, he knew nobody. He would get nothing. Once again I suggested he took advice. He lived there. He farmed. He should have his entitlement for repairs, for improvement.

I thought of the Sunday farmers gathered on the Pandy bridge, so neat, so God-fearing and prim and wondered nobody had felt called to break through his loneliness. He thundered an unflattering opinion of one or two folk in the village, punctuated by the names of the few who had been kind enough to give him a lift when he tramped down to Llanrwst. He walked there, disabled he might be, and insisted on walking and would not be beholden to anybody. In the old times one could go on pony down to Llanrwst for fair days, but today?

He seemed to grow taller, more worthy and dominant as he spoke. Three hundred years, he asserted, the Roberts family had lived here and kept a Sunday School for everybody around, and when things were bad, out they went, up into the cold to that miserable Ty Newydd on the top there above Frondeg – thrown out for the rent, after 300 years!

'So we know what independence is,' he growled, 'and I won't spend more than I have. No, I will not!'

We were standing beside the old ruin which Robert Roberts had described as a pleasant dwelling in autumn 1840:

Passing the garden we come to a large courtyard, or *buarth*, literally cow-yard, one side of which is bounded by the house, the other by various farm-buildings. A small paved court forms the entrance to the house, which we enter by a massive oak door of great antiquity. On the door frame above, we read in old characters J.R., A.D. 1584. Opening this door we descend a step, and find ourselves in a large room, low in the ceiling, and paved with blue flagstones. The chimney is a vast structure, the sides projecting far into the room, with a hob on each side of the fire wide enough to form a comfortable seat, and a 'settle' or screen large enough to contain the whole family when the day's work is done and they draw round to discuss agriculture, theology, politics, or folklore.

The furniture is all massive and heavy, like the door. First we notice an immense table that stretches along nearly the whole length of the room; it is formed of one great thick slab of oak, highly polished, and almost black with age, resting on rudely carved and turned tressels, and including roomy drawers. On the opposite side are the 'three-piece' cupboard, a sort of 'three decker', also of heavy oak, fantastically carved, dated 1587, adorned with immense pewter dishes ...*

Here for some years the *Great Scholar's* father had held a Sunday School, turning the whole cottage to make the only educational establishment in that valley of Cwm Cammas where as he tells:

'Shortly after dinner the neighbouring farmers and their families began to drop in, each with his Welsh Bible under his arm. They liked to come early that they might enjoy a little gossip before school commenced. Here they discussed the preachers at the chapel, the news of the week, and sometimes a little politics. When the kitchen got pretty full, my father would ask some 'religious' man to commence by singing a hymn and offering a prayer. They would then disperse through the house to their several classes, for the large kitchen would not hold them all. We had one class of women in the parlour, presided over by my grandfather; another occupied one of the bedrooms. Young and old were there, from my great-grandmother in my grandfather's class down to the young children of five or six who sat on the hob by my mother's side.

We stood there staring at the broken ruin with that one surviving beam above the old fireplace. A real man of the people had once lived there, but alas, a Church man, and like some scholars and literary men, one who tippled and who, alas, had illustrated the sad results in his own pulpit. How could they collect to have his cottage equated with the *Cartref* of the moralist Sir Henry Jones, the good Chapel man albeit deserting Wales for a Scottish university?

Somehow the luck of life is the strangest thing that one only recognizes with hindsight. The story of the present occupier of *Hafod Bach*, made into a mystery for no purpose, seems to carry far away echoes of that Wandering Scholar's isolation in his long struggles with compiling and pioneering the Welsh perplexities of words.

'*Pobdy Mawr*,' said David Evans again, striking the beam once

* *Life and Opinions of Robert Roberts*, Cardiff, 1923

more with his stick. 'That's what it was. And the family lived there too.'

And he turned to his own house. 'And that will come down one day,' he observed despairingly.

Remembering the words of Robert Roberts depicting the hive of activity once flourishing there, I could not help reflecting that others had read them also. Maybe those deacons on the bridge whom Mr Jarman had praised so highly, maybe they had striven to do one good deed and draw today's occupant of *Hafod Bach* into the chapel and into friendship. He was in no sense a conciliatory man and most likely would resent their patronage. It could possibly be their well intentioned efforts had long ago been rejected, perhaps more than once and the barbed wire defences erected in their repulse. I could not press this thought, nor enquire whether he ever paid 'dues' anywhere.

Promising to meet again, we shook hands. He showed me a private way to get dry-shod down to the road and I came away wondering in this valley of friendship where everyone helped, where everyone knows everybody, marvelling at this isolation that he preserved with such effort against all odds. I was deliberating also whether that strange shroud that overcasts the autobiography of the Wandering Scholar had come to hover in turn about him, that reluctance of the chapel folk to face the fact that Robert Roberts was not 'chapel' but 'church' and was just not the edifying example that could be idealized as could Sir Henry Jones. And for all his enthusiasm and talent, recognition from the Church was just as unforthcoming. Robert Roberts' grave for years went unmarked in Llangernyw Churchyard. Recently it has been located where it lay anonymously in the more crowded section east of the church, and probably because of John Hughes's interest, it has been marked by a small black tablet of new slate crammed close between two other graves. Below the numerals 1834-85 are four lines of Welsh verse (he himself actually wrote in English) which can be rendered:

He lived in the splendour of the morning,
But his day was closed by the clouds,
And his epic of far away inspiration
By memories of pleasure and pain.

22 *Religious Passions and Economics: Tithes*

The Wandering Scholar, a churchman, some would say a lapsing churchman, was keenly aware of the dreadful hostilities religion aroused in his day. Some sects would resist state education fearing it would interfere with their own Sunday Schools; learning for many meant no more than weapons to forge a chosen religion. Unless today one considers the quality of education then prevailing, it is difficult to realize how all these revival surges – Calvinists, Presbyterians, Methodists and so on – got into Wales from England and seized the population by the throat, even baptizing hundreds in the open rivers.

The Report of the Government Commission of Enquiry into the State of Education in Wales, published in 1847, disclosed that there was: 'bad, insanitary building, unsuitable furniture, a dearth of suitable books, – incompetent teachers ..., and the acquired information of the pupils [was] distressingly to seek'. Some might ask themselves how far the summary given by T.O. Phillips in his preface to *Y Sgolor Mawr** is true today: 'The root of the evil, according to the Report, was that the schools of Wales were clinging too closely to Welsh and neglecting to teach the children English, which, in turn, was impeding the moral development of the nation.' To the panjandrums of that time, expecting only complimentary sermonizing rhetoric this became known as 'The Blue Book Treachery', a mild enough censure to what it would be called nowadays if such a statement could ever see the light of day.

Of course, this sectarian bitterness was caused not only by the theology of that peasantry, however much the oratory of Thomas Charles and the printing of Gee's publishing house for *Y Faner (The Banner)* might enflame it, but by sheer economic distress. Tithe payments used to be demanded by the established clergy even during the occasional bad harvests. The life-style of the parish incumbent

* *Robert Roberts*, Univ. of Wales Press, Cardiff 1957

stood alongside the squirearchy's comparative magnificence and was resented. The squire might take rent as landlord, but to feed the clergyman, to give tithes to the Church when conscience demanded, dues to the Chapel – that was too much and, for the small farmer with his large family, was often impossible. The title deeds of these small properties, my own included, with their nineteenth-century history of loans, mortgaging and financial decline, are sad illustrations of this.

Here around Denbighshire there was not, as in South Wales, that early eighteenth-century flourishing of dissenters and 'secret' conventicles: indeed, there was violence towards the preachers, chapels were sometimes the target of mobs, and at least two (at Wrexham and Llanfyllin) were completely demolished.* Around my little cottage there are four places in the hills which are still remembered as old centres of dancing and celebrations for holidays and feasting. For the preachers to sweep these away was something hard to take. But they did, though older folk can name these summer locations where fiddling and dancing were once surviving even on Sundays.

It was towards the end of the century that the stronger propaganda of Thomas Gee began to engender action across Denbighshire and strange it seems to us now, in this peaceful, God-fearing land, to read how the Reverend Venables of Conwy received a letter threatening, if he did not agree to reduction of the tithe, to blow up his vicarage with dynamite. Later, on 31 October 1886, the Mission Church, Colwyn Bay, was burned down.

One great tithe battle had developed on 16 June 1886. As late as 1950 the well-known topographical writer of North Wales, Norman Tucker, was able to meet and take down eyewitness accounts and at the time the *North Wales Weekly News* published reports as dramatic as happenings in Ireland.

It was summer, and the Chief Constable, a retired Army major, had plenty of indication that trouble was afoot when he was advised of the intention of bailiffs to sequestrate cattle belonging to several farms at Mochdre. On the appointed day a railway train carried his party and made a stop close to Mochdre village where there was then no station. This party, huge for those days, of seventy-six constables ominously backed by seventy-six soldiers in red coats and carrying arms, lined up by the railway tracks. Their presence alerted all the scattered farms

* *Welsh Chapels* by Anthony Jones, Nat. Museum of Wales, 1984

on those hillsides. As arranged by the Farmers' Tithe Defence League, flags went up from Colwyn to the Conwy river. The crowds already in Mochdre village followed the marching soldiers toward Mynyddd Farm where the farmer, Hugh Roberts, expected them.

Up the narrow lane they went between banks and high hedges to the brow above. There the procession paused and looked down on the farm. Here the Chief Constable waited with the soldiers while he sent the bailiffs and some constables to try to persuade Roberts to pay his tithe. At last Mr Roberts came to the gate where the Chief Constable waited. As they talked and argued, the cattle could be seen grazing thoughtfully in the field adjoining. The crowd gradually swelled to some 500. At last it was clear to both sides there was no prospect of agreement. The order was given for the police to march down the hill towards the cattle. The crowd, now hugely increased, pressed forward; horns sounded and someone fired a shotgun. Down the narrowing lane they went, each man overtaking his fellows to be in the foreground as the police quickened pace. Resenting the pressure, the rear party of constables halted, faced about and began physically pushing the crowd back.

Seeing this, the party of onlookers dragging along the other side of the hedgerow concluded a fight had begun and hastened to join in, using their vantage point to shower missiles and brandish their sticks. Nothing loth, on came the men into that lane, rushing forward, charging on the police and driving them down. Stone-throwing is infectious, and at this threat the police drew their staves.

In the midst of such uproar, the farmer paid his tithes. But, as the police moved on to the next farm, the crowd, now blooded, had multiplied and the real battle had begun. As if drawn by some pre-arranged plan, many perhaps only intending to be spectators, more than 500 people had come together. Old Thomas Henry Jones of Plas Newydd Farm, though himself a cavalry man in retirement, mounted and joined the protestors on his horse. Here seemed the chance to display fulfilment of the pledges made at those many meetings of the Tithe Defence League, pledges never to allow a bailiff to seize and take away cattle.

The red coats of the soldiers, with the constables leading and forming their rearguard, inflamed the crowd as they marched out of the narrow lane and trampled through growing corn. At the mill known as Mochdre Felin, so tradition says, Farmer Owens in the mêlée beat down four constables with the great stick he carried. Across the struggle the military formed a line at the gate of Mochdre

Mill House. There, surrounded by police, a magistrate read the Riot Act.

The rifles of the military moved ominously. The snarl of indignant anger was hushed, as reluctant and slow, that crowd trickled away muttering with frustration. They left behind their wounded companions. These and the injured constables were dragged together into the granary and into the house for Mrs Lloyd to bandage. She would long recollect how the slate slab flooring of her front room was smothered red with the blood of her neighbours. Pandy Chapel was well aware of the political militancy. One significant entry in Deacon John Price's *Chapel Memorandum* Book records: 'Elias Hughes from Colwyn Bay failed to come to conduct the meeting in 1887 because of a wound he got in the tithe trouble at Mochdre.' It had been reported in the Denbigh Free Press 18 June 1887 that he 'was badly injured, his skull being cracked and his arm broken.'

Folk nearer the sea seemed bolder and more independent, though they had to pay in the end. In 1891, after an investigating Commission, an Act was passed which made it obligatory for the landlord to pay the tithe, though he was allowed to add the amount to his rent. Further inland, along my valley, people seem to have been more quiescent, acknowledging though avoiding where possible the power of the landlord and evading the Church. Seldom stirring the clergy from their torpor, they found their own true identity in the newer congregations of the chapels, even willingly paying towards their support. And so it is today.

'Oh, yes,' commented a respected neighbour at Pandy Tudur, when I enquired of a certain isolated and withdrawn resident who certainly never entered any place of worship. 'A very good man, and most reliable. He always pays his chapel dues!'

Whenever I think of it, the divisive nature of the Welsh Sunday fills me with regret. The disestablishment of the 'Church of Wales' has not led to any real awakening. Poverty haunts the old churches in their disrepair, ancient monuments though they are. The Gwytherin church in particular, on its historic, druidic mound with the four yew trees each probably older than both the church and the inscribed standing stones, shivers with its decay beset by the ghosts of the Dark Ages which only the brighter paint of the Lion Inn opposite attempts to drive away. All these ancient churches have had to group together to find cash enough to share an incumbent between them, and their social functions seem unattended by devotees of the Chapel. I attended recently a coffee morning under the auspices of St Digain's

Church for which the Llangernyw hall held a sprinkling only of parishioners. The well-known faces were not there, nor were they interested when I talked about it afterwards. The churchwarden told me they had no parson but by sharing with two other churches hoped to have one inducted within the next fortnight.

And as for Pandy Tudur, my village, once named Llandewi in glorification after its church, though the new chapel stands, smart and neat by the meadow below the bridge, the church of St David (*Llandewi*) exists alone, converted into a private house known as St David's Lodge, though there still remains the covered entrance porch with the original oak and pine door leading into the entrance hall. Worshippers once passed through, and weddings and funerals also. The vicarage close by has also been sold to be used as a guest-house. Noticeboards and invitations to stay for Bed and Breakfast proclaim its change of use. The Llandewi church was built in a flurry of development in 1867 when an enterprising builder began his ventures in Pandy. Most of the people who bought houses then were new to the district, and perhaps it was thought opportune to provide for them spiritually. The Nonconformist Chapel has won the contest, and the Church possessions have vanished. Coming through the village a year or two ago I noticed that new tenants, who had bought Llandewi in 1974 when it was a mere shell and converted it into their family home, had decided to sell and by now I believe it has changed hands again.

The Chapel, however, retains its popularity undiminished, as anyone passing through Pandy would know from the crush of cars and, when the service is over, from the parade of neat, dark-suited men who regularly take their stand on the bridge to put the world to rights in animated conversation. I used to wonder how many local reputations had been made on that spot or alternatively dragged down into mud deeper than the river below. On a Sunday it is difficult to get across the bridge without being drawn into some spirited discussion.

'No,' declared, a non-chapel-going reprobate, who certainly never 'paid his dues', 'I am not one to go upon the bridge, so I keep away at those times!'

There was certainly an intimidating severity about that line of Sunday suits and forbidding hats, and as in the ancient tribal days it was strictly a male preserve. No women walked or waited there or even gave it a second glance.

The first time I naïvely crossed that Pandy bridge, the leading deacon pounced upon me. He had just seen a display at some eisteddfod celebration illustrating the more ideal activities of Noah, and it had seized his agricultural imagination. The other deacons grouped round to listen to his exposition.

'What a wonderful farmer Noah has been, to save the animals like that! Where would we be today but for him? He knew his sheep. He chose the right time of year to save them. Wet land is bad for all. Indeed he was the best of farmers and deserved to win through.'

It had only been a children's pageant, but might have been a story arising from the Hiraethog Hills and the Conwy floodings. There was a smile on his face and his eyes were twinkling as he spoke, but the bystanders looked solemnly impressed!

Mr Jarman from the Pandy shop was always there. Tall and erect, his sense of humour showed by the merest twinkle of his eyes. Nobody had the interest of that village more at heart than he, nobody had better sweet peas or worked harder to win the 'best kept village' competition for attractive gardens, and he could bake better bread in his ovens than anyone anywhere. He believed intensely in his customers and especially in his fellow congregationalists. The regular minister, a former police sergeant had resigned and left the village. 'No matter,' Mr Jarman declared, when I was regretting that no successor had been appointed, 'we have such a good Committee, so dedicated a body of men that we do not need a minister. We can choose our own preachers!' Joking, brimful of energy, he had been showing me his rows of planted vegetables behind which the sweet peas would be brightening the little allotment. That very evening a stroke cut him down and he was no more. The little street, from shop to bridge beside the great apple tree has never been the same without his happy figure that was always hurrying to and fro across it.

23   Churchyard and Other Fairs

Though it was one enterprising builder who put the village in Pandy, others followed him, and even today there are three or four builders within the little cluster of houses. In the beginning everybody had to draw water from a natural spring on the hill. 'Pandy' means 'mill', and I used to look upon the huge millstone upon the millhouse front with some respect until a neighbour, Captain Hilton, disillusioned me, asserting that it was no more than a decoration brought from the real corn-grinding mill further up the stream. He had known Pandy Tudur from the end of the last war, when some folk were still drawing water from the well that is let into the roadside wall half way up the hill and now covered with corrugated iron, existing even today.

Whatever might be said about the fulling mill, he reckoned Pandy Mill had changed to grinding corn. Of course, the grindstone was there and the waterwheel also at the back which could still be fed from the stream. He remembered Harry 'Felin' (Harry the Mill) with his quick terrier dog that would sit beside him as the corn was being ground, watching and waiting for the rats. And before Harry knew the rat was there, the dog would have it dead in its mouth. Where did they come from? Ah, that very stream, of course. As soon as the corn was in the mill, even before the grinding, rats would arrive, for water carried the smell of it miles and miles downstream. And Harry *Felin* knew and his dog knew, and they were ready.

The History of Pandy Tudur, humorous as it actually is, has been written more as a parochial record of Methodism in which the names of chapel-goers are recorded by the Reverend E.J. Jones BA,[*] each individual being noted by his ecclesiastical position in the hierarchy of the congregation. But the old name Pandy Budur embarrassed him for it signified *Dirty Mill* as no doubt as a fulling mill it once was, but how inappropriate for the clean neatness of Methodism, so the Reverend

[*] *Hanes Methodistiaeth yn Nosbarth Llangerniew*, 1926

E.J. Jones labours on to find 'a diligent researcher of the correct history of the parish, a former dweller, who recalled one Tudur Huws keeping this same mill and work as a fuller there. The most melodious name and the most pleasant is this name Pandy Tudur, and it is this name that the Methodists continued'.

Nevertheless, Pandy was once a fulling mill. The peasant weavers would bring their cloth to the mill straight off their hand looms. Here it would be washed, treated with fuller's earth and soaked for hours, after which the natural oil had to be pressed out. The cloth when taken out of the water would be spread and tightly stretched to dry on frames beside the mill. Then it was pressed between iron sheets with weights suspended, while a smouldering fire of turf and dried cow dung sent up drying fumes through the material. The process resulted in the cloth being shrunk sometimes by as much as a fourth of its length.

Tudur's Mill – then who was Tudur? Despite the fertile ground for folklore, no one thought much of Huws and no Tudur ever ground there. The truthful name was Pandy *Budur*,* that Dirty Pandy, Dirty Mill, as travellers passing through well knew, especially in the far-off days before the bridge when there was a great pool and a ford with all its mud and stones. The wool washed in the running water above, when spread along the walls to dry, presented a long line of muddy colour slandering the attractions of the valley, as did the fumes from those slow-burning drying fires – all of no use to the builder who was erecting houses, improving the bridge and attracting outsiders to live here. '*Budur*' easily became 'Tudur', a legendary patron of the village, and despite the old references and in spite of the parochial Church of Llandewi, 'Tudur's it was, and 'dirty' was out, for all agree that the mill eventually went over to grinding corn, and there stands the millhouse with its millstone and the millstream and waterwheel to prove it.

In these later years of the twentieth century, thanks to new earth-moving equipment, more modern builders have placed a couple of rows of neat bungalows on the hilltop where they can look right into Pandy Street and have larger gardens than in the village just below them. These houses, however do not attract outsiders today for nearly all are occupied by Pandy's own people, some retired, who can look back and remember the days when a line of Pandy women would go walking down to Llanrwst on Fair Days, their great baskets of eggs carried steadily above their heads, and most older men recall when,

---

* Budr ... adj Dirty

before the new curve swept a modern road round the hill, the way went straight up by Bryn Aber, and the younger farmers would test horses by driving them hard up the steep, either for a racing challenge or to achieve some sale.

Down in the village the post office doorbell constantly rings. Sometimes Siop Pandy seems to centralize the locality for here as in the older days contacts and friendships reach out across the whole valley. A builder now lives in the millhouse between which and the post office he has been for ten years erecting a grand new mansion, ten years because, as is mysteriously explained, it becomes worth more by standing empty – inflation being what it is – than if it were finished and sold.

When he departed, not to be replaced, from Pandy Chapel, the Reverend Pritchard was remarking that perhaps he had not accomplished much against the influence of television in every house along with other modern influences that appeared to be creeping upon the village. But even on 21 May 1750 the Reverend John Kenrick, Vicar of Llangernyw, was writing to his bishop complaining that,

> It is what has prevailed and been connived at a long time in these parts of the diocese but now somewhat less. It is Fiddling and dancing upon Sundays in the afternoon upon our Hills or Country where a great number of young men and women meet and thereby the Evening Congregations become thin and God's worship is thereby neglected. Our Churchwardens, I think, ought to prevent such irregularities but they never do it – the Civil Magistrates' assistance, I believe, would actually suppress it but they don't mind it. So it is continued in some part or other. For these things we are reproached by the Methodists who say they assemble on our hills to worship God, but we to dishonour him and to profane the Lord's day."*

Poor John Kenrick! He was not altogether a spoilsport, nor so garrulous and plaintive as the tone of his correspondence with his Bishop might suggest. From being schoolmaster at Llanrwst and curate of Capel Garmon, fifteen years a schoolmaster, he had come to be vicar of Llangernyw by the favour of Bishop Hare, his patron. He was in good hope to better himself but found he had only succeeded an incumbent who, having married an heiress, had no need to rake in the proceeds from that living and so had left the Glebe House uninhabited for twenty years and allowed dilapidation everywhere, for which John Kenrick found himself responsible. In one letter asking

* *Transactions* Denbigh Hist. Soc., Vol. 18, T. Fthall.

permission to absent himself from the parish in order to accompany his son for obtaining admission to Oxford University, he mentions how his wife had died fifteen years before and of her seven children only four were still living, the youngest having been only two years of age when her mother died.

When he left the steady task of schoolmastering to live in Llangernyw, he must have been almost overwhelmed, and not only by financial stringencies. In 1750, when his Bishop was far away at the other end of the Diocese, a potentate secure in the ease of his palace at St Asaph, he 'was shocked at the unhappy customs and irregularity that then prevailed; it troubled me extremely,' he wrote, 'for they not only, as of late, marketted in the Church yard but even the Church door was open for them to pay and receive money, and I have been told, but did not see it, that they drank their ale and smoked their pipes in the lower end of the Church, but all this I immediately put a stop to, by having the key of the Church in my own custody, but was not of consequence enough to discountenance other practices which was always an eyesore.'*

There had been a visitation in 1749 when matters had come to the notice of the Rural Dean and it appears pressure was brought upon Kenrick to sweep away those practices accepted by the locality as ancient tradition and tolerated by his negligent predecessor, especially that market held in the churchyard. 'In this little pitifull village,' he continues, 'where there are not above 3 or 4 thatched houses,' persons sometimes since, had the curiosity to number the horned beasts at one market and found them upwards of 2,000.'

After the Bishop's visitation he prevailed on the churchwardens before the next Great Fair on 18 September 'to concurr and assist in keeping all persons and things out of the premises, by first nailing up the Gate of the Churchyard Porch and setting the Clark and some other stout fellows upon the stiles and other avenues to hinder their entrance; upon this we endured many bitter and sharp reproaches, as if it had been a custom immemorial and as it was suffered in other Churchyards within this as well as the Diocese of Bangor with a deal to this effect, but against all their attacks we maintained our ground that day'.

At the next fair, of 18 November, he again repeated his firm stand but persuaded the people 'to retire to a spot of ground about two stone cast off, where they now buy and sell (I'm ashamed to say it) what

* *Transactions* Denbigh Hist. Soc., Vol. 18, J. Ethall

was bought and sold time out of mind in the Churchyard'.

Twenty years John Kenrick lasted as vicar, and it required some strength to take this unpopular action. By expelling important markets from his churchyard he was giving the lead to other such bans. Next year he claimed credit for this, writing on 21 May; 'I have the further pleasure to acquaint your Lordship that keeping Fairs in the Churchyard is discontinued in other places for at a Fair in Llansannan (3 miles from this place) on the 7th instant both Buyers and Sellers were cashiered out of the Churchyard, nor did I hear that anybody grumbled much at it.'

Of course such local fairs are now things of the past, for in districts such as this the auctioneers have a hand in them and organize the cattle sales with the co-operation of the National Farmers' Union. On Fair Days at Llanrwst you can be sure of meeting almost everyone you know. All roads lead there, and the journey is downhill. The big livestock sales are in October at the autumn change over from hill pastures to the lowlands when the turnover of cattle and suckling calves can run to over four figures. Buyers come from the Midlands and from the far away Lleyn peninsula as well as from Anglesey, the interest being in Charolais and Welsh Black crosses which have come to predominate other breeds.

Sleepy little Llanrwst can take Fair Days, even the seasonal sales, with hardly a hiccup now, so convenient is the transport of livestock by road. Once the herds that did not come down on their own hoofs used to arrive by special train the previous evening and be driven out from the railway station to spend the night in pens and stables, some being taken through the congested streets to selected fields. Today everything is highly organized even as compared with the first Llanrwst Show I attended in 1946. Heavy horses, especially from Anglesey, made a big display then and contrasted with Miss Brodrick's ponies, while a schoolmaster, obviously selected as the man with the most durable voice, ran around unpedagogically dressed in white breeches, encouraging the sheepdog trials with a megaphone.

Arthur Williams of Ty Celyn, Pandy Tudur, a farm close by Ty'n-y-Llidiart, was showing three ewes for which the First Prize was only 20 shillings. For the 'Grand Athletic Sports' that evening, admission was one shilling, 'Entries taken on the Field'. Every year since there has been a colourful pony and trap section, 'the gentleman's turn-out competition'. Of course electronic communication has superseded the megaphone and made for precision. The disappearance of the running man and waving megaphone has unfortunately erased a great deal of humour. I well remember one Summer Show at Llangadock in mid-Wales where the schoolmaster's megaphone, enforcing rules bilingually, vibrated over the heads of competitors and spectators alike, but trotting horses, half in control, grew confused in either language until he threw up his megaphone in despair as he searched for the word to which horse and driver might respond. Then, waving his fists aloft, he ran round bellowing, 'Disqualifio! Disqualifio!'

For the last few years the organizers of the Llanrwst Show have been concerned to attract other than just four-footed entries. In 1983 for example Mr Glyn Owens declared: 'We try to cater also for those wanting to enjoy themselves at a large scale event!' So, besides the sheep-shearing with New Zealand experts contesting, Llanrwst was treated to its first wrestling show for twenty years, but this time with a girls' bout between Klondyke Kate ('Barnstorming Bombshell') and Tina Starr ('Beautiful Teenage Wondergirl') along with turns by Orig Williams (*El Bandito*), Mighty Chang, Amazing Kung Fu, and Dynamite Kid Cullum! Whatever would those mild canine entrants for the dog obedience demonstrations think, supposing they could get admission to view such human antics? The great chapel doors between the Greco-Roman façades are closed on Saturday nights and there is no one to cry, 'O tempera, O mores!' until Sunday. The discos absorb the younger folk and the surrounding villages are peaceful. John Kenrick would have today little more than the increasing number of road accidents to lament, when, all those who can, stream out of Liverpool and the Midlands to view Snowdonia.

24   *Eisteddfodau, Singers and Harpists*

Try as may the preachers in their chapels to give a religious cloak to cultural aspirations, it is the Eisteddfod that blends the past into the present. Sermon and *cymanfa canu* (singing meeting) have their part, but it is the eisteddfodau that today really hold the heart of the Welsh nation, both uniting its knowledge of cultural history and promoting rather than fossilizing its progress. Each local eisteddfod flourishing in village, chapel or school, has over it the national splendour of the Annual Welsh Eisteddfod with its fame, its competitive rivalry and the complicated and often disputed history from which it springs.

That history can produce facts and dates enough: first, Prince Unien Rheged's eisteddfod at Oystermouth in AD 517, then Maelgwn Gwynedd's at Conwy in 540 about which the fourteenth-century bard Iorwerth Bel wrote a *cywydd** to instance the Prince's preference for his bards over the harpists. He sings how the contest was arranged at Deganwy Castle, which involved a crossing of the river. The harpists found their harps warped by the water and the strings all twisted, whereas the bards competed unaffected by such difficulties. The next date usually instanced is Lord Rhys's Meeting at Cardigan Castle in 1178, but the really definitive event seems to be in 1523, for which Henry VIII, a harpist himself, is believed to have issued a Royal Warrant. After that time the Renaissance and foreign travel caused interest in ceremonies of bardic culture to flag amongst the nobles and squirearchy.

The eighteenth century, however, evoked an interest in criticism and metrical composition. The latter prompted pedantry of argument and open disagreement until in 1792 Edward Willams (*Iolo Morganwg*) — in London of all places and on Primrose Hill — designated the historic meeting of the Gorsedd (high seat or throne). His researches led to the publication of the tenets of the Gorsedd and the eventual formulation

---

* A rhymed couplet of seven-syllable lines

of the procedural rules. He was seventy-two years of age when at Carmarthen in 1819 he attached his Gorsedd to an Eisteddfod. He took pebbles from his pocket and arranged them on the ground there, thus initiating the circle of upright stones, said to be inspired by Stonehenge, although local people declare it was rather the circle of stones above Penmaenmawr he instanced. Only as late as 1937 was it decided to merge the Gorsedd and the Eisteddfod into one governing body known as the Court, but as early as 1860 a governing body had been set up and accepted the proposal to hold eisteddfodau alternately in North and South Wales.

Criticism, scandal even, the National draws upon itself, in its beginnings no less than today. In 1896 when the Eisteddfod was held at Llandudno the magazine *Wales* was sneering: 'The *Gorsedd* that has attached itself to the National Eisteddfod is the creation as Professor J. Morris Jones has conclusively proved, of a few Glamorganshire bards who vainly imagined they knew something about the druids ... The ritualistic institution which has attached itself to the Eisteddfod, the *Gorsedd*, will be decked with new tinsel and gee gaws at Llandudno ... What a privilege it is to be able to describe the theories and the thoughts of the "druids" as if one had been in the closest personal contact with them ...' Finally the editor prophesied: 'The *Gorsedd* will evidently remain a cautious old humbug to the last.'*

Even recently, when the Eisteddfod Committee preparing for the Rhyl National Ceremony in 1985 appealed for assistance, they met with disapproval despite the fact that such an event would bring trade and prestige to a town that badly needed it. The thirteen stones of the Bardic Circle erected in 1904 near the site of the so-called 'Sun Centre' had since been buried by sand. The stones for 1953 once put up in Coronation Gardens had disppeared, giving place to children's swings. A plaintive appeal that 'Anyone with information about these stones should contact the Eisteddfod Office' met with no response. Though Rhyl Council might have been considered to have some responsibility, when asked for £1,800 towards the work of replacement they refused, Councillor Richard Edwards being reported as declaring that *Gorsedd* Stone Circle a 'Pagan Anachronism' and 'only slightly pretty'.

All the valleys going down to Llanrwst, as well as those from far back into the Hiraethog Hills, have continued a community spirit delighting in the pleasures of music. Llanrwst itself once took pride of place with its craft of harp-making. The gravestone of its eighteenth-

---

* '*Wales*', ed Owen M. Edwards, MA, July 1896

century harp-maker David Roberts lies in St Grwst's Churchyard with its harp emblem boldly carved thereon. The town was noted in the seventeenth century for its harps. William Camden had noted: 'This town, small and ill built, is famous for its harp-makers.'

The old Celtic harp, once used to accompany the bards, came to be superseded. It was tuned in the Doric mode, ie to a scale of D without sharps and flats, a mode in which the old folk-music and songs were written. As the desire and, indeed, the fashion of the Welsh to sing in harmony grew, the Welsh harpists adapted the Celtic harp to play accidentals, making use of the triple harp with three rows of strings, the two outer giving the diatonic scale and the inner the diatonic semitones. Welsh music became no longer modal, and the harp evolved to accompany pennillion singers and even choirs, growing in popularity. The need was felt then for an instrument giving greater volume, so the double-action pedal harp introduced by the Frenchman Sébastien Erard became adopted as providing this while at the same time being easier to play and keep in tune.

The eighteenth century has been described as the golden age of the harp in Wales for it was said there would be one in every house playing music of quality. Names of the great harp-players became part of the folk-history. The Tudors took the skill to England. Lord Petre, the Catholic Secretary of the Tudor kings at his Ingatestone Hall in Essex, had a Welsh harpist in his retinue, while John Jones of Llandderfel became harpist to a Prince of Wales and much later John Parry of Denbigh became musical director of the famous (or infamous) Vauxhall Gardens.

Unfortunately the Methodist movement disliked secular music and instruments associated with it, regarding the harp as linked with the Devil. It was not until, towards the end of her reign, Queen Victoria appointed John Thomas as her Royal Harpist and, as professor at the Royal Academy, he arranged so many Welsh airs for the harpists' repertoire that the instrument came back into popular esteem and use, just as today the delightful old Welsh dances are returning to cognizance at last.

In 1961, apart from a semi-private workshop, there was only one orchestral harp-maker in Britain, John Sebastion Morley in South Kensington, a firm founded in 1816, and, as Mr Morley said, no orchestral harps had been made there for forty years, he and his three assistants having to devote all their time to repairing old ones. Since then not only has a flourishing Welsh Harp Society been formed but twenty years later, when they displayed an exhibition of harps at

Ruthin Castle, twenty-five craftsmen were in their employ. When, however, eleven-year-old Glenna Foulkes of Cefn Isa, Llanfair Talhairn, came with her people to the exhibition in order to place an order for her harp, the price was £3,700! Today a glance through local newspapers indicates how, since the inception of the Welsh Harp Society, *noson llawen* (entertainment evenings) and pennillion singing have spread along the Conwy Valley.

It is these small concerts and eisteddfodau that are the life blood of the tradition, formed as they were in local groups before the splendour of the National Eisteddfod had materialized. Actually when the Gorsedd attached itself to the organization of the National Eisteddfod towards the end of the nineteenth-century, not a few were irritated to notice that another Gorsedd was being held on the shore of Llyn Geirionydd in as poetic a locality as anywhere, with the great monument to Taliesin at the head of the lake. In 1896 the medal for the essay, 'the medal of the silver tongue', was then given 'for the first time during these last four hundred years'. Claiming that its competitions and music were of the highest standard and 'more like the ancient Eisteddfod than anything we have at present', it set itself up as a deliberate rival to the official Gorsedd of the national ceremony.

Today the large and green-lichened monolith to Taliesin stands at the western end of Llyn Geirionydd, deserted and solitary as the lonely mountains. Here Gwilym Cowlyd (né William John Roberts in 1827) called himself 'Chief Bard Positive of the Institutional Bards of the Isle of Britain' and from his headquarters there presided over his open-air eisteddfod. He had graduated as a bard at Denbigh in 1860, after which in the very next year he had won the Chair at the National Eisteddfod at Conwy. He was the seventh son of a seventh son, a circumstance which inspired him with delusions of magic power. His *Gorsedd* was regarded as divinely instituted, and his claims were of unlimited extravagance. Of course, his neo-druidic fancies and other eccentricities were tolerated only because of his unusual ability and individual poetic genius. The englyn describing the surroundings of his bardic haunt is an example.

> Silent and green the lakes: about them stand
>   Their rampart mountains, ranked in close array;
> While hour by hour the sun with burning hand
>   Upon the water draws the shape of day.*

Gwilym Cowlyd died in 1905, but the previous year he had been

---

* *Poems from the Welsh* translated H. Idris Bell. Welsh Publishing Co 1913

visited at his home by J.H. Davies, Principal of the University College of Wales, Aberystwyth, who purchased the bundle of books and handwritten papers which years later he edited and published as the *Life and Opinions of Robert Roberts, A Wandering Scholar*. But for this, the advent of 'the Great Scholar' might have remained unknown. Cowlyd had also preserved and published the writings of his uncle, Ieuan Glan Geirionydd (the Reverend Evan Evans), educated like himself at the Free School, Llanrwst, and born in 1795 beside the brook flowing out of Llyn Geirionydd, so both these poets must have known the 'Great Scholar', being to an extent contemporary.

Not only around Trefriw and the Conwy Valley were there these little groups of self-proclaimed bards gathering. The account of the Hiraethog Poets, a Sunday School of rustic bards up on the high moorlands far beyond my own hearthstone, is fascinating.

Around the vast Hiraethog Hills the memory of these unorganized groups is preserved in the record of Twm O'r Nant, the so-called 'Welsh Shakespeare' whose adventurous life, in and out of debt or gaol, writing interludes and satires, seems, although passed in the eighteenth century, like that of a medieval pilgrimage in its search for learning in the bookless but oral world among people who measured prowess by spoken poetry:

> I became friendly with an old cooper who was very skilful in copying the works of poets such as songs and carols, and shortly afterwards I became friendly with another one who had the same inclination towards book collecting, namely, an old man in Pentrevoelas who was a lay reader in the church on Sundays, and was a clogmaker at other times ... Later I became friendly with another poet who was unable to read or write, and who had remarkable naturable poetic facility in the three and four bar measures. He was known as Twm Tai yn Rhos. However, I had the honour of acting as secretary to the old poet; when he completed a poem he memorised it until I came to him. And when the old man declaimed his composition, I would sometimes initiate a discussion with him, but it was better the other way; he almost appeared jealous in case I was attempting to offer destructive criticism of his work.*

This clogmaker of Pentrevoelas, Sion Dafydd, welcomed the many literary wanderers who came that way exemplifying an ancient culture, Doric in character akin to that of the antique

* Sir O.M. Edwards, *Gwaith Twm O'r Nant* (Cyfres y Fil 1909)

Peloponnese that lived by the spoken word of the shepherd. Twm O'r
Nant could look back to it in after years in the loneliness of reality,
saying:

> *Hyn o gyfeillion heini*
> *Fur a'u sain yn fy oes i;*
> *Wele 'rwyf, wae alar wynt,*
> *Heno heb un ohonynt.**
> [Those active friends were loquacious in my lifetime,
> But behold, here am I, mournful wind, this night without any.]

Along the Hiraethog Hills there flourishes a peculiar dialect of which
the distinctive soft musical quality exists to this day. Indeed, not only
does it exist in the native Welsh, but it transmutes its pleasant
characteristics in the English that is spoken there, an English which
delights and can immediately be distinguished from the harsher
sharpness of tongue south of the Berwyn Mountains.

The tuition that was given around the hearth of Sion Dafydd
Berson, the clogmaker, was typical, and the tradition continues in folk
memory today. Morris Owen (Isaled) as the son of Griffith Owen of
Gwytherin could recall how his mother saw the aged poet Twm O'r
Nant as, scaring the children, he passed by on his aged white pony,
journeying to the Pentrevoelas clogmaker. Now of course today the
playwright's interludes are not merely performed by the Urdd but
adapted for celluloid and indeed shown on video.

No one today can visit the smallest village eisteddfod without
feeling sympathy for the clogmaker's injunction:

> *Gwiliwch na chollwch Jaith hen, di esgus,*
> *dysgwch bawb ei darllen:*
> *deydwch siaredwch heb sen,*
> *a chenwch eich Jaith ych hunen.†*
> ['Beware that you do not lose the old language, there is no excuse,
> everyone should learn to read it; say; say, speak and sing your own
> language without rebuke.']

There is the nostalgia that permeates all the singing, a joy which can
be thoroughly appreciated to the full by those English folk who, few
indeed and probably to pass some examination, have mastered the
spirit of such as the ancient Anglo-Saxon verses. But only the shadow

---

* Emyr Wyn Jones. Transactions. Denbigh Hist Soc Vol 30
† *Ibid.* Vol 30

of that joy can fall amongst the topography of eastern England, for neither that language nor its metre lives any longer.

Every chance I get, I go to the local concerts and eisteddfodau, the fertile fields from which grander concerts of the media and the National Eisteddfod spring. Perhaps they are in themselves justification for the pressure which intensifies in competition after competition to raise rustic standards to an international excellence.

'How is this?' I asked a friend at the Llangernyw-Pandy Eisteddfod. 'How does the village produce such talent? Is it really home cultured?'

'Not at all,' he asserted. 'The moment a boy or girl shows real promise, it is spotted and off to the coast they go for tuition. They are provided the best teachers there, and the whole family will impoverish themselves to pay whatever the cost. Music is everything to us, everything!'

In Llangernyw Community Hall I would listen to the adjudicators giving their criticisms of each competitive item, long discourses from which I revolted, repelled by both the exultation and domineering authority of each adjudicator as he or she held audiences captive with the wisdom of platitudes worn out by the centuries from the times of ancient Helicon.

'Why, oh why do they drag on?' I whispered in a despairing protest. 'They are not competing. It is as if they are the main event and not the artistes!'

'The main event is just what they are!' my companion replied. 'The adjudication is exactly what everyone has come for, the most important value of the day. Every word, every phrase! Look at them listening!'

He was right, as was proved when I stared around through each long evaluation that was sometimes read, more often declaimed in a paean of balanced criteria that exalted the critic.

'Why not do this in writing and hand it out as a report?' I queried, but was silenced with 'They want to hear it said, and so do I.'

Today the prize is the spur and personal triumph the glory. Very few are those like the Hiraethog poet John Thomas of whom it was said: 'He did not compete with a view to winning a prize, but for his own personal enjoyment and the entertainment of his neighbours.'*

I did find it possible as I grew accustomed to the local organization to avoid these long examining expositions, by munching thick slices of bread and butter or cake, drinking huge cups of tea with other folk as

---

* *John Thomas, Pentrevoelas*, F. I. Roberts, *Cymru*, Vol 25 (1903)

lacking in critical faculties as myself, for there it was possible to chat and discuss sheer enjoyment of performance, the blossoming of young talent and the families from whence it sprang, the local folk associations of the delightful chosen songs, and, spiciest of all, the careers of those semi-professional eisteddfod chasers who travel from event to event, eating their ticket value in refreshments each time and feeling sure of a prize-money income.

Sometimes, apart from the regular Spring Eisteddfod, I would be fortunate enough to attend a performance of a more relaxed character supported by choirs from the surrounding villages. They would appear in a uniformity of costume along with their choirmasters or conductresses, pursued by no other criterion than applause and not unaccompanied by that amusing Welsh taste for satire. I well remember the relish given when a stalwart team of Welsh lads played an interlude in which the ceremonies of the Gorsedd were burlesqued and the Dance of the Flower Maidens was vulgarly done by brawny fellows in green costumes obviously more suited than they for druidical ritual, with a can-can finale learned rather from the Moulin Rouge.

25　Betws-y-Coed – Tourist Town and Elgar's Home

When on some bright morning I leave my hearthside and go down the valley and on towards Betws-y-Coed, the change in the population shouts its evidence of holiday time. Often the pavements are full of tourists, young people from the Midlands in summer clothes, staring wide-eyed and lounging as if waiting for bizarre appearances, earnest, brawny lads and lasses off to the mountains and retired and sedate thinkers recapturing, as they walk on, the Victorian grandeurs that have vanished. Recollections of the little town seem to amalgamate a history of reactions to holiday travel.

In the eighteenth century, with its concern for landscape, classical or romantic, controlled or horrific, and the dogmatic lessons of antiquity as depicted by Pennant or Bingley, this 'Gateway to Snowdonia' opened a view that came to be supplanted by the bouncy interest which Borrow evoked, an interest in personality, humour and human activity – the chitchat of encounter and conversation – which when pursued by later travel writers can become patronizing and quite wrong in its search for the Welshness of Wales, especially here in Betws-y-Coed, where the television aerials are everywhere and the boarding-house windows open to release the loud accents of Lancashire, sophisticated voices of trippers who, though they might covet the souvenirs in the many gift shops and buy local books of fable and legend, would never fall for those lads of long ago selling painted jackdaws in cages as Welsh parrots!

Bradley, writing in the last years of the nineteenth century about, as he asserts, 'the most famous mountain village in Wales', remarks that 'Betws-y-Coed may be said for a century to have been more or less exploited by the British public.' He observes how convenient it is for enjoying the best Snowdon scenery: 'One enters the place with relief and thankfulness that it is still a bower of foliage beneath which two bright and rushing rivers, the Llugwy and the Conwy mingle their waters. There are four or five hotels, it is true, but with woods behind and trees before them they are almost inoffensive, while a single street of stone cottages that have been so long given up to the business of entertainment that with the aid of art and nature and a quiet respectable antiquity, they are really anything but unattractive, completes the havoc of civilization.'*

His observations hold good today, except for the mass of humanity which automobiles and coach tours, cycles, caravans and the railway bring in daily, but which evening or rainstorms or the season duly evict with tidal impetuosity to leave forest, mountain and riverside in their accustomed places.

The genius of David Cox had flourished here in days before the planting of tar-green conifers smudged the mountain landscapes. He began visiting the Royal Oak Hotel in 1844, arriving from Birmingham. The signboard he painted is still retained in the hotel to record his delight in that tree which, when allowed, thrives so splendidly above the Welsh valleys. Betws-y-Coed hosted an artists' colony in those days and even nowadays feebly tries to withstand the horrors of commercial afforestation. Only one success can be registered against the philistines of the Forestry Commission. The village anger rose fiercely enough to prevent the destruction of that mature beech wood known as 'Artists' Wood'. These trees remain to stand in a shrine of glory through both spring and autumn, continuing to denigrate the bombastic assertion upon a stone erected within this very wood, a stone upon which the commission boastfully commemorates the planting of the first 100,000 conifers in North Wales.

Many years ago, I was fortunate enough to be able to stop and see the work of excavation at Caer Llugwy, the Roman fort that lies in a level meadow beside a delightful old wood south of the main A5 highway. The garrison here was actually manned by Asturian legionaries from North Spain and guarded the network of Roman roads, so disputed by local historians, that connected with the more famous Sarn Helen. If one glances at the old house, mistakenly named Ty Hyll ('Ugly House') where it stands by the bridge below this Caer Llugwy, it becomes obvious that the quarried blocks of ancient stones, all very heavy ancient masonry, could have come from the old Roman fort. The story that two bandit brothers erected their dwelling between sunrise and sunset, evoking the ancient law to light a fire within and secure

* Highways and Byways in North Wales, A.G. Bradley Macmillan (a) 1898

possession of freehold against the landowner is ridiculous. Such a task could hardly succeed with today's use of modern machinery.

In recent years the house, soundly built and with five acres of land, was offered for sale at £60,000. The owner had tried unsuccessfully to get a grant for roof and timber repairs for £20,000. He quoted a turnover of £12,000 a year from 19,000 visitors in 1983. As 'Ugly House' it had attracted crowds of tourists which 'Beautiful House' could never have drawn, but as a dwelling, alas for giving a dog a bad name, nobody, not even the boldest publicity seekers, came forward to buy!

Most popular guidebooks on the famous waterfall give some cheap explanation that the name 'Swallow' Falls is based on a mistranslation of the Welsh word for 'foaming'. George Borrow wrote:

'The Fall of the Swallow is not a majestic single fall but a succession of small ones. First there are a number of little foaming torrents, bursting through rocks about twenty yards above the promontory on which I stood. Then came two beautiful rolls of white water, dashing into a pool a little way above the promontory; then there is a swirl of water round its corner into a pool below its right, black as death and seemingly of great depth: then a rush through a very narrow outlet into another pool, from which the water clamours away down the glen. Such is the Rhaiadr y Wennol, or Swallow Falls, called so from the rapidity with which the waters rush and skip along.'

The very intensity of Borrow's description evokes another age, for he was writing of course in summer when the thunder and the volume of spray from the single cataract at flood time did not upset tranquillity of observation and when he had no elbowing crowds to jog his pencil. Today the summer coaches disgorge their contents to crowd that promontory where he once stood. Instead of pencils and notebooks they clamber and press with cameras at the ready, and it is their buzz of excitement as much as the spectacle that takes one's breath away.

Borrow accepted his Welsh much as he heard it, not having our modern dictionaries, where I read *gwennol* as swallow and the adverbial use 'foaming' as *cwynnog.** And why call this fall 'foaming'? They all do that! And how unoriginal, amongst all the beautiful waterfalls of Wales, falling from the heights they do, each with

---

* *Y Geiriadur Mawr*, 11th ed. Gwas Comer, Llandyssul 1983

cascade on cascade of foaming flood, to call this of all of them, in native Welsh, 'the foaming falls'! The fact is that the cascade of this river today, just as when Borrow watched, divides at times, not once but severally into the white swallow tails or even spreading wings from season to season. And if not in Wales, there do exist more southerly legends, the legends of the White Swallow. Nothing makes men more pedantic than linguistics.

The legend that exists here is rather that of Sir John Wynne of Gwydir MP, the magistrate with his own dungeon by the Conwy at Llanrwst, whose oppression terrorized the valley, a black legend that the old harpers would sing on the spot as they played to nineteenth-century visitors outside the Betws-y-Coed hotels. His spirit lies, they sang, chained in the blackest pool below the falls, doomed to haunt the darkest depth until limitless time should purge away his sins and allow his purified soul to rise again.

Time passes. This is a rationalizing age. No one stands in the street to sing a ballad today. Hotel staff or police would soon move such itinerants on. Betws-y-Coed Council has erected a security railing to protect tourists, steps to the Falls have been carefully cut, and a booth with turnstiles and attendant to collect the money that so largely reduces the rates of the little town. But, however white may be the water over those rocks, the stench of the sewage a few yards below the car-park hits one like the black stroke of a bludgeon as it passes on towards Llanrwst, drifting by the salmon waiting to ascend. Is there anything to help them pass the falls, I wonder? Locals leaning against the parapet of the Pont-y-Pair* have often assured me that very early in the morning one can see them jump above the rocks, yet if those fish have to wait for the rising water among the sewage, the anglers and the poachers, how small are their survival chances!

The Rivers Llugwy and Lledr are today the only ways by which they can reach their spawning grounds, for the old salmon ladder up the Conwy Falls has been derelict, broken from time out of memory, some say by flood or as others whisper, broken up by dynamite to hold back the fish and improve the hotel waters. Now that the building of the Conwy Road Tunnel for the new coastal Expressway has made people fear a possible silting up of the downstream river, the Water Board considers the progress of salmon might be impeded there and to improve the fisheries has promoted a scheme to replace the shattered ladder by a modern fish pass along which the fish can swim to reach

---

* Bridge of the cauldron

the higher tributaries. One glance at the map shows the possibilities of this opening up all the spawning beds as far as Pentrevoelas, the Hiraethog Moors and from Penmachno to Isbyty Ifan. This could double the salmon stocks of the Conwy. Yes, but only eventually, for salmon stocking is a long-term project and in the meantime fish would not be held up to await anglers in the famous pools at Betws-y-Coed, nor would so many pass into the Lledr and Llugwy. Anglers from the hotels might find the fish had travelled on. Though in the newspapers not a mention of this appeared, loud and clear arose the protest that the beauties of the Conwy would be desecrated by concrete ladders.

Conservation societies began to publicize a forgotten beauty overgrown by time which the Tourist Board had ignored because of its inaccessibility, and they grumbled to such good effect that the Water Authority was forced to adjust its expenditure of £200,000 by 'landscaping' with trees and 'rough finishing' with concrete surfaces to attract mosses and lichen.

These Conwy Falls lie at the head of the 'Fairy Glen'. In the days when all the tourist views of Betws-y-Coed were priced at 2d, when so many more believed in fairies than nowadays and the glen could be priced, I sought it out. The farmer, a stalwart fellow, dressed to face all weathers and walking with a threatening stick, stopped me with the challenge, 'Are you for the fairies?' The challenge accepted, he took my money and issued me with a small, printed and perforated ticket torn from a spool. This allowed me to walk with the fairies up the glen on that one day as far as the falls.

The Glen is unchanged today, but so deserted! I can never meet any farmer with his tickets, and there seems no encouragement to look for fairies. The tall cliffs stand over the river, a few pools have shifted and altered depths as they do in rivers with the passing of years. The torrent hurls itself over the rocks where an immense boulder breaks it, dividing into two cataracts between which the remains of the old salmon ladder have lodged, wedged irretrievably.

Back in Betws-y-Coed the three waters combine to make the great easy-flowing river of the Conwy Valley. The old church, 'the bede house in the woods', always seems gloomy as do the pools between with their history of drowned tourists, who with the recklessness of street-bred people ignore the depths of mountain water and trust slippery rocks. Even the paintings of St Michael's by David Cox only seem to emphasize a gloom. Whenever I passed by I found the church closed, superseded as it has been by the new Victorian St Mary's in the centre of the town. Appeals go out for conservation of the older building, so obviously in need of repairs for which one or two paintings done by the Victorian master in that very churchyard would easily settle. Locked up as I have always found the fabric, only the guidebooks tell how in the chancel remains the stone monument of David Goch recumbent in armour, fortified by the old Latin prayer: AGNU DEI MISERE MEI. He is reputed to have fought with the Black Prince. Fedw Deg, the house where he once dwelt above the Lledr Valley is no more than an old farmhouse now, but is still occupied.

Legends, always welcome at holiday times, proliferate along the river and its larger pools. So it is with the Beaver Pool, over which the bridge goes now. The great beaver, lured to the land by a fair maid singing, was netted by strong men and dragged out from the river by a team of oxen and pulled out of the Conwy Valley. The men named and marked all the places they passed and the names are remembered today, but even then it escaped them across the mountains! Whether the tale contains echoes of a dolphin struggling up the Conwy at some distant time of flood water, captivated and enchanted by a maiden singing long ago, or merely a poacher's memory of an otter struggling with a salmon in the half light of the dawn mist, let us wish the tale well and send it on its way, for the creature escaped its captivity and the seductive maiden was unharmed.

Downstream from the pool stands the 200-year-old riverside house 'Minafon'. Substantially built, dating from the early prosperity of the little town and in pleasant grounds, it became the home of Sir Edward Elgar. At the beginning of this century the dwelling was owned by Alfred E. Rodewald, the cotton broker and Liverpool patron of music who had founded the Liverpool Orchestral Society. Here Elgar worked on his monumental composition *The Apostles*, which was performed at the last pre-war National Eisteddfod at Denbigh.

Elgar's 'Pomp and Circumstance March No. 1', containing 'Land of Hope and Glory, was dedicated to Rodewald's Society, and was performed at Liverpool in October 1904, unfortunately a year after Rodewald's death, surely, however earning the patron a niche in that Temple of Fame for which today so few qualify in the footsteps of Maecenas. The river here flows on, slow and quiet, on and on, as it must have done when Elgar opened his windows on the riverside lawn and mused peacefully in those days of uncrowded roads.

Further down the valley other legends arise, like that of the giant Ifan Goch, who, bearing the fierce name 'Red Evan', would sit on the great rock as on a chair and cool his feet in the Conwy river, or indeed, stand with one foot on his cliff chair and the other on the opposite bank while he stooped down to wash his hands in the water, maybe taking a salmon out at the ebb of the tide. No doubt such tales symbolize the fear of travellers passing below those wooded clifftops whence a flight of arrows would be powerful enough and deadly. Looking across from the foundations of the Roman town beside Caerhun Church, the cliffs would be menacing in the extreme, though nowadays on the near shore hawks and harriers stroll peacefully among the sea fowl taking their pick from the tide. Thomas Gray must surely have known these cliffs when meditating the lines for his magnificent ode: 'On a rock whose haughty brow frowns o'er cold Conwy's foaming flood'. The National Trust rules today with a more benevolent protest, and grants a glorious panorama to its members who take the footpath from Maenan School up to the 'Chair'.

26 *Clwyd. Forgotten Haunts of Doctor Johnson*

How idle it strikes me as I sit listening to the cruel wind ceaselessly howling over my roof with the noise of an express train, cutting across the quickthorn bushes, biting through the tunnel of mountain ash trees and tearing down my lane, how idle of me who only yesterday was lounging by the West Shore dreaming against the setting sun, how idle to write about these mountains and moorlands as if bardic pleasures, metrical compositions and the delights of pennillion were the stuff of their lives, when they are hardly even the luxuries of the few and many of those today, ministers of religion, schoolmasters, professionals such as are employed by the Media.

I have drifted through those bucolic regions along the Balkans and through to Greece, I have seen the shepherds in their pastoral settings on the slopes of Mount Helicon, crouching under thick coats against the bitter cold of midwinter, cherishing their thoughts against the bleak weather and meditating of better times or past misfortunes in words that are provocative of poetry. For the climate there soon dries and the sun can shine through a day of storm as in the old days of Theocritus. Up in these Clwydian Hills, however, the rain and the clouds come down and stay, wet and damp, the cold wind brings sleet, the sheep become rain-soaked as the ground freezes, the shepherd can hardly dare go home. No wonder so many would choose the jovial companionship of work with friends in the quarry or the mine and opt to live in a terraced house in a street of mining folk.

'I would not take the small farm,' declared such an exile to me years ago. 'I would not leave my wife to the chickens and animals while I went to Dolgarrog on shift work. It is a life of poverty and chapel and not for me!'

Today of course there are grants for buildings and fencing. Land Rovers and tractors have replaced the drawn plough and the pony, while the Banks come forward to extend the grasp of the major farmers and extinguish the smaller holdings, but for all that, existence is hard. True, as Lloyd George told the future Edward VIII: 'All Wales is a sea of song!' But realities of the present are severe. Tourist presentations and fantasies of history hardly exhibit the grim struggle of the ordinary man.

'You are here in this cottage really only because you have bought it,' commented a local man looking me in the face, 'but these folk, they are here because they were born here and with their holdings and their sheep; they were all born here, and that's what it means!'

And the stones of my little farmhouse and the fire on its ancient hearth, all are suggesting the same. I am no farmer like those who laid these stones together. I should understand the realities, the truth of existence between this earth and these skies.

Robert Roberts was no farmer either. If the climate was much the same, the times he described in Pandy Tudur were harder than today though he liked to think of them as happy. Ty'n-y-Llidiart, as shown by the Ordnance Survey, is at 965 feet, compared to Robert Roberts's Hafod Bach at 675 feet, so according to his descriptions my cottage should be on the way to a climatic blight. Robert Roberts lived in the next century after Doctor Johnson. His ambition was modest. He only sought to be a compiler of words, and to do this he had obtained a curacy from Bishop Short of St Asaph at a stipend of £30 a year, to be stationed at Cwm, some three miles from St Asaph and to the south, only three miles from Bryn Bella where Doctor Johnson often visited Mrs Thrale. Here in the Clwyd Valley it would be dull to presume he had never heard of the great lexicographer who had been so befriended by the best families of that district from St Asaph to Denbigh and Ruthin. The friendship with Mrs Thrale at Ben Bella, the association of the Middletons, must have held memories which lingered and inspired throughout the region.

Today the Great Lexicographer's influence is in eclipse all along the Clwyd. In the recent eisteddfod (1985) at Rhyl his name and local habitation, alone of all the poets, received no mention, either verbally or on the illustrated map. No doubt when the great man announced: 'Wales is so little different from England that it offers nothing to the speculation of the traveller,' he was presenting a feature that to him was admirable! There is little doubt that for him the beauties of Denbighshire must have been as near as he could get to paradise. Boswell has written: 'Johnson has said gruffly, Instead of bleak and barren mountains, there are green and fertile ones; and one of the castles in Wales would contain all the castles that he had seen in Scotland!'*

There is no mention by Robert Roberts either of the Great Dictionary or of the *Lives of the Poets* but no 'Wandering Scholar' in the mid-nineteenth century could have failed to know of them.

Certainly Robert Roberts was as captivated by the classic beauty of his new landscape as the learned Doctor had been. He wrote of his new curacy:

'About a mile before that valley of beauty expanded into the plain or marsh of Rhuddlan, the Flintshire hills receded for about a mile and formed by the bend the lovely hollow of Cwm. Moel Hiraddug, a high bald hill protected it on the north and the Marian or plateau of Flint rose on the east. On the west and south it sloped gradually till it reached the meadows where the Clwyd and Elwy met. A lovelier spot did not exist: the view was magnificent extending from the Irish Sea and Rhuddlan Marsh in the north, over the wooded glades of Bodelwyddan, Trefnant, Cefn, to the hills of Yale in the far distant south. The majestic remains of Longshank's Castle of Rhuddlan appeared on the right. The grey towers of St Asaph rose in front – a little further frowned the grey ruins of Denbigh Castle and away southward the red pile of Ruthin towered above the plain. All around was beauty, fertility, wealth. So far as outward appearance went, my new home was a delightful spot: the eye never tired of gazing on beauty everywhere, near, afar off, right, left, around: move ten yards in any direction and a new panorama opened before you, more delightful if possible than the last.'†

And miracle of miracles, his words written about 1870 hold as true today. More credit to those sagacious friends of Dr Johnson who lured their literary lion to those Elysian fields higher up the valley where the Afon Ystrad speeds down to by-pass Denbigh before joining in the main river.

Puzzled by the fashion in which topographical pundits and even County Records have tended to gloss over the theme of Dr Johnson in Wales, I resolved to seek out the location he loved. I had tried several times over the years, but though clearly marked on the Ordnance maps, Dr Johnson's cottage is incredibly inaccessible. Faint-heartedly and short of time, I had always turned away, but this year, stimulated by the absence of all reference in the National Eisteddfod programme

---

* Boswell, *L of Dr J. III*
† *Life and Opinions of Robert Roberts*, p 381

and its literary topographer, a celebration held only nine miles distant, I resolved to devote a whole day to the search. It happened that long ago my wife's Aunt Peggy, from her own house in Denbigh, had actually rented the cottage as a holiday home, and as a child my wife had often stayed there. Perhaps I had heard so much of her happiness, and of the friends and relatives who would come and stay, that I felt I knew the place almost as well as she. Her father was an expert at tickling trout and would get them out of the stream across the opposite meadow.

As the cottage was well sheltered with the woodland rising behind it, they could stay there in winter time as well, though she remembered how, when the spring on the hill froze, they had to fill up the kettle with snow.

After one winter, when returning in early summer, they found a dead owl lying on the hearthrug, and in the living-room everywhere was total chaos with debris scattered destructively. The poor creature had come down the chimney and in frantic efforts to escape had knocked away all before it, china, and ornaments, thrown with feathers and fragments into a sad confusion.

We had a coloured postcard showing a neat two-storeyed house with its plaque over the front door, the outbuildings and the little gate between trim garden hedges. There was a cowl visible upon one chimneypot, a good roof with clean guttering and creeper on the wall. The picture was marred only by a caption wrongly spelt: 'Dr Samuel Johnston's Cottage, Denbigh!'

Though the little dwelling and Gwaenynog, the seat of the Middletons who hosted Johnson and provided him with the cottage, are both clearly marked on the popular maps, there is no route shown linking them. When my wife and I drove to the bridge over the Afon Ystrad, our enquiries to passers-by met with blank faces, so she decided to ask at the house positioned before the drive up to Segrwyd Hall.

Mrs Hooson came to the door and was most helpful. Not only did she give directions, but offered to telephone Dolhyfryd to make sure they knew we were coming and would show the way. She advised walking up by the drive, as then Mrs Bathurst would be ready and expecting us. And a delightful, level walk that was, through the meadow just above the stream with the great trees lining the banks and swaying in that summer breeze. We found Mrs Bathurst in her courtyard. She let us through the garden wall by unfastening the gate, promising to keep it unbolted until seven o'clock.

Alas, she told us, the cottage was gone, though the monument was there still. Captain Martin had taken the plaque from the cottage wall and was giving good care of it. She was afraid we would be disappointed for there was nothing of the cottage. It had not been occupied for fifty years!

We walked on to pass Dolhyfryd, where it spread across the narrowing valley, its many chimneypots making a pattern of pleasant living and its windows shining out fresh and clean. Not for nothing had the house been named 'Pleasant Meadow'. The house meadow sets the level floor in a line of meadows that provide a valley guarded to north and south by woods in fringes of deciduous trees, with the Afon Ystrad close to its southern side. As in the old days, the way was even wide enough for a pony and trap to pass along, travelling half way up the northern slope right through the trees and surveying such a landscape as would have delighted the most severe of eighteenth-century artists, a landscape which was so sheltered the wind could not reach it nor disturb its tranquillity.

At last the path came down upon the meadow and there, close to the hillside, was the ivy-covered ruin. Saplings, briars and brambles with greedy hands had clutched it back into the hill. Hedges and gate had gone in a tangle of nettles. No slates, no roof at all was there, but the walls stood alone, stark and sere. I found the lintel where the door had once been framed and broke my way beyond the briars and the barbed clutching tentacles of brambles. Old beams and spars stuck up through fallen stones.

I had my camera ready to take pictures when the pile of ruin gave way beneath and I fell headlong over the nettles and the rusty nails sticking up from old floorboards. The upper floor had long ago fallen in and I found myself sitting upon pieces of it, staring at the old iron bedroom fireplace high there in red rust upon the bare wall. Directly below, straight in front of me, was the great arched hearth at which Dr Johnson must have sat warming himself, drinking his tea made with Welsh water, and talking with friends away from the noise of the coffee-houses, far from the tensions of Fleet Street, in a paradise of seclusion and happiness.

The arch of the old hearth cast a spell upon me. I forgot the stinging from those nettle beds and the drip of moisture from remains of the showering rain and sat in an empty pondering of wonder at the passing away of time, the shadows of old dissertations, the *obiter dicta*, the conversations, sometimes mere chatter, that had fallen vanished into the air between those walls, vanished as utterly as the people had gone. It was a big hearth round which tea could well be sipped, that tea which is so much better made with boiling Welsh water, and I sat dreaming there beside the ruined hob, thirsting for something that could not be supplied, until a wood pigeon above grew impatient, annoyed at my intruding presence, and flew from her nest with a startling clapping of wings, and my wife called anxiously from beyond the brambles and the nettles.

I had no business to be meditating there. The Cheshire Cheese, off Fleet Street, is the place where remembering Johnson is allowed, with good clergy folk and bookmen with books, of course it is!

Another loose lump of wood caught me as I gingerly extricated myself over the stones in the overgrown doorway, a shaky rock rolled back so that to protect my camera I again had to suffer another fall into the briars and nettles.

Out on the meadow once more we both ruefully surveyed the derelict pile before taking the long, long footpath through the woods and grassy fields to reach the celebrated Monument which we might never have found at all had not a labourer assured us it was just another quarter mile within railings at the riverside. And so it was, the end of the sage's walk after he would have traversed the woods and the pleasant meadows, reciting as loudly as fancy took him the verses and quotations he cherished, an adequate stroll among these hills between the purling stream and the classic groves, a stroll that was as easy and level as a London pavement.

The urn is substantial, described as Grecian though *savants* today would term it Roman in style, and is mounted on a high pedestal protected by a good railed enclosure. There, still as clear as can be, is the inscription so typical of the veneration by which his contemporaries surrounded him. The sage's grumpy rejection of the monumental compliment was characteristic, as he wrote to Mrs Thrale: 'Mr Middleton's intention looks like an intention to bury me alive. I would as willingly see my friend, however benevolent and hospitable, quietly inurned. Let him think, for the present, of some more acceptable memorial.'

There, however, the Monument stood reminding us: 'This spot was often dignified by the presence of Samuel Johnson LL.D.' etc. Outside the woods, on the very edge of the swift stream where the green hill lifts away towards the open sky, it provides a mystery of its own. Antiquity absorbs it as a memento of the sage's reflections in such a beautiful location. Turning to go away, my foot struck a loose stone. I stooped to pick it up. There, as a marvel provided, I had in my hand a

Stone-Age tool, some $6\frac{1}{2}$ by $2\frac{1}{4}$ inches in size. Below its crust of dirt it was neat and polished, made with a good thumb-grove. Had it been disinterred when they dug out the earth for the Monument. Had the learned Doctor himself picked it up and discarded such an uncivilized item, *vanitas vanitatum*?

As we returned to the bridge, bolting the garden door of Dolhyfryd behind us, a gardener was making his own way home. We joined him, lamenting the cottage, its dereliction, its ignominy. He sympathized.

'They used to get a dozen patients from the Mental Hospital to clear it,' he declared, 'but it was not enough. It always got worse then, much worse. And they wouldn't sell. And no one would live there for good. With a house, you've got to have some one in it to keep it standing. Oh yes, you get some one in it, if it belongs to them they won't leave it. Look at the old lady with the cottage below Brenig Reservoir. Eighty-five years she was, and wouldn't move for all that Water Board. Only the highest Law could move her. Get someone the likes of her in that cottage, it would be there still. Put the life in a place and it stays, and if some one is born there. Of course' – and wisdom came to him – 'that was it. No one was ever born there! So why should they stay?'

He stopped at the bridge but went on talking. He worked at the Mental Hospital. He was born at Brook House. No, he would not leave Denbigh, not he. Just like the old lady at Brenig, they would have a job to move him! She had stayed through the terrible winter of 1947, snowed up and frozen up, but no one could move her. Not even when the ambulance came for her, she would not move! And nor would he. If you are born in a place, that makes it different. They can't understand that!

He left us on the brink of some deeper philosophy: as is the sheep on the sheep-walk of his birth, is so man on his own moorland? Is there a deeper underlying force that even the dowser can only guess at?

And I myself, after occasions of trying through the years, had at last come to this place, once occupied by my wife's aunt and where she herself had often stayed as a child, had come as if drawn there, I myself with the host of family recollections of collateral association with the great Doctor from my eighteenth-century forbears with their farms and packs of hounds by the Devil's Punchbowl in Derbyshire and the oft-quoted family tradition of the great man's visit when he came to see Warley Camp and called upon them at their farm nearby, their eldest sons for generations being christened Samuel and the silver spoons all engraved S.J.

Eryri, the cluster of the Snowdon Mountains, offers the visitor a suggestion of the sublime, whether white against the blue winter sky or standing in the softer moist light of summer. In the last war its clouds and mist presented the young men who were learning to manage aircraft or returning from operations over enemy territory the grimmest of threats.

Though swift, noisy and very low flying aircraft often fly over my moorland, skimming hilltops or threatening slated roofs, they always take account of the weather and never fly when the clouds come down, those stationary clouds full of moisture that mountains can gather and let drop with incremental darkness into the valleys. War-time exigencies, however, used to compel flying in all weathers. Returning planes would sometimes be caught in unfathomable cloud before a mountain wall like that of the Carnedd Llewellyn, when weather, speed and height, light and dark jumbled as the dice of fortune, of life or death. I walked over the moors just after World War II towards Llyn Dulyn, one of the grimmest lakes in the range. Foel Grach and Foel Fras surround its western sides with a high, threatening precipice.

Skeletons of wrecked planes shone out from the high ledges, a charnel-house of war planes, some wrecked on training sorties, some on active operations, and some, it was said, German planes which had lost track of their route to bomb Liverpool. Here and there on those wide moors that lead across to the precipices I could stumble over fragments of aircraft, and there were one or two racks of bombs, high explosive and incendiary which had been hastily jettisoned. They had struck into the soft earth, sinking through the seasons into the spongy peat, where they remain for ever. On those wide, empty spaces, details were not so easy to record as in Denbighshire, but the Snowdon Aviation Society maintains a history of which the following is a typical selection.

On 12 July 1944, at evening, the plane Anson MG. 804 took off from Anglesey for an exercise flight. At 02.00 hours wireless signals were received from it indicating there had been a crash. By 02.45 approximately its situation had been worked out and the Mountain Rescue team were informed. No further information came. The medical officer joined the advanced Mountain Rescue party to conduct a search of the crags at Foel Fras. They left the station sick quarters for Tyn-y-Groes police station in the Conwy Valley where PC Jones met the party and they all hastened to Tal-y-bont. Here they turned up to take the mountain track to Foel Grach. It was 5.45 when they reached the area. Adverse weather conditions had set in, and visibility was no more than twenty-five yards. They therefore fanned out in a northerly direction and moved towards Foel Fras. Here they found their quarry. Though the front of the fuselage and the starboard wing had been smashed when the plane glided into the cliff side, the remainder of the aircraft was relatively intact.

On the ground at the port side of the aircraft the air-bomber was lying, delirious and shouting. He was given morphine and covered with blankets. Upon the arrival of the Mountain Rescue team three other members of the crew came out of the aircraft; all three were suffering in one way or another. The staff wireless operator was lying inside the aircraft near the door and had apparently died of shock and concussion shortly before help had arrived on that scene, though he had managed to summon the rescue party. A radio call sent out to Llandwrog brought a stretcher-bearing detachment of ten men at 18.30 hours. They took their journey back along the plateau between Dulyn and Melyn Llyn, $1\frac{1}{2}$ miles down to the road, then on to Llandudno Hospital. The lonely and sad little party did not arrive back at Llandwrog till 00.35 hours on the 13th. The air-crew member who died was buried at Heneglwys near the air station in Anglesey.

Earlier in the next year, on 1 February 1945, another accident occurred to a United States bomber that had come all the way from its base at West Palm Beach, Florida, via Brazil, Dakar, Marrakesh and Cornwall. Strong winds had blown the plane to the west of its track and, flying in cloud at 3,000 feet, it crashed into the side of Y Garn, one of the Snowdon Elidyrs. Time does not dispel the aura of such a tragedy that rises again intensified when one sees the names of the air crew on the memorial plaque in that lay-by on the Llanberis Pass, their lives snatched away from the warmer climes – Texas, California, Utah and Dakota.

To those who know, that long dark line of the Glyders and

Carneddi Mountains symbolizes the dangers of those war-time flights – thirty Anson aircraft alone being lost there because of the poor navigational aids available then.

For the folk around my own hills, however, memories are centred on those German bombers who mistook their targets and dropped bombs at random, such as the unexploded bombs that fell into the Ty Hwnt i'r Afon fields at Gwytherin on 3 April 1940, or the two high explosive bombs and a flamenburg on Highfield Park, Abergele on 3 October 1940. What the old farmers really remember is the light in the north-eastern sky when Goering began despatching 160 bombers at two-minute intervals for the four-day attack on Liverpool, 176 on the second night and 145 on the last, making an incessant noise across the Hiraethog moors.*

For some reason the little valley from Pandy Tudur to Llangernyw was also particularly unlucky for aircraft. On 13 September 1942 a plane crash-landed $1\frac{1}{2}$ miles south-west of Llangernyw police station and next year on 6 July a Lancaster crashed again just $1\frac{1}{2}$ miles south-west of the same police station and was completely destroyed, the entire crew of six being killed. In May of the following year, 1944, also in Llangernyw, a Wellington bomber crashed in Plas Ucha field, caught fire and blew up. Again all the crew of six were killed. During war time such events are only whispered and one passes on in the tumult, expecting worse happenings daily. Only in the aftermath, in time of peace, do such disasters become history, to be contemplated dispassionately.

I think of the First World War particularly, when people expected danger not so much from the air as from the sea. There was then a prisoner of war camp in Llansannan. One of the prisoners had been repatriated in the summer of 1915, but he had maintained contacts with his fellow prisoners by arrangement and using carefully coded letters. No time was lost. That very August, 1915, three prisoners made their escape and managed to find their way, at least ten miles from the camp, to the shore at Llandudno. Off the coast here two submarines, the U27 and U38, were lurking, waiting patiently, signalling and making rendezvous with the assignated cove. At great risk they stayed on for three nights consecutively, completely ignorant that the three Germans were watching and waiting in the next bay. Then, assuming that the prisoners had failed to escape, the commander of the submarines abandoned the rendezvous. Famished

---

* Denbigh Hist. Soc. *Transactions* Vol. 26, 1977

and worn out after the tramp from Llansannan and three days of ceaseless vigil and hiding, the three trudged back to Llandudno. (Only after the war did they discover how near they had been to rescue.)

Nonplussed in the Welsh seaside town, Korvetten Kapitän Hermann Tholens from the German cruiser *Mainz* was reconnoitering for the others in Mostyn Street, where, unshaven and derelict, he aroused the suspicion of PC Morris Williams. One wonders whether the constable challenged him in Welsh! At any rate he was at once arrested and the alarm was raised. The other two were loitering at the pier gates by the cab stand where Alfred Davies was watching them from his cab. When he challenged them, they offered no resistance and were arrested. They were important re-captures: von Hennig having been the commander of the submarine U18, von Helldorf was a cousin of the Graf von Helldorf, the eventual Head of the Storm Troopers and participant in World War II in the unsuccessful plot to assassinate Hitler. As for the submarines, though the U38 outlasted the war, the U27, only six days after leaving Llandudno was prowling around the Scilly Islands where it was sunk, trapped by the 'Q-Ship' *Baralong*.

As the facts are considered, one wonders whether those escaped prisoners had help on their way from the Llansannan camp, so remote and so isolated. Spy stories are so common and sophisticated these days that those of World War I seem distant and naïve. Information also passed less swiftly and incidents must have slipped from public knowledge. The story of Miss Mountsey, for example, which I know only as, from her friends, may account for the submarine commanders lack of topographical knowledge.

Living alone in one of the large houses overlooking the bay at the bottom of Meiriadog Road, Old Colwyn, she seemed to become more and more anxious in the post-war years and would induce friends to stay with her at night. She would often tell how she used to see a man sketching the coastal scene on the edge of the shore at Rhos-on-Sea. As she saw him so continually moving along the coast, it occurred to her he was carrying out a systematic plan and was no mere sketcher. In those days of World War I there were fields where now stand the housing developments of Penrhyn Bay, and near the golf links the shore was usually deserted except for him. Gradually Miss Mountsey braced herself to tell her suspicions to the police, whereupon the man was arrested and after investigation proved to be spying for Germany. She was never told his final fate but always said that if she had (been) told, it would have been better for her. As it was, not knowing, she was afraid. Would he come back? Would he challenge her? She would not leave her home, but desperately tried not to be alone in it, worrying her friends and becoming a nervous recluse, afraid of the nights and the dark.

Not all the prisoners of that Llansannan Camp wanted to escape: several succumbed to the charms of the district, not necessarily those of a landscape or climatic nature. When wandering through Gwytherin churchyard where stand the ancient stones with their large incised Roman lettering, I noticed the graves of the farmers beside the yew trees, important stone graves of men who had stayed in Britain keeping their German names in the post-World War I years, making themselves with the help of their local wives as prosperous as anybody.

At the end of World War II there were so many prisoners and prospects for escape to the Continent were so hopeless with the widespread retreat of enemy forces that tense captivity was relaxed; Germans and Italians, appropriately dressed as prisoners, were allocated to farm work. The playing-field of Dyffryn Conwy School, Llanrwst, was the camp for the numerous Italian prisoners. In a summer of that time I went up to fish in Llyn Crafnant and found the western hill slopes sprinkled with Italians gathering in the hay. Not all of these went back to sunny Italy.

Vicenzo Algieri did go back to see his family in distant Calabria, but after fourteen months he returned to marry Beth, daughter of a Llandoget farmer, whom he had met while on his way to and from that school playing-field camp to which he had been brought after capture at Tobruk, North Africa, in 1944. Now he farms at Plas Iwrygle, high above the Conwy river, managing there without electricity or piped water. He has prospered in true Italian style with seven sons, two daughters and twelve grandchildren!

Toni Schiavone's father was another who married a Welsh girl, and now he himself lives in Pandy Tudur with his wife and two children, Owen Rhys and Gwennan Mair, and none more Welsh than he, standing as he does as the candidate for Member of Parliament to represent Plaid Cymru. Not only does he work for the local electors whether win or lose, but energetically backs Dafydd Iwan, Plaid Cymru's prospective candidate for the North Wales Euro-seat, and with full local support they have declared Pandy Tudur a Nuclear-Free Zone!

The editorial of the *North Wales Weekly News* with raised eyebrows and relaxed pen observed: 'The Continent is extremely large, whereas beautiful little Pandy is the kind of place that makes the average hamlet look like a metropolis ... If on the other hand they proudly announce in Brussels that Pandy Tudur has unilaterally disarmed, they are likely to be mistaken for a Monty Python Sketch.'*

Be that as it may, years later the notices declaring the village's Nuclear Free status meet every entering vehicle. The press photographers no longer chase about for copy and the check-points to picket cars have been abandoned, though across the field below my cottage a neighbour has painted a 'Ban the bomb' sign visible to passing aircraft.

Maybe it is a difficult task, but Pandy Tudur has attempted it, and good fortune go with Toni Schiavone and all who fight such quixotic battles with giants whether or not on Rozinante across La Mancha.

Since then, irony of ironies, the deadly cloud from the Chernobyl accident in far-away Russia has reached these rain-filled hills, sales of lambs have been banned and some local farmers face impoverishment – a savage reminder that world involvement reaches everywhere.

* *North Wales Weekly News*, 1 March 1984

28   Hiraeth: *Exiles Return*

Early one fine morning in the Spring, I saw two figures coming down my lane, a man and woman passing through the daffodils and narcissi. They paused and looked around from time to time. The man was smoking contentedly, and there was something possessive about the approach of both of them, as if they were contemplating a purchase or indeed actually already owned my farmhouse. Until I understood, I found the comfortable, easy way they walked the lane irritating, even aggravating.

Trying not to appear vexed by such a trivial annoyance at their presence, I approached and introduced myself. How staggered I was to be told how he, Otto Zeise, had lived here during the War and that his wife Mair had been brought up in this very house! They had read in the *North Wales Weekly News* of my struggle with Council officials in getting the farmhouse restored* and on impulse that fine Sunday morning they had driven over from Buckley to see what was happening.

I was delighted to make them welcome and most amused by their surprise at what I could show. Otto Zeise, as a German prisoner of war, had been allocated to Ty'n-y-Llidiart to work on the little farm. He had the use of the gun and went with the dog shooting over all the land around. And, of course, there was Mair Davies, the daughter of the house, his future bride, to gladden his life. Later, when he had a motor-cycle, the dog would know of his approach the first of anyone, making a commotion as he recognized the far-off noise of that engine and barking almost before Otto came into the lane.

They both expressed sorrow that all the pigsties and poultry houses had gone, but marvelled at the cottage interior – the great beam making the bressummer over the hearth astonished them, as did the slant of raw poles upon which the old roof was laid, all of which were

* *NWWN* Tony McIntyre, 22 February 1979

new to their eyes, as in their time it was pasted over by green matchboarding or layers of wallpaper. The lofts above were gone, and the ladders to them. Mair told how she would lie awake at night and identify and count the great rats as they trundled their bodies over the boarding after dark; one could distinguish them by their size and speed of running, the females and the males. The field at the back was then level with the roof. Small mammals could creep into the cottage beneath the very slates, and they did, running overhead the whole length from the dairy into the cowshed.

'Ah, no,' commented Otto with his broad smile, 'I rescued her from that.'

Bland and of prosperous appearance Otto Zeise visibly expanded as he walked around smiling. 'Yes,' he agreed, 'you must be happy here. For me, I enjoyed the work all the time. The happiest days of my life, I spent them in this place.'

Mair's father, Ebenezer Davies, had been the postman as well as running the little farm with his wife, known to everyone around and still remembered by the older folk. It was a difficult job for him before the days of Land Rover cars and often meant tramping for miles or cycling. Sometimes, in deep snow, he could not pick up the mail at Pandy shop post office. Then the postmen would walk together to the crossroads at Glan Rhyd to meet the mail van on the Abergele road, making difficult times in the shorter days and bitter weather.

More cattle were kept then and the cowshed at the end of the farmhouse was always occupied. Besides making their own butter, surplus milk could be taken to the cheese factory near Hafodunas. Ebenezer Davies would get out his cart, harness the pony and take it down to Llangernyw. Even if the price was low, there was always whey to be brought back to feed the pigs; besides, swill could be loaded up from the Stag and other pubs down there. One of the troubles was to find enough food for these pigs that seemed for ever squealing in the sties. The cheese factory by Hafodunas closed down when the depression came, but there were others in Llangernyw who kept cheese-making going. Llangernyw cheese could be taken to Abergele and be sure of a sale. The factory work was a boon to the young women of the villages; sometimes as many as a dozen would be in work there, despite the long hours and low pay, cycling into Llangernyw from the farms to reach either Hafodunas or the factory at the far end of Pandy Tudur. When the main factory finally closed, it was a real blow, not just for the bigger farmers who had put money into the Company but for all the women who had grown to depend on it. Then the small farmers reverted to traditional sheep-rearing as the price of cattle became less dependable, and naturally the few scattered cheese presses petered out. Those were the days before World War II, when times could be really bad.

Mrs Davies, Mair's mother, also worked hard and even harder after her husband died. Her only recreation seemed to be standing by the gate, gazing across the farms on the opposite hills, staring above them long into the far moorlands, as if remembering.

W. Trevor Jones remembered Mair as a pupil and called to mind the well-kept gardens when she lived at Ty'n-y-Llidiart with her parents. There were rows and rows of blackcurrant bushes and always hams and bacon hanging in the farmhouse. There were other advantages of country life in those days that are not shared today – the salmon and the rabbits.

Down in the valley below Ty'n-y-Llidiart, the Cleydwyn river runs through pools and shallows. Salmon-poachers used to know the way down through my lane and on towards the lower farm past Tyddyn Ucha, an easy, secret way by night or after dawn by which they could avoid bailiffs and police. They would go quickly by with torches shaded and hidden gear, making for where the salmon lay below the mill weir or along the gravel shallows. In season or out meant nothing to them. A good fish or two would be left at Tyddyn Ucha or Ty'n-y-Llidiart as a bribe of silence. But the activity was so lucrative that quarrels began among the poachers over priorities. People living at the waterside were frightened by the disputes, the noise of shouts and blows in the dark of night and they decided to have no more. Weirs and dams that held back the fish were blown up with explosives so that the fish spread along the river, becoming difficult to find. Gates that had been idly shut became unaccountably locked, a bull tended to be turned into the riverside meadows to graze. After many blank expeditions poaching became too difficult, following as it did a hard day's work. The pursuit lost its appeal and came to be forgotten.

Sometimes, knowing this past history, I would hear noises and creep unobtrusively from my cottage to listen, half expecting to see a group of bold fellows hurrying down the fields, but always it would only be the sheep bleating or the owl over by the sycamore trees.

Bryn Castell, the little cottage I had once wanted to buy, always attracted me where it stood opposite the entrance to my lane. Year after year it deteriorated. The roof lost slates and became ragged, hedges grew and the deserted garden struggled to pull the house down. The crumbling chimney had been filled with twigs right down to the oven below, for it belonged to the jackdaws who flew away in a pack as one entered. An old double-barrelled gun, stockless, lay about, surely some poacher's weapon. It rusted away by the hedge where gooseberries ripened and roses tried to grow large in summer. Several owners and clients had, after buying or tendering, given up in despair on being refused planning permission and having appeals rejected.

Nevertheless, ever optimistic, as are all estate agents, Bob Parry listed it each time. This last year its photograph appeared in the local newspapers above the invitation:

PANDY TUDUR Derelict single storey cottage situated in a roadside position with pleasant rural views. Offers invited over £6,000.

I could seldom resist at least once in a while stepping inside. The summer-time swallows would fly out and perhaps a blackbird leave its nest, and in the evenings bats would be mysteriously there, easy to see against a light sky but quickly disappearing into a private seclusion of their own. Bryn Castell, obviously on a more ancient site, was some 200 years younger than my own cottage. The nineteenth-century windows each had four large panes of glass, and there were no antique beams, but as against Ty'n-y-Llidiart, everybody knew of it, for Johnnie Morris, the tailor, had brought up nine children there.

Where the hedgerow was no more than a couple of feet high, he could be seen sitting cross-legged on his table catching all the light he needed to make suits, jacket and trousers, and even costumes for ladies; every farmer for miles around had bought one of his suits, but he was more renowned for one greater gift he possessed. All Pandy respected his fame, and children then unborn still heard account of it. He possessed a marvellous tenor voice. Mr D.J. Davies of Ty Gwyn talking of him as an example to the Pandy Male Voice Choir, shook with regret whenever he was mentioned. 'If only there had been a tape,' he would say, 'if something had been done in those days – a record made or something! Now that voice is gone for ever! Even those who heard it can do nothing, nothing about that!'

One day I was surprised to notice someone trying to penetrate the hedge into Bryn Castell. It turned out to be Johnnie Morris's daughter, now Mrs Weekes who, with members of her family and some grandchildren, and come upon an annual memorial visit to her childhood surroundings. They were sharp-eyed, those grandchildren.

One had surprised me by pointing into the sky, crying, 'Look, a vulture!'

Sure enough, higher almost than sight could follow, the buzzard was hovering, one moment invisible in the sunlight, next, as he turned appearing as a tiny dark shadow, identified by the boy from his television knowledge of the passengers through eastern skies.

My new acquaintance was kind enough to lend me her father's account books of payments charged for his tailoring, the prices for suits and trousers (noted as 'trs') neatly listed, suits priced mostly at one guinea! One of nine children, she recalled the delightful garden for which he had won prizes in local shows, she remembered also those trials of early life which none thought of as hardships at the time, though they lived by lamplight and candlelight and there was no water in the home unless it were carried by the children from the wells in the great field, Cae Delyn. In summer their well sometimes dried up and they would have to go and share the lower well with Ty'n-y-Llidiart, for that never dried.

Mrs Weekes sent me photographs, including one of the famous Pandy Tudur Choir, taken at the very climax of their success, with her father standing fourth from left in the back row, and the choir grouped with some of the awards they had won, the three Eisteddfod Chairs in the centre and their conductor and accompanist also. Between 1922 and 1930 they had won fifty-nine out of sixty-four entries for which they competed in the surrounding eisteddfodau. On the great stage of the Pentrevoelas Eisteddfod Sir Hugh Roberton, of Glasgow Orpheus Choir fame, had specially congratulated them as having all ages and voices blending in one choir, each individually living through a life of song. With this in mind that photograph proves a perfect monument to a triumphant excellence in that village music culture for which all Wales strives.

Mrs Weekes had gone to England into domestic service and married there. Her sister had sold the cottage for very little then, unfortunately, for now she Mrs Weekes, would like to own it, though in these days it would be priced away from her. She walked down my lane with me, showing where the winberries grew still, though more sparsely than in her time, and she grieved for the days gone by.

I told Gwilym Jones, my neighbour at Cefn Castell of her visit and surprised him for he on the contrary had stayed all his life on his hilltop farm and never budged away from it. His mother was a Welsh colonist from Patagonia, speaking Spanish and Welsh but no English at all, but of course in Pandy Tudur one does not need English. No, not a word of English could she speak as Gwilym Jones's own sister at Capel Garmon could vouch. Gwilym himself had been a talented guitarist at one time with a good singing voice also, but he had become reticent of recent years although quite different at sheep trials where he came forward and won prizes. He had the knack of picking and training sheep-dogs and had a reputation of getting the best out of them. His mother had come back to Pandy because she had inherited Cefn Castell, but it is fair to say Gwilym was a contented man and by no means ambitious, for he had divided up Ty'n-y-Llidiart when it came to him, only adding a field or two to his Cefn Castell farm, and letting the rest go to Tyddyn Uchaf and to Trevor Roberts the builder, whence to me. He had a smiling, shining sense of humour, so likeable if only I could extract it, and link his satire and fancy with reality.

From time to time the owners of Bryn Castell continued to fret and worry about its deterioration. Inspired also by the increase in property values, they stirred themselves and their agents to re-advertise the derelict building. Energetic folk came along to appraise it with other motives than Mrs Weekes and her family. One evening I looked up from gardening, disturbed by a large estate car full of a numerous family driving down my lane. It pulled up sharply before Ty'n-y-Llidiart. Two or three boys jumped out and, like young foxes laying a spraint to mark possession of a boundary, instantly began relieving themselves, the youngest held out by his mother to do so.

The driver came forward, brandishing maps and plans. He was a flourishing man, collarless, with prosperous red-brown moustache on rosy cheeks, dressed in a workmanlike jersey with sleeves rolled up. He motioned me to him. He scrutinized me fiercely as if he would buy me out on the spot.

'I'm buying cottages!' he declared. 'Is this supposed to be Bryn Castell?'

He showed the advertisement with the newspaper Sale column and the photograph as I denied and disclaimed ownership, but he persisted, with impatient gestures, waving his literature at my cottage with impatient gestures, demanding, 'What about this then? What's this? Come off it, now!'

I refused intention, denied interest and at last convinced him that he had passed Bryn Castell, telling him how to get through the hedge and see the place. Nevertheless he renewed his approach, using all the devices of a buyer who suspects some bargain covered up. Persuaded ultimately, he became confidential. 'I buy cottages, holiday cottages,' he declared. 'Get them! Do them up, work the garden, clean and plant it. Open out the windows to make people happy! I've got ten, but it's not enough. I must expand! This is a good place for a base. I could expand from here!'

Friendship expanded from him as he began to talk money. He blossomed with confidential information, and though there was no one to hear, his voice dropped to a whisper, '£6,000 they want,' he confided. 'I might offer £5,000. Would that do it?'

I told him the story of how many years ago they refused to sell it to me at all. 'Yes, offer five,' I chatted glibly. 'It has been waiting for years and will go on waiting. Offer five and see what five will do!'

He took me as some kind of prophet. The verdict pronounced, away they all drove, leaving me wondering whether I really wanted neighbours, and such neighbours from the Midlands in such quantity as he would supply.

'Ten cottages is not enough for me,' he had asserted sagely. 'To live you've got to expand these days!'

29 'As far as the Mountains' – Echoes and Reflections

Years go by in a dwelling before it becomes such a friend as to seem part of oneself, enhancing one's life, imparting a sympathy that is more than the warmth of four walls. Only with time do the windows shine their smiles out of the stones surrounding them, and the trees, the planted shrubs and the flowers all blend to give a ready greeting.

The sacks and sacks of bulbs, daffodils, jonquils, and narcissi, all rose to accept their flowering time and glorified the boundaries. All along the lane they spread in massive sheets of colour. Crocus, white, purple and saffron, flourished in the grass while the snowdrops stayed like waving clouds in their appointed places. The primroses excelled and threw fertile seeds which sprang up unexpectedly where I would never have planted them.

Nothing could be more pleasant than to arrive in such a welcome and await the coming of the swallows after the procession of Spring, to relish the early summer, when one could sit in the doorway and watch the birds flying low over the grasses. Sometimes, after I returned from Spain, it would seem that I myself had raced back and arrived before them, for surely they were among the flocks I used to see massing above the valley at Medina Sidonia. A chaffinch would always be singing loudly from the top of the silver birch, and when beds of bluebells shot the lane with colour once more, the spotted flycatchers took their own perches upon the wire fence. Wagtails came to bob beside the waterpools. Chiffchaffs and migrant warblers would call unseen from the thickening depths of hawthorn. Redpolls that would scarcely be noticed in my Essex garden, here take on a gleam from the clean air and flash their red spot. Even the wind, when the season changed to stable, used to drift on with a softer, kindlier gesture and no longer thrashed the avenue of mountain ash trees.

Regularly at their proper time of day the buzzards came to fly on patrol, sometimes, if they required to descend lower, being savagely mobbed by crows. At the change of weather the curlews would arrive mysteriously from the coast to choose nesting sites, while here and there protesting, querulous lapwings flapped across the meadows.

If I had started a book diary of birds, I could have recorded the first time the cuckoo landed on my roof and then in midsummer those warblers feeding their monstrous cuckoo chick at the end of the hedge, and not least interesting, the swift little merlin that came out hunting, flying from the pine trees above the old quarry just down the hill.

In the beginning I used to labour through early summer, now I leave everything uncut and persuade myself that tall, blossoming grasses swaying in the wind, all heights, all shapes, all kinds of shadows, are better for me, better to look at, certainly better for the grasshoppers and the multitude of smaller creatures, existing as they do only as breakfast for each other or for the birds.

A year or two ago I was delighted, when I arrived, to see the hare get up and peer with ears erect before darting to the back of the house. Next morning there he was lolloping through the field gate. He knew something was different and would not come near, but spied and listened, ears uplifted, from below the bank in the lane. He was learning he had a human neighbour and made off. Now he is sure of that for, at a footstep, away he goes like an arrow. I do have to suffer on his behalf, for last year he, and perhaps a friend or two, stripped the bark from my apple and plum trees up to three feet from the ground. Now I must wait years for the stumps to resume growth and in the meantime provide essential protection.

When I stand beside the two fallen stones and look over that great field, *Cae Delyn*, a sadness comes over me. The field has been ploughed and modernized with the usual fatal results towards emptiness. I delight to watch the larks in the sky there singing, not just in the daytime, but rising higher in the failing light of evening higher and higher with their knowledge that only clear over the western mountains was the sun ever shining bright and worthy of song. I would see them, etherial larks in the late moonshine, not one but many shadowy spangles ascending the moonbeams above the darkening fields, filling all the mists below them with their music of joy. It is always eerie, standing there into the night, with the larks singing towards the dying sun beyond the mountains, a sun that they can see but I cannot. They have sung that song their lives through as their forebears sang it through the thousands of years when it was sung to the men and maidens travelling the 'knights' causeway' that is now my lane, walking the ramparts, carrying water from the ancient well-heads, with none knowing the last singer or hearing the last song, only feeling the chill from the mountains and the cold of the moon.

So I am waiting always, till I hear the clean, pure evening air replete with song and see those beautiful tiny shapes climb the moonbeams again. Often in the late summer evenings when the mist climbs over the meadows and the moon is strong, I go out searching in hope to see a lunar rainbow. It only needs a thin hovering shower against the moon. Surely one night in the mist rising thinly from the autumn fields I shall see it as I look down and southwards towards Llansannan, or take my walk northwards towards Llangernyw. Often the marvel has been seen making a great pale white bow across the Conwy river by Deganwy usually when there is very fine rain like the parting of the mountain mist before a full autumn moon. For a few minutes with the spread of the shower across the full moonlight it comes, light pastel shades of the prism, an almost colourless rainbow, or a broader white like finest gauze, they say, the *Iris Lunaris* that so many Conwy Valley folk have often seen but which, in the antique land, Aristotle himself only observed twice.

One must have the moon at full, strong and clear, with the running mist departing into thin showers and the bright moonbeams darting through. It is a delight in store for me, though maybe I shall have to go on watching the larks for a long time yet and perhaps by that time the purple orchid will have returned to the roadside. One midwinter the snow-plough churned it entirely away. Surely by then my cob-nut hedge will be in bearing and the apple trees bowed with fruit.

I had been inspired by indigenous survivals round the cottage: – the clump of age-old yellow daffodils surviving beside the roots of departed trees, the little wild Welsh pansies, and, wonder of wonders, the plum trees that grew in the hedge and must one time have dropped their round fat little fruit into the pigsties below. Every autumn they were dark with ripe plums as if to remind me that despite those late seasons plums would flourish there, and I remembered the ripe, so-called 'Denbigh' plums that grew in Aunt Peggy's garden in Old Colwyn.

Determining to plant such a 'Denbigh' Plum, I was surprised to find no nurseries stocked it, nowhere in Denbigh or Flint, not in all Clwyd. Nor could I buy the tree in England where I was treated to the typical response, 'They all want Victorias. That's the plum!' Only in Denbigh market, in the middle of the town did I get a positive response.

'What did you say was the name of the plum?' asked the gipsy stallholder. 'Did you say Denbigh?'

As I assented, he turned and shouted to his wife, 'We've got all them Denbigh Plum trees in our nursery, haven't we?' Then, after a pause, 'You know, them Denbigh Plums?'

The woman looked at him and still hesitated. Some unseen gesture passed between them. He took an answer from her out of the air, not waiting for either assent or denial. 'Oh yes, plenty of them!' he pretended to echo.

'Come next market day,' he assured me. 'I will have one saved for you. Yes, next market day. We've got plenty of them sort. I'll tell you the price, then, I will.'

His pleasant effusiveness contrasted with his wife's gaping scowl of disgust which said silently unconsciously but efficiently, 'What a liar!'

So I never came back to Denbigh Market nor sought to buy from such itinerant vendors again. Nothing is worse than to tend a tree until it matures and gives fruit to declare itself as the wrong variety.

The Royal Horticultural Society came to my rescue. I had seen in my old pre-war catalogue of Bunyard's Nursery the Denbigh Plum listed as Cox's Emperor, it having been discovered and produced by one Cox, a nurseryman in Denbigh. The Society had two such trees at Wisley and if I could not obtain one from the nurseryman they mentioned, would let me have cuttings for grafting when the season came round.

I was lucky. Scott's Nurseries of Merriott in Somerset sold me a fine tree which now stands protected from the rapacious winter appetites of hares. Now perhaps I can boast I have the only Denbigh Plum in all Denbighshire!

'Let us now praise famous men'. The adjuration of the old psalmist has seldom been taken to heart more than in North Wales, where every valley seeks out and cherishes its notables, not merely the ancient great ones of the times of the Mabinogion, or of Llewellyn and others in battles against the Norman-Saxon invaders, for they are only heroes of the school-room histories or the tourist guidebooks.

The real famous men are those who towered almost within living memory. No chance is lost of celebrating them, but they must have 'a local habitation and a name'. How so, when the name may be Jones or Williams or Hughes? The name of the location is more adequate, so John Jones becomes Talhaiarn after his village, Hugh Hughes, Derfel after Llandderfel Bala, Gwilym Hiraethog after his mountains and so on. It is the location from which they spring which is significant and nowhere more so than in this valley from Pandy Tudur to Llangernyw

(Cwm) where even the great Professor Sir Henry Jones becomes 'Harri'r Cwm'.

At the last National Eisteddfod at Rhyl the Gorsedd showed in print their allegiance to the custom of deference to location pages where 31-40 of their programme were given to biographical notes – *Panel Enwogion* (Panel of the Renowned) – stressing the location of bards in their vicinity to Rhyl, in which topographical pride in personages really excelled, from Tudur Aled (1480-1526) who was born at Llansannan up to Thomas Gwynn Jones (1871-1949) of Betws-yn-Rhos.

When at evening I stand above the Pandy hills and gaze across the ridge of Snowdon's mountains, they blacken as mist comes into the valleys, and transient humanity crouches away within houses and meadows. The great heights overwhelm with their sense of awesome power as the light disperses after sunset. Staring across I remember other poets beyond the far-away ranges – *Glaslyn* (Robert Jones) beside whose cottage I camped as a boy, and then his poet biographer *Carneddog* (Richard Griffiths) of Nantmor. Folk came at that time to tell me how *Carneddog*, stricken by domestic tragedy, must leave his mountains. Would I help him, they asked, by buying some of his books? On the way uphill to his farm, I met the representative of the National Library of Wales coming away with two cases of literary spoil. (Richard Griffiths had been a popular columnist with a style that made him for forty years one of the most widely read of Welsh journalists.) Despite the bardic sign over the lintel, the house was desolate, and the poet also. I came away that night sensitive to his despair, and wrote:

IN MERIONETH

Moelwyn's grass is green at evening
But Cynicht's slopes grow grey,
As a song bereft of gladness
Takes the darker way.
Step upon the mountain meadow,
Bound the brook and pass you by.
Never heed the branches broken,
Blackened, gnarled and dry.
Never heed in crook of mountain
Bard of darker years;
Bygone storms have left him withered,
Bygone suns have dried his tears.
Let the seawind sing of summer,
Bend ripe apple from the leaf.

Bide not for the wind of winter
Biting chill with grief.
Moelwyn's grass is green at evening
But Cynicht's slopes grow grey,
Darkens now the further mountain
Though bright your seaward way;
Stay you not beside that mountain
Like the bard or broken tree,
Worse than wind will bleach or blacken,
Strike you as those branches be;
And when crook of mountain empty,
And wood from wall away,
Moelwyn's grass grow green at evening
But Cynicht's slopes be grey.*

This attachment to location has a history to itself which is associated with the Welsh Saints who so aggravated the sponsors of the Methodist revival. The Reverend Jones, in his book already mentioned on Pandy Tudur Methodism, insists on the early difficulties in preventing the worship of these saints and even of sun and weather worship!

One imagines the missionaries late in Roman times travelling on their task of conversion and finding a pleasant vicinity with a refreshing well, beside a cave or ruin where they could become hermits, accepting as their due in final years of wisdom the veneration due to a saint, so transferring to that profession. Only thus can the multiplication of these Celtic saints be explained. Both the early Church and the Methodists found the veneration of these 'well saints' almost impossible to eradicate and inveighed against it, associated as it was with older mythologies. But during the nineteenth century the Gorsedd, the organizations of eisteddfodau unwittingly resolved the problem. For the preachers and schoolmasters, all that could, became bards and the chapel took over the magic mysteries of the wells and became revered indeed.

I know I have fallen into the weird bewitchery of these hills and I go to the local eisteddfodau spellbound, glad that hymns and folksong with choirs and pennillion have snatched the precious inheritance from what A.P. Graves called 'the silent lips of a vanishing generation' in

* Moelwyn and Cynicht: two opposing mountains on the other side of the Glaslyn valley from Tan yr Allt, Shelley's temporary home. *The Mundane Tree (Fortune Press, 1947)*

thoughts such as George Borrow translated from 'Twm o'r Nant' (Thomas Edwards, Tom of the Dingle).

> God's wisdom has made every part to avail
> With wonderful wisdom the Lord God on high
> Has contrived the two lights that exist in the sky:
> The sun's hot as fire, its ray bright as gold,
> But the moon's ever pale and by nature is cold.

The greatest of the modern Welsh poets is acknowledged to be Thomas Gwynn Jones, and his genius also sprang from his own location. The spirit of Wales rather than the records of Israel lives within his verses whether in simple poems or those strict metres so incomprehensible to most non-Welsh speakers. In spite of his foreign travel and studies, the *Mabinogion* and the Welsh countryside are the sources of his inspiration.

It happened that, as he was married to my wife's mother's cousin Margaret Jane, my wife was often a guest at his house, Buarth, in Aberystwyth, for he was Professor of Welsh Literature when she was a student there. Before he moved to the smaller house in the village called Bow Street, he would often take a stroll beside the sea, leisurely walking with his wife to the end of the promenade and looking out across the ocean. There were bardic chairs unobtrusively placed in his house. He never tired of talking about Old Colwyn, where my wife was living with her aunt, for he had moved with his parents from his birthplace in Betws-yn-Rhos to the farmstead there, just where Peulwys Lane joins the Llanelian Road, standing high above the lane. The small stream runs down to the road and continues under a little bridge where he often used to play in childhood. He would smile with delight as he described the rare and tiny red pebbles he could pick up and collect out of that rivulet, taking them from the water and watching the glistening colour fade as he gathered them.

True to the spirit of location by which North Wales venerated its bards, the school on that Llanelian Road nearby is named Ysgol Gwynn Jones, and, much as when he was born there, his birthplace, *'Gwyndy Uchaf'*, can be found today. The 'Upper White House' with its stone barns and the pine trees nestles sheltered in the dell by Betws between beautiful river valleys lined with oak trees, its meadows halfway between sea and moorland, a location where genial surroundings, rich and pastoral, themselves could provide the makings of a poet.

What a contrast it poses to that older poet's cottage above Ty

Gwyn in Pandy Tudur, high up and almost on the bleak moors of Wenlli, doomed to be famous for one poem known everywhere but his name hardly mentioned.*

Llwybr Troed (The footpath)
Rwyn hen a chloff ond hoffwn am unwaith
Gael myned pe medrwn
I'm bro, a rhodio ar hwn,
Rhodio lle gynt y rhedwn.

The poem, an englion, celebrated as the winner in a major eisteddfod has now been carved on a stone slab before his bungalow, renovated to modernity where it shows no trace of that footpath between the woods, but everyone knows of it and the spirit behind those sparse words: 'Old am I and lame, and long to go home, but where I used to run may hardly walk.'

Standing there and turning away from reading the stone tablet, I could see Siabod, pyramid of mountain, and due southward the green meadows changing to brown as they crouched below the stark Hiraethog moorland. I resolved to go on to Nebo, to see the cottage I had chased some ten years before.

There was that empty dwelling on Oerfa, the green paint blistering on its woodwork, closed to humans, shuttered against animals with no sign of feet ever going to the door. And down the hill, that ruin, which Mrs Kerry had refused to sell me, more ruined still. The stream at which the old lady was noted for doing her washing and filling kettles to make tea ran just as sadly, for the chimney had broken from the house, the walls were shaky and dangerous, no one would wash anything there, nor smile, nor sleep, nor go out shopping as they had done for hundreds of years.

And as for Bryn-y-gwynt, from where I had hoped to have under my eyes the wide panorama from Hiraethog to Snowdon, a dismal black bullock stood in the entrance, dripping water, for a rainstorm had set in. The walls stood firm upon their huge rock bases, but the oak lintel over the doorway was thinner now and frailer. As for my own window sills, at least there were no piercing nettles to leap across them, nor mosses upon the cottage floors. My walls stood firm and the roof upon them was weather-proof. As for the windows, they looked out upon the distant meadows away to the moorlands, seeking panoramas which 'went on and on as far as the mountains'.

* J.T. Jones, 1894-1975

Index